RAVES FOR GEORGE A. ROMERO'S
Night of the Living Dead

George A. Romero's debut set the template for the zombie film, and features tight editing, realistic gore, and a sly political undercurrent.
> —Rotten Tomatoes

Romero's grainy black-and-white cinematography and casting of locals emphasize the terror lurking in ordinary life; as in Alfred Hitchcock's *The Birds* (1963), Romero's victims are not attacked because they did anything wrong, and the randomness makes the attacks all the more horrifying.
> —American Movie Classics

I saw *Night of the Living Dead* first-run at a drive-in. *Night of the Living Dead* was scary.
> —John Waters

There's never been anything quite like it. . . . *Night of the Living Dead* establishes savagery as a necessary condition of life. Marked by fatality and a grim humor, the film gnaws through to the bone, then proceeds on to the marrow.
> —Jim Gay, Amazon.com

If you want to see what turns a B movie into a classic, don't miss *Night of the Living Dead*.
　　—Rex Reed

Since this was twenty years before CNN would be showing body parts during prime-time television, I was totally blown away by how graphic Romero's movie was.
　　—Lloyd Kaufman, president of Troma Entertainment

Over its short, furious course, the picture violates so many strong taboos—cannibalism, incest, necrophilia—that it leaves audiences giddy and hysterical.
　　—*Village Voice*

One of the best films ever made, and possibly the most influential horror movie of all time.
　　—*Time Out*

There's a brute force in *Night of the Living Dead* that catches one in the throat.
　　—Lucius Gore, *ESplatter*

A doozie.
　　—Emanuel Levy, EmanuelLevy.com

Graphically gruesome!
　　—Fandango.com

At AM, we love a good zombie movie, and we are eternally grateful for this classic piece of celluloid. It's true *horror*, plain and simple.
　　—AskMen.com

If the American Film Institute's list of the classic movie quotes had been voted on by Pittsburghers, somewhere among those one hundred would have been "They're coming to get you, Barbara."
—*Pittsburgh Post-Gazette*

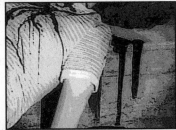

Second only to *Psycho* among influential horror films.
　　—*Entertainment Weekly*

The best thing is that *Night of the Living Dead* isn't over-composed—it just hurtles ahead with all its gruesomeness.
　　—*Los Angeles Times*

Minted in chilling black-and-white, George A. Romero's indie classic manages to be scary as hell, funny, and political all at once.
　　—*Premiere*

It's rare when a movie transcends pop culture's usual fifteen minutes of fame and becomes a time-tested classic. *Night of the Living Dead* redefined a lackluster monster and gave rise to both a new genre in horror and a new image in the public consciousness. There's no denying it, *Night of the Living Dead* is THE archetypal zombie film . . . a bona fide classic, inspirational, thought-provoking, and most important, still very scary after all these years. Thanks for the nightmares, George!
　　—Classic-Horror.com

Night of the Living Dead is one of my first favorite movies. Every week, for the first six years of my life, I watched *Night of the Living Dead.* . . . It was the first film that I had memorized. It scared me away from wanting to ever frequent cemeteries. **I DECLARE** *NIGHT OF THE LIVING DEAD* **IS ONE OF THE GREATEST HORROR MOVIES OF ALL TIME!!**
　　—Harry Knowles, *Ain't It Cool News*

Night of the Living Dead establishes savagery as a necessary condition of life. Marked by fatality and a grim humor, the film gnaws through to the bone, then proceeds on to the marrow.

 —Amazon.com

One of the best and most influential horror films ever made. George Romero packed *Night of the Living Dead* with shocking horror, brilliant filmmaking, complex themes, and a controversial social commentary of the times.

 —Bloody Disgusting.com

With its radical rewriting of a genre in which good had always triumphed over evil, Romero's first feature shattered the conventions of horror and paved the way for the subversive visions of directors like David Cronenberg, Tobe Hooper, and Sam Raimi.

 —*Time Out*

Nobody could have imagined when *Night of the Living Dead* was playing off unheralded second feature drive-in dates in 1968 that going on fifty years later it would have become a cultural touchstone every bit as potent as the most famous mainstream movies of the era. It's partly the lack of slickness, the newsreelish presentation with unknown actors that still gives it its power. It's like a documentary about the end of the world.

 —Joe Dante

NIGHT OF THE LIVING DEAD

NO ONE
WILL BE ADMITTED
WITHOUT A STOMACH
DISTRESS BAG!

GALLAGHER THEATER
THURS 7:30

NIGHT OF THE LIVING DEAD

BEHIND THE SCENES OF THE MOST TERRIFYING ZOMBIE MOVIE EVER

JOE KANE
THE PHANTOM OF THE MOVIES®

CITADEL PRESS
Kensingon Publishing Corp.
www.kensingtonbooks.com

CITADEL PRESS BOOKS are published by

Kensington Publishing Corp.
119 West 40th Street
New York, NY 10018

All Kensington titles, imprints, and distributed lines are available at special quantity discounts for bulk purchases for sales promotions, premiums, fund-raising, educational, or institutional use. Special book excerpts or customized printings can also be created to fit specific needs. For details, write or phone the office of the Kensington special sales manager: Kensington Publishing Corp., 119 West 40th Street, New York, NY 10018, attn: Special Sales Department; phone 1-800-221-2647.

First printing: September 2010

10 9 8 7 6 5 4 3 2 1

Printed in the United States of America

Library of Congress Control Number: 2010924999

ISBN-13: 978-0-8065-3331-5
ISBN-10: 0-8065-3331-5

For Nancy Naglin,

Without whose indefatigable love,

assistance, and support—

Fughedaboudit!

Welcome to a night of total terror!
—Trailer, *Night of the Living Dead*

One thing that seems clear to me, looking back at the ten or a dozen films that truly scared me, is that most really good horror films are low-budget affairs with special effects cooked up in someone's basement or garage. Among those that truly work are *Carnival of Souls, Halloween, The Texas Chainsaw Massacre, Night of the Living Dead,* and *The Blair Witch Project.*
—Stephen King

We made it a good film. The fans made it a classic.
—*Night of the Living Dead* producer Russell Streiner

CONTENTS

FOREWORD

A *Night* to Remember:
What the *Living Dead* Means to Me

by Wes Craven

Seeing George's masterpiece for the first time is a vivid memory for me. I was just newly in New York, working at some lowly position, not yet having directed, when a friend of mine asked if I'd like to go see this film called *Night of the Living Dead*. "Sounds dumb," I said, not knowing anything about it, and having never seen a horror film in my life. "But it's supposed to be fun," my friend said. "A happening." So I said okay, and off we went to the Waverly in Greenwich Village. The theater was packed, even though the film had been out a long while already. Everybody was buzzing with excitement, running up and down the aisles for final Cokes and popcorn, leaning over the seats talking to each other. Then the lights went down. And that brother-sister duo started their scene, arguing over their dad's grave, or whatever it was. So what's the big deal, I thought. And then I saw that strange, lurching figure in the deep background appear. Coming toward these two rather annoying people, the first yells started—and then screams and nervous laughter. I realized I was scared already—*something about that guy is not right!*

Well, you know the rest. He attacks, the annoying guy is toast, and as all hell breaks loose, the screaming girl begins running for her life. An hour and a half or so later, after countless yells, screams, and hoots—plus huge laughter—there comes the moment of realization that, hey, this movie is *about* something as well. And beyond all of that, there's the fact that I'd never, ever been in a theater where that kind of energy, delight, and raw fear took over 300 people and welded them all into one big quaking blob of humanity *in extremis* and *loving it*.

Unlike anything I'd ever experienced before.

That movie, more than anything else I can think of, liberated me to make *Last House on the Left*, because I knew that after that there was a whole new kind of film blossoming in American cinema. It was something hybrid that mixed terror and laughter and social comment into one heady, totally unpredictable witches' brew of entertainment unlike anything I'd ever experienced before.

I was hooked, and it's George's fault.

ACKNOWLEDGMENTS

Special thanks to (in alphabetical order) Tim Ferrante and Roy Frumkes, good friends and film scholars who went above and beyond the call in helping with the creation of this tome, and my editor Gary Goldstein.

The entire *Night of the Living Dead* team, with super-loud shout-outs to Judith O'Dea, George Romero, John Russo, Kyra Schon and Gary Streiner.

Also . . . filmmakers par excellence and fellow *Night* fans Allan Arkush, Danny Boyle, Max Allan Collins, Wes Craven, Larry Fessenden, Frank Henenlotter, Peter Jackson, Lloyd Kaufman, and William Lustig.

Plus . . . Brian Boucher, Paul Bresnick, Jeff Carney, Jim Cironella, Jeffrey Combs, Joe Dante, Eric Danville, Terry & Tiffany DuFoe, Rob Freese, Paul R. Gagne, Stuart Gordon, Kevin Hein, James Karen, Lynn Lowry, Joan Kane Nichols, Gil Reavill, Debbie Rochon, Tony Timpone, Tom Towles, Scott Voisin, Calum Waddell, Tom Weaver.

ACKNOWLEDGMENTS

NIGHT OF THE LIVING DEAD

ANCESTORS
OF THE LIVING DEAD

I didn't mean to invent the new zombies. I never called
them zombies. *They* were those big-eyed cats in the
Caribbean. —George Romero, *Zombie Mania*

Don't say that living dead stuff, boss. I'm one of the living
living. But you give me the feeling that if I stay around
here, I'm gonna be one of the dead dead.
—Nick O'Demus, *Zombies on Broadway*

The living dead didn't suddenly spring forth, fully formed and famished, in
1960s Pittsburgh. On the contrary, they have been with us, in
one incarnation or another, nearly as long as life itself. Of Western Civ's five cornerstone pop-culture creatures—Dracula and
vampires, the Frankenstein Monster, the Mummy, zombies, and
werewolves—all save the last mentioned, technically, fit into the
living dead category. The concept of the zombie represents the
newest of the group, initially popularized by sensationalist travel
writer William Seabrook, the print equivalent of jungle explorers
Martin and Osa Johnson, whose lurid, often casually racist and
generally xenophobic celluloid safaris (e.g., *Baboona, Congorilla*)
flourished on 1920s and '30s screens. Seabrook's influential 1929
book *The Magic Island* told of deceased Haitians, frequently victims of voodoo vengeance, taken from their graves and forced to
toil as slaves for their rapacious re-animators.

At the time, Universal Pictures ruled as Hollywood's

1

unchallenged fright-film frontrunner. The studio even surpassed Lon Chaney's fabled silent reign as Gaston Leroux's *Phantom of the Opera* (1925) and Victor Hugo's *Hunchback of Notre Dame* (1923), among other fantastic characters, by bringing Bram Stoker's *Dracula* and Mary Shelley's *Frankenstein* to the sound screen in 1931, *The Mummy* the following year, and introducing two new terror titans to replace the by then late Lon—Boris Karloff and Bela Lugosi. But it was the independent Halperin brothers, director Victor and producer Edward, who surprisingly beat that mighty Tinseltown outfit to the zombie punch with their classic and trendsetting *White Zombie* in 1932.

The film adheres fairly closely to the zombie rules set forth in Seabrook's book. In this creepy shocker, *Dracula* alum Bela Lugosi cuts a memorably menacing figure as evil-eyed zombie master "Murder" Legendre. He employs a powerful powder to reduce the living to a catatonic state (a fate that befalls drugged ingénue Madge Bellamy) and keep revived corpses obediently working in his sugar mill: The sight of those eerie, dull-eyed drones endlessly pushing the creaking mill wheel remains one of the most indelible images in the whole of horror-film history. Unlike George Romero's future living dead to come, these early zombies function with no will of their own, killing only on command from their human overseers.

The Halperins struck out in their second undead at-bat with the insufferably dull *Revolt of the Zombies* (1936), a tale nominally about living-dead troops on the loose in World War I Cambodia—but mostly a static yakathon shot on a few cheap sets. Far more frightening are the ghostly war dead who rise to trouble the conscience of a self-destructive humanity in Abel Gance's dark World War I fable *J'accuse!* (1938). Fear-film fans also fared better with a pair of back-from-the-grave Boris Karloff shockers, 1936's *The Walking Dead* (wherein Karloff sports a tonsorial style to rival his striking *The Black Cat* look) and 1939's *The Man They Could Not Hang*. In each, Karloff's reanimated character operates outside then-established OZ (Original Zombie) rules: He can think, act, talk, and, despite a few physical alterations, was *not* transformed into an entirely new being.

Traditional native zombies received a bit of a boost in the

1940s, resurfacing, to alternately comic and surprisingly scary effect, in the Bob Hope frightcom hit, set in Cuba, *The Ghost Breakers* (1940). The following year witnessed the release of Monogram Pictures' Mantan Moreland showcase *King of the Zombies*. Although later maligned for being politically incorrect, it highlights the inventive African-American comic's oft-improv'd interactions with the titular living dead. The subject was played solely for laughs in *Zombies on Broadway* (1945), a fitfully funny vehicle for Abbott and Costello wannabes Alan Carney and Wally Brown, with a major assist from Bela Lugosi as an unstable (what else?) scientist. Elsewhere, the deceptively titled *Valley of the Zombies* (1946) offered only one eccentric, vampire-like living-dead fellow (Ian Keith).

Probably the first screen zombies to resemble Romero's ghouls can be briefly glimpsed staggering, arms outstretched, in the 1942 Lugosi vehicle *Bowery at Midnight* ("They're coming to get you, Bela!"). Unfortunately, these creepy Caucasian apparitions are granted criminally scant screen time in a largely crime-centric ca-per. And on the subject of ethnicity,

> **"One day we'll all be dead; then we'll finally have something in common."**
> —*Zacherley*

mad scientist John Carradine may have been the first to integrate the homegrown zombie ranks in 1943's *Revenge of the Zombies*. In this film undead Anglos and African-Americans un-live to-gether in apparent blank-brained harmony, bringing to mind TV horror host and once and future "Cool Ghoul" Zacherley's im-mortal line: "One day we'll all be dead; then we'll finally have something in common." Rather passive voodoo-struck female zombies, meanwhile, supply the supernatural angle in 1944's *Voodoo Man*, wherein Monogram springs for three top terror tal-ents—Bela, Carradine, and the drolly sinister George Zucco.

Zucco scores solo lead honors in the second-best zombie movie of 1943, *The Mad Ghoul*. This ingenious, wryly scripted (by Paul Gangelin, Hans Kraly, and Brenda Weisberg) scarefest de-tails the adventures of one Dr. Morris (Zucco) who, assisted by a clean-cut, All-American boy med student named Ted (David Bruce), works on a series of seemingly harmless experiments.

Little does the ever innocent Ted realize, however, that the doc is actually planning to create slaves to do his ruthless bidding by perfecting a gas designed to induce zombie-like trances. Soon Ted is led by Dr. Morris on nocturnal graveyard visits, where he practices his surgical techniques, removing the hearts from recently buried cadavers in order to sustain his own increasingly worthless life. *The Mad Ghoul*'s mix of genuinely creepy over-the-top horror and deadpan gallows humor qualifies it as one of the era's best and brightest fright flicks.

Even *The Mad Ghoul*, however, pales beside RKO producer Val Lewton's and director Jacques Tourneur's atmospheric masterpiece of quiet horror *I Walked with a Zombie* (1943). An extremely fetching Frances Dee plays a Canadian nurse assigned to care for Christine Gordon, the comatose wife of plantation owner Tom Conway, on the gloomy Caribbean isle of San Sebastian. Here, locals "cry when a child is born and make merry at a burial." Is Gordon really a zombie, victim of a voodoo curse? Finding the answer to that question provides viewers with one of horrordom's most haunting cinematic journeys.

In the 1950s, the zombie took a cinematic backseat to radioactive mutants and hostile E.T.s, though exceptions proved the rule in the Dean Martin and Jerry Lewis romp *Scared Stiff* (1953), a retooled *Ghost Breakers*. The largely dull Boris vehicle *Voodoo Island*, the static, subaqueous *The Zombies of Mora Tau* (1957), and bargain-basement schlockmeister Jerry Warren's *Teenage Zombies* (1959), which was the first flick to feature a zombified ape, as well as your typically overage titular adolescents, brain-zapped to serve as Stateside pawns of the International Commie Conspiracy.

> Teenage Zombies *(1959)*, was the first flick to feature a zombified ape.

Ed Wood's deathless *Plan 9 from Outer Space* (1956, unreleased until 1959), is justly lauded in many circles (including this one) as the best bad movie ever made. It merged zombies with a more contemporary trauma, the ever-present alien threat. While slow to implement (to put it mildly), the invaders' insidious scheme calls for the resurrection of the deceased via "long-distance electrodes shot into the pineal and pituitary glands of the recent dead." As dedicated Edheads know, the interlopers manage to re-animate all of three zombies—played by slinky erstwhile horror hostess Vampira (a.k.a. Maila Nurmi), massive Swedish wrestler and Ed repertory troupe regular Tor Johnson, and chronically underrated chiropractor Tom Mason, subbing for the actually, inconveniently dead Bela Lugosi. The group ambulates in a manner much like Romero's future living dead.

The lobotomy-scarred *Creature with the Atom Brain* (there are actually several in number) were scientifically revived corpses in the service of a crazed ex-Nazi (Gregory Gay), in league with a deported gangster (Michael Granger) who's looking to rain vengeance down upon his enemies. While lacking *Night*'s zombie autonomy, these are possibly the most violent and arguably the scariest deaders seen onscreen to that point (1955). They're capable of snapping human spines and, with the help of those handy atom brains, even blowing up stock-footage airplanes.

Edward L. Cahn's cheap but occasionally chilling *Invisible Invaders* sees transparent aliens commandeer earthly cadavers for the usual sinister purposes. Of all the '50s zombies, these most closely resemble those in *Night of the Living Dead*. They don't boast the latter's age, gender, and occupational variety—all are business-suited, middle-aged white guys who look like they suffered simultaneous seizures at the same sales convention. But they're honestly unnerving dudes for 1959 as they stagger in stiff, hollow-eyed tandem down a cemetery hillside.

Kicking off the next decade, 1960's *Cape Canaveral Monsters* repeats *Invisible Invaders'* riff of aliens reanimating and inhabiting expired Earthlings, in this case bodies retrieved from a car crash. An admirably nihilistic ending supplies the lone attribute of this shoestring sci-fi effort by director Phil Tucker, who fails to recapture his *Robot Monster* (1953) magic. Another notoriously penurious entrepreneur, minimalist sleaze merchant Barry (*The Beast That Killed Women*) Mahon, went the traditional voodoo route with his obscure New Orleans-set outing *The Dead One* (1961). It's the first Stateside zombie movie lensed in color, the better to accentuate the pale white title character's sickly green visage. Connecticut-based auteur Del (*The Horror of Party*

Beach) Tenney headed south to the Caribbean, by way of Miami Beach, to create the nearly thrill-less black-and-white zombie quickie *Voodoo Blood Bath* (1964). A.k.a. *Zombie*, the film wouldn't widely surface until 1971 when aptly named distributor Jerry Gross resurrected it as the cheatingly titled *I Eat Your Skin*. The film doubled up with his much more explicit *I Drink Your Blood*, a blatant bid to ride *Night of the Living Dead*'s cult coat-tails.

AIP produced a more lavish living dead story in Roger Corman's 1962 *Tales of Terror*. The Edgar Allan Poe-based trilogy highlighted a reanimated Vincent Price in *The Facts in the Case of M. Valdemar* segment, a tale George Romero would tackle nearly thirty years later in the Dario Argento collaboration *Two Evil Eyes*. The most creative of the period's drive-in-targeted active corpse flicks, though, came from Las Vegas and the fertile mind of the late Ray Dennis Steckler. His 1964 *The Incredibly Strange Creatures Who Stopped Living and Became Mixed-Up Zombies* not only boasted the second-longest title in genre-film history (after Corman's *The Saga of the Viking Women and Their Journey to the Waters of the Great Sea Serpent*) but arrived as the first zombie musical (in fact, Steckler billed it as the "First Rock'n'Roll Monster Musical"). Del Tenney's *Horror of Party Beach*, unleashed earlier that year, actually offered the first zombie rock *song*, the Del Aires' "The Zombie Stomp." *The Incredibly Strange Creatures . . .* scores more points with its wildly surreal, pre-psychedelic extended-nightmare sequences than with its rather uninspired rubber-masked zombies.

Other countries likewise contributed to the screen zombie ranks, often tinkering with traditional zombie rules. Mexico delivered *Santo vs. the Zombies* (1962), a.k.a. *Invasion of the Zombies*, pitting that most exalted, eponymous masked wrestler against energetic dead men in the employ of a criminal mastermind. That pic proved popular enough to inspire Santo to join forces with fellow grappler Blue Demon in *Santo and Blue Demon Against the Monsters* (1968), *Santo and Blue Demon in the Land of the Dead* (1969), and *Invasion of the Dead* (1973). Zombies would likewise surface in the Jess Franco-directed French/

Spanish co-production *Dr. Orloff's Monster* (1965) and Germany's *The Frozen Dead* (1966), the latter fleetingly elevated by Nazi scientist Dana Andrews's death-by-zombie-arms-protruding-through-a-wall. The tableau is similar to the nightmare sequence that opens Romero's *Day of the Dead*, though executed with far less flair.

Britain took its zombies a tad more earnestly. Sidney J. Furie's *Dr. Blood's Coffin* (1961) is a slowly paced *Frankenstein*-like affair, while the bleak doomsday quickie *The Earth Dies Screaming* (1965) offers some atmospheric shots of terminated townsfolk raised (once again) by alien invaders. The Hammer period piece *The Plague of the Zombies* (1966) represents the first film to show ghouls rotting before viewers' eyes (unless you count Vincent Price's famous facial meltdown in the earlier cited *Tales of Terror*).

> **Plague of the Zombies** *(1966) represents the first film to show ghouls rotting before viewers' eyes.*

It might be argued that Herk Harvey's brilliantly terrifying art-house horror *Carnival of Souls* (1961)—with its relentless nightmare quality and haunting nocturnal images of zombie-like phantoms in perpetual pursuit of alienated heroine Candace Hilligoss, in a movie created by the operators of a Lawrence, Kansas, commercial/industrial film house—served both as *Night of the Living Dead*'s spiritual progenitor and basic business model. But the film that acted as its true template was the 1964 American-Italian co-production *The Last Man on Earth*. Based on Richard Matheson's celebrated doomsday novel *I Am Legend* (also the inspiration for the 2007 Will Smith blockbuster of the same name as well as the 1971 Charlton Heston showcase *The Omega Man*), *The Last Man on Earth* arrives replete with slow-moving human corpses-turned-predators, boarded-up windows with the creatures' hands thrusting through them, an infected child, human bonfires, and many other key elements that would soon surface in *Night*.

But no matter how groundbreaking the walking dead imagery, even *Last Man* lacked the insidious black magic that would make *Night of the Living Dead* the most terrifying and enduring zombie movie ever.

———

> I caught that on television, and I said to myself, "Wait a minute—did they make another version of *I Am Legend* they didn't tell me about?" Later on they told me they did it as a homage to *I Am Legend*, which means, "He gets it for nothin'." George Romero's a nice guy, though. I don't harbor any animosity toward him. —Richard Matheson on *Night of the Living Dead,* as told to Tom Weaver

DUBIOUS COMFORTS: INTRODUCTION TO *THE LIVING DEAD*

They're coming to get you, Barbara!
—Johnny (Russell Streiner) in *Night of the Living Dead*

It was a dark and stormy night, Halloween season, out in rocky Montauk Point, Long Island. We had just left a wedding reception and had driven several blind blocks, through a drenching rain, powered by gale-force winds. Finally finding shelter at the Memory Motel (earlier immortalized by the Stones song of the same name)—and already three sheets to the wind and counting—I wanted nothing more at that exhausted moment than to fall into bed for a solid eight.

First, though, from force of lifetime habit, I instinctively turned on the telly. And what grainy sight should greet my booze-befogged eyes? None other than Johnny and Barbara's car just starting its doomed journey down that forlorn road to the old Evans City Cemetery, where the eternal, infernal nightmare would begin anew. As lightning and thunder thrashed outside, I obediently settled on the edge of the bed, instantly scared sober by that flickering tube. I dreaded every frame I knew I was about to reexperience, but I was powerless to resist.

That night time-warped me to Times Square, more than a quarter-century before. I had glimpsed *Night of the Living Dead* adorning Deuce marquees, circa 1969, but, despite that cool title, took it for just another fright flick, one I was always too busy to drop in and see. When *Night* resurfaced in June 1970, however, at the Museum of Modern Art, where I had a student membership, it seemed a sure sign that this black-and-white indie from the Steel City had been deemed something special. This time I surrendered, eagerly joining an anticipatory audience of art-house lovers and horror hounds in MoMA's auditorium.

The film opened, natch, the same way it would on the Memory Motel TV, and as it had at several midnight shows I attended at New York City's Waverly Theater during the '70s, on VHS in the '80s, DVD in the late '90s, and during countless other broadcast airings and streaming video Internet showings: As soon as we sight that lonely vehicle, we sense we're going on a journey and, given that title and bleak autumnal landscape, we're pretty sure it won't be a pretty one. As the car follows the gray brick road to the graveyard, we get the feeling we're not in Pittsburgh anymore.

Next, we peek inside and pick up on a conversation in progress between impatient big brother Johnny (Russell Streiner) and his prim little sis Barbara (Judith O'Dea). The tedium of their long and, in Johnny's eyes, pointless drive to pay a perfunctory graveside visit to their deceased dad has reduced the twenty-something siblings to regressive role playing, with Johnny's teasing Barbara and Barbara chastising Johnny for his immature antics. Sans a single excess frame, the scene perfectly encapsulates both the pair's longstanding relationship and present situation.

As with all of *Night*'s major characters, the viewer voluntarily fills in the rest of their backstories based on the few key clues provided. Johnny, we surmise from his suit, tie, and protruding pocket pens, is likely a low-rung white-collar worker. His acceptably longish hair, slightly stylish specs, and driving gloves indicate that the '60s have encroached on him in a distant 'burb way. But he's essentially a pretty straight dude, the type who would much prefer watching the Steelers on TV rather than visiting the grave of a father he claims to barely remember. Johnny is relentlessly, even deflatingly pragmatic, but also a bit of a joker.

Barbara, with her conservative coat and proper demeanor, is probably a secretary or similar office support person. We determine that she's somewhat repressed, almost certainly single, and a virgin. Both siblings, it would appear, still live at home with mom. And, most crucially, neither is played by a recognizable Hollywood thespian; both look like people we see in real life. Already, the film has taken on a distinct documentary feel.

An almost subliminal hint of impending danger is subtly conveyed via a static-interrupted radio broadcast. Johnny, shrugging, switches it off, convinced that what he's heard is merely a temporary technical glitch. While the siblings place a wreath at the gravesite, Johnny recalls a similar moment from their shared childhood, when his attempts to scare young Barbara aroused their granddad's rage, provoking their elder to angrily predict, "Boy, you'll be damned to hell!"

When Johnny senses Barbara's growing anxiety, he reverts to the same puerile behavior, mischievously invoking Boris Karloff, lisp intact, and uttering *Night*'s signature line, "They're coming to get you, Barbara!" If we hadn't guessed already, we *know* we're in deep nightmare territory when Boris himself, or an unreasonable facsimile thereof, suddenly materializes, as if by black magic, behind them.

At first, the film teases the viewer with that distant apparition: Is the figure important? Menacing? Or merely set decoration? We soon learn the answer when he clutches a vulnerable Barbara, stunning us with one of the primo shock moments in horror-film history. Johnny races to sis's rescue, engaging the mysterious aggressor in a furious fight that seems all the more frightening for its raw, random choreography. This isn't a Hollywood stunt show; this is an awkward, brutal battle to the death. When Johnny's head hits a cement cemetery marker with an accompanying thud, the image chills with its abrupt finality. Barbara reacts just as instinctively, running to their car and, despite her terrified state, retaining enough composure to release the emergency brake and roll downhill, even as the single-minded killer shatters the window with a heavy rock.

Alas, Barbara's escape attempt lasts but a few yards as she plows the car into a tree. There follows a frenzied flight, shown in a blur of multi-angle images further spiked by a panicky soundtrack, as Barbara zigzags down the graveyard road. She never pauses, not even once she's outdistanced her erratically loping pursuer. In a standard horror film, her nearly three-minute sprint might well tax audience patience. But *Night* ingeniously ups the terror ante with each frantic footfall, hitting such a hyper pace that the opposite effect takes hold, forcing jangled viewers to share Barbara's suffocating fear.

When she escapes into an appararently empty farmhouse, Barbara keeps cool enough to lock the door, dial the phone (it's dead), and snatch a protective knife from a kitchen drawer. A frightened peek outside reveals that two additional fearful figures have joined her brother's attacker. Shell shocked, Barbara decides to explore upstairs, only to be stopped dead in her tracks by the grotesquely grinning skull of a rotting corpse.

Draped over the banister, Barabara half-slips, half-slides down the stairs. Now she's freaking out in earnest. She staggers to the front porch, where headlights freeze her, fawnlike, in their blinding glare. Without warning, a face pops up out of nowhere and into frame—a *black* face. Help or another threat? For the moment, Barbara doesn't know—and neither do we. When the intruder hustles her back into the house, we realize he's on her (and our) side. Still, trapped in the imperiled farmhouse with a black stranger while killers mill outside, Barbara's mental meltdown accelerates.

The man identifies himself as Ben, but there's no time for personal details or pleasantries. Ben quickly sizes up the situation and takes control, questioning, with little success, the now silent and useless Barbara. He also tries the phone, which emits a weird, faint electronic hum. He, too, discovers the corpse at the top of the stairs and mutters a stunned, "Jesus." When he stumbles downstairs, Barbara briefly assumes a prayerful position as if responding to Ben's religious "plea." But it doesn't look like any deus ex machina's on the way to save these souls caught in a sudden living hell.

As Ben moves about the house, we also imbue *him* with a sketchy backstory never spelled out in the film. We can tell by his speech and comportment that he's intelligent and highly competent, but his casual clothes suggest that, as a black man in 1968 America, he probably works a job that's somewhat beneath his abilities. We also suspect, from the otherwise white (and, in the case of the attackers, downright pale) characters we've encountered thus far, he's probably not native to the immediate area but just "passing through."

While Ben scours the house for food, blood from the ceiling drips on Barbara's hand. Seeking Ben's solace, she locates him in the kitchen and absently fondles his tire iron. Her hysterical query—"What's happening?"—could have gotten a laugh, given the jargon of the time, but it never did at any screening we attended. Ben doesn't know the answer.

Outside, the zombie ranks continue to swell. The walking dead seem more focused now, hefting stones and systematically smashing Ben's headlights. He takes his trusty tire iron to one of the creatures, then another, crushing their skulls (at this point, they're out of frame, though the scene is accompanied by emphatic soundtrack thumps).

One zombie enters the house via the back door and creeps up on Barbara, but Ben swiftly intervenes, wrestling the crippled-looking fiend to the floor. This time the camera doesn't cut away, and we see the gruesome results of Ben's handiwork—a large, lethal hole in the zombie's forehead. Ben dispatches another deader in the doorway. The first zombie's eyes fly open. Ben commands Barbara, "Don't look at it!" He drags the body outside and sets it on fire as the other zombies back away.

Stifling his impatience, Ben exhorts Barbara to help him find boards to block the windows and reinforce the doors, vulnerable points of entry the zombies appear determined to penetrate. Barbara is hypnotized instead by a tinkling music box, a genteel reminder of a recent, abruptly smashed past. Ben locates lumber conveniently stashed under the kitchen sink and, working alone, begins boarding up the house. Barbara lends an ineffectual hand in a slow, nearly wordless sequence that again could have bored audiences. By this time, however, most viewers with active pulses are too hooked to fidget; they're thoroughly fixated on every move, no matter how slight, the screen protagonists make.

While dismantling a table, Ben relates the tale of carnage he'd witnessed at Beekman's Diner: "I was alone. Fifty or sixty of those things were just standing there." Once Ben completes his horrific monologue, Barbara begins to tell her story, albeit in the voice of a traumatized child. She trails off, complains of the house's heat, tugs at her clothes, and again grows hysterical, irrationally insisting they leave and look for Johnny. When Ben opines that Johnny's dead, Barbara slaps him. In another culturally trailblazing moment, black Ben delivers a solid punch to the white woman's jaw. He gently places an unconscious Barbara on the couch, then clicks on the radio.

As Ben continues to seal up the house, a newscaster reports an "epidemic of mass murder by a virtual army of unidentified assassins" plaguing the "eastern third of the nation." Spooky sci-fi theremin music nearly drowns out the announcer's droning tones.

As people were wont to do concerning the ubiquitous, nerve-numbing news accounts of the latest Vietnam casualty stats, political assassinations, civil unrest, and other routine outrages of the era, Ben only half listens as he dutifully pursues more practical matters. Having discovered the fiends' fear of fire, he pushes a chair out the door and sets it aflame; the zombies stiffly retreat.

In a hall closet, Ben finds a rifle—and a pair of women's shoes. He bends down to put the shoes on an awake but frozen Barbara, a gesture that hints of both intimacy and servility; to Ben, the act is purely pragmatic, though we do sense his growing empathy for the terrified girl. The radio reveals that the hordes of unknown slayers are "eating the flesh of the people they kill." Ben goes upstairs and drags the female corpse down the hallway.

Suddenly, the cellar door swings open. Two men burst forth. Barbara screams. Having assumed the job of Barbara's protector, Ben rushes downstairs, ready to do battle. He angrily asks the men why they didn't help them if they knew the two were on the floor above.

The older man, excitable, middle-aged Harry Cooper, responds with equal rancor. Their argument escalates immediately, reflecting the toxic generational discord of the 1960s (where families argued over issues ranging from racism to Vietnam politics to basic life values). Many viewers instantly peg quintessential square Harry, with his bulldozer approach to dissenting opinions, as a petty, bullying know-it-all dad and authority figure. Ben, on the other hand, is a defiant black man, standing in and up for the country's alienated youth, segregated minorities, disenfranchised poor, and all the oppressed.

Then the Great Basement Debate commences. Should the survivors hole up in the cellar, isolated and blind, as Harry insists, or remain on the first floor, where the enemy's movements can be monitored and dealt with directly? With Harry representing the Old Right and Ben the New Left, the argument flares with the same intensity that fueled the repetitive political arguments that marked those confrontational times.

The divisive squabble seems to drag on interminably, with each side loudly reiterating its position with no signs of compromise or progress, each more interested in proving its point than coping with a common problem. Tom, meanwhile, plays the role of the undecided youth who listens to both sides and gradually leans toward Ben. That heated discussion is abruptly interrupted by a classic jump scare when, as Ben brushes by, clutching zombie arms suddenly thrust through the boarded window gaps.

Ben and Tom hurriedly beat them back, and then Ben grabs his gun and fires through the window. Bullets, we see, are ineffective against a persistent zombie until Ben drills him through the head. Buoyed by his kill, Ben informs an unhelpful Harry: "You can be the boss down there. I'm boss up here." Midnight-movie audiences often cheered that moment of underdog defiance.

When her beau summons her from the basement we next meet Tom's fetching squeeze, Judy. (Like the late Johnny, the two have been lightly touched by slowly spreading '60s styles, with Tom sporting modest sideburns and Judy bedecked in hip denim jacket and jeans.) As Harry prepares to descend the stairs of ignorance, Tom pleads: "If we work together, man, we can fix it up real good." But, then as now, that's not happening with Harry and his kind.

In the basement, we meet the rest of our cast—Harry's frustrated wife, Helen, and their sick, supine daughter, Karen. When Harry apprises Helen of his unilateral decision to defend their underground Alamo at all costs, Helen spits out, "That's important, isn't it? To be right and everybody else to be wrong?" The disenchanted spouses struck many younger viewers as the types who'd likely married for the wrong reasons (sex for Harry, security for Helen) and now, in early middle age, are in too deep to go their separate ways. As soon as Helen hears about the upstairs radio, the basement debate rages anew in what's becoming one of the most fractious films to surface since *Who's Afraid of Virginia Woolf?*

Tom calls down that they also found a television. Judy agrees to take Helen's place in the cellar and look after Karen. Helen thanks her with a heartfelt, "She's all I have." (Harry, understandably, doesn't fit into her equation.) When Harry announces his intention to take Barbara downstairs, Ben grows more fiercely protective: "If you stay up here, you take orders from me—and that includes leaving that girl alone."

TV reports, meanwhile, elaborate on the earlier radio bulletins about "creatures who feed on the flesh of their victims." Viewers are strongly advised to burn their unburied dead—immediately: "The bereaved will have to forgo the dubious comforts a funeral service will give." The locations of emergency rescue stations appear on screen, while speculation about a "Venus space vehicle" spreading radiation adds to the panic. We see a live remote from Washington, D.C., where waffling authorities can't agree on the significance of those rumors while they're trailed by a crew of desperate newsmen.

Inside the farmhouse, everyone is in momentary agreement that they should hie to the nearest rescue station. To accomplish that goal, they need to unlock a gas pump to fill Ben's borrowed truck. The plan calls for scattering the cannibals by tossing Molotov cocktails into their midst. Ben and Tom volunteer to undertake the risky mission.

Before that happens, the film breaks for a rare mellow interlude, a sentimental dialogue between young lovers Tom and Judy. As their exchange unfolds, they calmly prepare the Molotov cocktails, not unlike contemporaneous real-life radicals, a parallel not lost on the movie's midnight viewers.

Harry throws a few flammable jars from an upstairs window. One zombie catches fire, while the rest scatter. Ben and Tom make their move, with Tom hustling to the truck. Judy impulsively decides to join him, running out of the house amid the predatory dead. Not a good idea.

Ben attempts to hold the creatures off. When he shoots the lock off the pump, his torch is left burning on the ground. Tom clumsily swings the hose, spraying the torch and spreading the fire. Ben tries to tame the burgeoning blaze with a blanket as Tom and Judy scramble for the truck. Too late: The engine ignites. Tom manages to tumble out the door, but Judy's jacket gets caught on the handle. When Tom dives back in to rescue her, the truck explodes and the lovers are consumed in an instant inferno.

Ben then back-steps his way to the house, wielding his torch for protection. At first, Harry refuses to open the door, then relents and aids Ben in boarding it up. More transgressive moments for the times: Black Ben proceeds to beat the tar out of white Harry, while the flesh-famished zombies—former friends, neighbors and just plain folks—enjoy an alfresco Tom and Judy barbeque, visually conveyed via unprecedented gut-munching close-ups. (While Florida exploiteer and gore movie co-inventor [with partner David F. Friedman] Herschell Gordon Lewis had been splattering the screen with more explicit grue since his 1963 breakthrough *Blood Feast*, his campy, borderline amateur films furnished none of the impact of *Night*'s terrifying tableaux.) The feast, meantime, can be—and, in midnight circles, often was—interpreted as a destructive society literally devouring its young.

Back in the house, order is temporarily restored. Ben, Helen, and Harry discuss the possibility of finding the Coopers's abandoned car, a notion the battered Harry predictably dismisses out of hand. We also learn that little Karen has been bitten by one of the "things." Further TV reports confirm Ben's empirical findings that a "ghoul" can be destroyed by a bullet to the head ("Kill the brain and you kill the ghoul"). On screen, roving cops and posse members—who look like the types frequently seen beating up black and youthful protestors on nightly news segments—scour the countryside on a search-and-destroy mission.

Inside the farmhouse, the electricity goes out; the zombies take advantage by launching a fresh offensive. Helen holds the door shut, while Harry again hangs back. When Ben drops his rifle to help Helen, Harry grabs the gun and orders his wife down into the basement. Ben tackles him. A fierce struggle ensues. Ben gains control of the weapon and, drained of patience, shoots Harry in cold blood. Harry staggers down the cellar steps. In his dying act, he tries to touch daughter Karen.

Then we shock-cut to one of the reigning money shots in horror-film history: A zombified Karen chowing down on her dead dad's severed arm.

Upstairs, Barbara snaps out of her trance and pushes herself against the door, enabling Helen to break free. Then we shock-cut to one of the reigning money shots in horror-film history: A zombified Karen chowing down on her dead dad's severed arm.

When Helen appears, Karen abruptly drops the hunk of raw father flesh and stalks mom, who falls during her disbelieving backward retreat. Karen retrieves a trowel and gets busy, stabbing mom to death as blood splashes the wall.

We're down again to the original two, Ben and Barbara, trying to halt the zombie assault. Johnny makes his dramatic zombie entrance and reclaims sister Barbara, pulling her out the door into the cannibals' midst; instinctively, she wraps her arms around her brother, half-resisting, half-succumbing.

Now Ben is the last of the farmhouse Mohicans. As the zombie from the opening-scene cemetery climbs through a window, Ben belatedly follows the late, hated Harry's advice and barricades himself in the basement, though not before tossing little zombie Karen across the room.

Once downstairs, Ben wearily, warily surveys Harry and Helen's bodies. Suddenly, Harry's eyes pop open and Ben seizes the opportunity to kill him again, pumping three bullets into his brain. This time, the act carries no sense of triumph. Moments later, he's forced to do the same for Helen. Upstairs, the thwarted dead mill aimlessly, sans purpose or direction.

Outside, the scene resembles a post-combat Vietnam morning; as a helicopter buzzes overhead, we can almost smell the napalm. We see an aerial view of Sheriff McClelland's posse crossing the field on foot, guns at the ready. A newsman intercepts the sheriff for an on-the-spot interview, leading to the following deathless exchange:

NEWSMAN: Chief, if I were surrounded by six or eight of these things, would I stand a chance with them?

SHERIFF: Well, there's no problem. If you had a gun, shoot 'em in the head, that's a sure way to kill 'em. If you don't, get yourself a club or a torch. Beat 'em or burn 'em, they go up pretty easy.

NEWSMAN: Are they slow-moving, Chief?

SHERIFF: Yeah, they're dead. They're . . . all messed up.

Cut briefly to Ben in the basement, then back to the posse and police systematically executing the retreating zombies, whose nocturnal uprising looks to have faded with the morning light as authorities easily quell the rebellion. Ben hears the activity and, with measured hope, climbs the stairs. When he peers out the window, a rifle shot from a posse member terminates his life. All that remains is the mop-up, as Ben is dragged, "another one for the fire," to a mass funeral pyre in a crushing photo montage as the stark credits appear.

The zeitgeist had been captured in a low-budget film can. In the parlance of the day, *Night of the Living Dead* had crawled out of nowhere to liberate the horror movie. That is indeed The End for the devastated viewer. But how did this dark cinematic miracle begin?

SHERIFF: *Well, there's no problem. If you had a gun, shoot 'em in the head, that's a sure way to kill 'em. If you don't, get yourself a club or a torch. Beat 'em or burn 'em, they go up pretty easy.*

BIRTH OF THE LIVING DEAD

> I thought George was kidding. People eating people!
> —Rudy Ricci

It was a cold and snowy day in January 1967 when three twentysomething principals of a modest Pittsburgh commercial/industrial film house, The Latent Image, Inc., repaired to a local eatery for a late lunch, well-lubricated with equally cold beers. The three— George A. Romero, John A. Russo ("Jack" to his friends), and Rudy Ricci—were bemoaning their business struggles. Russo, like the others a frustrated filmmaker, suggested they undertake a feature-film project for the drive-in circuit. Little—make that *nada*—did they know that such a seemingly whimsical notion would, less than three years later, result not only in a completed movie but an international pop-culture phenomenon that would endure decades into the future, still with no end in sight.

Meanwhile, back at the drawing board, or lunch table, major obstacles loomed. On the upside, The Latent Image HQ harbored all the basic equipment needed for low-budget feature-film production. The group had already produced such commissioned mini-epics as *The Calgon Story* (quite possibly the first detergent-oriented sci-fi film) and *Mr. Rogers Gets a Tonsillectomy* ("probably the scariest movie I ever made," Romero would later declare). But the company could only loosen some $6,000— and *that* with a little help from its friends—to fund filming. Even in 1967 Pittsburgh, six grand could barely buy a 30-second local commercial, let alone bankroll a marketable movie. What kind of feature could be lensed, or at least begun, on so low a budget?

"How about a monster movie?" Russo suggested.

While certainly a thought in the right direction, that inspired

> "How about a monster movie?" Russo suggested.

query didn't immediately lead to the creation of the immortal *Night of the Living Dead*. Russo recalls:

> The first concept—one that we all liked—was about monsters from outer space, only it was going to be a horror *comedy* instead of a horror drama. Some teenagers "hotrodding" around the galaxies were going to get involved with teenagers from Earth, befriending them, while cartoon-like authority figures stumbled around, trying to unearth "clues" to the crazy goings-on. The outer space teenagers were going to have a weird, funny pet called The Mess—a live garbage disposal that looked like a clump of spaghetti; you just tossed empty pop cans, popsicle sticks, or whatever into The Mess and it ate them. There was also going to be a wacky sheriff called Sheriff Suck, who was totally inept and kept being the butt of all the teenagers' jokes.

Make that a *long* way from the *Living Dead*. Indeed, that initial concept hewed closer to an earlier indie horror hit likewise lensed in the wilds of Pennsylvania, Irwin S. "Shorty" Yeaworth's *The Blob* (1958). "The main reason this project got scrapped," Russo elaborates, "was that we couldn't afford the props and special effects that would have been required to pull off the spaceship landing, The Mess, and so on. We had to scale our thinking down a little in terms of logistics." In this instance, lack of budget may have actually saved the day, or at least rescued The Latent Image crew from ongoing obscurity.

Fueled by such fave fright films as *Forbidden Planet* (1956), *Psycho* (1960), and especially the über-creepy *Invasion of the Body Snatchers* (1956), Russo began exploring a darker idea: A boy runs away from home following a fight with his brother—the same basic setup employed by an earlier, gentler indie film, Morris Engel's Brooklyn-set *Little Fugitive* (1953). The similarity ends there, however: Instead of frolicking at Coney Island like the latter film's titular runaway, Russo's young hero arrives at a clearing in the woods, where he discovers large panes of glass covering rotting bodies. "Ghoulish people or alien creatures would be feeding off the human corpses," Russo remembers, "setting them under the panes of glass so that the flesh would rapidly and properly decompose to suit the ghouls' tastes." Russo further determined: "Whatever we did should start in a cemetery because people find cemeteries spooky."

Russo relayed his bare-bones idea to Romero, who, a few days later, "amazed me by coming back with about forty really excellent pages of an exciting, suspenseful story. Everybody in our group loved it. We all decided this had to be *it*—the movie we would make. It was the first half of *Night of the Living Dead*."

Those forty pages described a new breed of screen monster. "George had the dead cannibalizing the living," says Russo. Some of those pages were adapted from an earlier prose effort. Romero states, "I had written a short story, which I had basically ripped off from a Richard Matheson novel called *I Am Legend*." In any case, according to Russo, "It clicked. It had action, tension, and horror. It turned us all on."

That turn-on resulted in the formation of Image Ten, the Latent Image-spawned outfit that would produce the group's feature-film debut. Beyond the three "R"s—Romero (director), Russo (co-writer), and Ricci (actor)—the company consisted of Latent Image cohorts Russell Streiner (producer) and Vince Survinski (production manager), cousin Rudy Ricci (actor), sibling Gary Streiner (sound), friends Karl Hardman (co-producer, actor) and Marilyn Eastman (makeup, actress), as well as partners in the industrial/commercial sound studio Hardman Associates, Inc., and attorney Dave Clipper.

Says Russo: "We agreed—and later it turned out to have been a critical decision—that Image Ten would be chartered to make only one feature motion picture. This was our way of guaranteeing the investors that we wouldn't tie up any profits by sinking them into a new project of which some of the group might not approve. In other words, if our very first venture made money, we would be obliged to pay it out to the risk takers who had supported us."

While eager to produce a feature film, not *all* of the ten were entirely enthused about going the straight-ahead horror route. As Russ Streiner, who would achieve scare-screen immortality as Barbara's brother-turned-zombie Johnny, noted, "Deep down inside, we were all serious filmmakers and somewhat disappointed that we had to resort to horror for our first film." Rudy Ricci was likewise unmoved by the undead cannibal concept. "I thought George was kidding. People eating people!"

Still, the premise ultimately earned enough support among the consortium to keep the project rolling. Romero's early draft for the as-yet-untitled horror film (known simply as Monster Flick during production, it would later acquire the obscure working title *Night of Anubis*, a reference to the Egyptian god of death; it then switched again to *Flesh Eaters*) pleased his partners for another reason. It had a small cast, "not counting extras," Russo points out, "and was within logistical constraints that could be kept within our ridiculously small budget."

> *Originally, Barbara was to emerge alive from the zombie onslaught after Ben drags her down to the cellar.*

Several Image Ten members, including Romero, Russo, Russ Streiner, Hardman, and Eastman, brainstormed the second half of the grisly tale, with actual scripting tasks falling to Russo: "I rewrote what George had written, changing whatever needed to be changed, and then wrote the second half of the script." During that process, several key changes were effected. "In the first script there wasn't a young couple," Russo reveals. "There was a middle-aged gravedigger named Tom. Then we decided the movie needed the young, good-looking girl in it. We made Tom younger and made him the boyfriend. That was all written in after the fact."

But the most notable alterations involved the ending. Originally, Barbara was to emerge alive from the zombie onslaught after Ben drags her down to the cellar. Ben's dire fate, however, was present from the get-go. Says Russo:

> We figured it would shock people and they would hate it, but it would make them keep talking about the picture as they were leaving the theater. Karl Hardman suggested a third possibility:

He wanted to see the little girl (Kyra Schon) standing in the foreground as the posse members finished burning the dead bodies and drove off. There would thus be one ghoul still left alive.

With the basic script in place, directorial chores were assigned to Romero, who'd grown up a committed movie addict in the Bronx, New York. Intellectually precocious, of Cuban and Lithuanian-American heritage and a bit of a loner, young George found refuge and inspiration in the local theaters. There he was enthralled by such screen wonders as the *Frankenstein* and *Dracula* re-releases, sci-fi greats, such as *The Thing (From Another World)* and *The Day the Earth Stood Still*, and his all-time fave, Michael Powell's and Emeric Pressburger's enchanting dance fantasy *The Tales of Hoffman*, all from 1951. The last-mentioned had aired on New York City's *Million Dollar Movie*, a TV series that emulated a movie theater by hosting multiple showings (as many as 10) of the same film over the course of a week. George caught them all. He later said, "I think that film made me want to make movies more than any of the other ones."

> "The Thing *was the movie that drew me to the genre. I was the right age, it was exactly the right time, and it had exactly the right effect on me."*
>
> —George Romero

As for his attraction to horror, Romero specifically credits Howard Hawks's above-cited sci-fi trailblazer, *The Thing*—complete with documentary-style overlapping dialogue—wherein characters trapped in a remote locale are forced to battle a powerful unidentified enemy. "*The Thing* was the movie that drew me to the genre. I was the right age, it was exactly the right time, and it had exactly the right effect on me."

"George Romero was absolutely wild about movies—wilder than any of the rest of us—and he started making them sooner than any of us, too," Russo recalls. Romero's filmmaking "career" in fact dated back to age eleven when his rich physician uncle, Monroe Yudell, presented him with an 8mm camera. Says Romero, "I used to take the camera out and mess around. I actually made my first little film at age eleven, *The Man from the Meteor*."

That now-lost science fiction effort, which reportedly bore more than a passing resemblance to Edgar G. Ulmer's *The Man from Planet X*, released earlier in that same year, 1951, provided a spark but didn't quite light a professional filmmaking fire. "I never went beyond thinking I could make a little movie, splice it together, and show it to the neighbors. It was playtime. It was like kids saying, 'Let's put a rock band together.' With absolutely no idea there was any sort of professional future in it for me."

The Man from the Meteor also marked the lifelong maverick's first run-in with authorities—not meddling producers but unamused security guards who intervened after the young director tossed a flaming dummy off a rooftop for the sake of his art. Along with underground legends George and Mike Kuchar, creators of such homegrown fare as *Sins of the Fleshapoids* and *Pussy on a Hot Tin Roof*, Romero likely ranked as the Bronx's leading teenage auteur—even if few beyond those fledgling filmmakers' families and friends were aware of it.

Later, at Suffield Academy, which Romero attended for a year after graduating high school at the tender age of sixteen, he made a more earnest film, a documentary entitled *Earthbottom*, which earned him an award *and* membership in the Future Scientists of America.

Those experiences, amateur though they may have been, supplied Romero with some much-needed know-how, the kind one couldn't easily acquire outside of specialty film schools like UCLA, certainly not at Pittsburgh's Carnegie Institute of Technology (later Carnegie Mellon), which Romero entered at seventeen to pursue an art degree. "In those days," he remembers, "a film appreciation course was all you could take. Which meant you watched *Battleship Potemkin* and talked about it."

Beyond his teenage 8mm efforts, later, ultimately abortive projects included *Whine of the Fawn*, a proposed art film in the vein of Ingmar Bergman's *The Virgin Spring* (also the basis for Wes Craven's influential 1972 feature-film debut *The Last House on the Left*). Romero wrote his own screenplay draft for *Whine of the Fawn* and, prophetically enough, interviewed then-adolescent future makeup effects collaborator Tom Savini to play the lead role.

As Savini recalls, "George came to my high school to audition people. Later I approached him about doing the makeup for his *Night of the Living Dead*. He was so busy I was following him around the studio flipping pages of my portfolio. He said, 'Yeah, man, we could use you.' Unfortunately, they called me to go into the army right before George shot. So when he did that, I was *in* Vietnam." Another Romero project, an offbeat 1960 comic anthology entitled *Expostulations*—boasting a budget of $2,000 and starring actor friend Ray Laine—was actually filmed but the soundtrack never completed.

Romero had even dipped a toe into the cinematic mainstream, working as a go-fer on a pair of major Hollywood productions that would play a significant role in shaping his negative view of the industry. First up was Alfred Hitchcock's 1959 *North by Northwest*, which left a teenage Romero less than wowed: "I didn't see him [Hitchcock] much, but I did see him some, and the way he worked was just so mechanical! There was no vitality on that set." His experiences assisting on the Doris Day comedy *It Happened to Jane* later that year only strengthened his deprecatory 'tude. "I really think that was the one that did it. It seemed so clearly like one of those things that was just a *deal* and nobody gave a shit about what was going on."

> **"I didn't see Hitchcock much, but I did see him some, and the way he worked was just so mechanical!"**
>
> —George Romero

The aspiring auteur gained far more useful knowledge working at Pittsburgh film labs and delivering news footage to local TV stations. Says Romero, "I just went down and hung out at one of these film labs. My first job as a P.A. was literally bicycling news; news was on film. These journeyman guys would be splicing this stuff together while smoking cigarettes over flammable glue pots! It was like a pressroom. It was in one of those labs that I learned the basics."

Feature filmmaking had been Romero's goal since cofounding The Latent Image in 1963. After dropping out of Carnegie Tech and leading a restless boho existence for a couple of years, Romero and former college bud Russ Streiner opened the production house in a $65-a-month office that doubled as the pair's crash pad. John Russo was invited to join them but opted instead for a two-year army stretch. Says Russo: "George and Russ told me they were going to start a commercial film company and if they were doing well by the time I got out, I could come to work with them."

The Latent Image ranks increased to three when local roller-rink owner Vince Survinski bought his way into the outfit in a bid to fulfill his own long-simmering celluloid ambitions: He hoped to produce a fact-based Rudy Ricci script about an East German prison escapee/defector named Aberhardt Doelig. While that project fell through, Survinski stayed on.

At first there wasn't much shaking beyond wedding and baby pictures. Romero would sell an occasional oil painting for fifty bucks or so, enough to allow the three to purchase a pet monkey (!) and a table-hockey game. In the beginning, they spent more time playing with both than meeting nonexistent clients' imaginary demands.

Armed with a 16mm Bolex and some rudimentary lighting equipment, the three scored their first significant gig creating a cost-conscious TV spot for Pittsburgh's Buhl Planetarium, depicting a rocket ship landing on the moon. Romero painted the backdrops, while Streiner molded the clay that formed the lunar surface; Rudy Ricci's brother Mark chipped in the toy rocket. The ad took off, so to speak: The client loved it, forked over $1,600, and the spot even played during local drive-in intermissions, marking Romero's first big-screen exposure.

That effort proved successful enough to attract bigger players like Iron City ("The Beer Drinker's Beer") and Duke beer. In the latter spot, a proto-redneck of the sort that would join *Night*'s posse greedily gulps down not only *his* Duke brew but his understandably bitter half's too, leading the miffed missus to moan, "And I had to pick a natural man!"

After The Latent Image secured a thirty thou business loan and relocated to a more expansive office space, larger Pittsburgh-based corporate clients, like Alcoa and Heinz, came calling. This resulted in a workaholic lifestyle for the group. Russo recalls: "We had gotten a reputation in some circles of being an energetic nucleus of creative maniacs who could make good films for those who couldn't afford—or didn't want—to spend very much money. We were fiercely proud of our work. But most of the time, we were broke, frustrated, and physically and mentally exhausted."

It was *The Calgon Story*, however, budgeted at a lofty $90,000, that brought much-needed cash into the company coffers, allowing the lads to spring for their first 35mm camera. It also injected them with the confidence to plan their feature-film plunge in 1967. Though the imaginative ad, a spoof of the hit sci-fi film *Fantastic Voyage* (1966), received but a single airing due to Calgon's sale to a new corporation, Romero cites it as a major turning point. "The Calgon spot, in fact, was the trigger. It gave the company a little money to be able to take the time to get something going. We probably would have eventually gotten it up some other way, but that's really what enabled us to make *Night of the Living Dead*."

> "We couldn't afford to buy or build a house to destroy," Russo recalls, "since the $12,000 had to cover all the costs of production."

But a long day's journey into *Night* yet awaited. While the group had attracted an additional ten investors, swelling the budget to a skeletal twelve grand, they still needed to procure the film's crucial main setting, the farmhouse where the bulk of the zombie and human horror would unfold. "We couldn't afford to buy or build a house to destroy," Russo recalls, "since the $12,000 had to cover all the costs of production."

Luckily, a young Latent Image intern named Jack Ligo provided a critical lead. Says Russo: "A large white farmhouse in Evans City, Pennsylvania, was going to be bulldozed because the owners were intending to use the property as a sod farm. It looked perfect. The owner agreed to rent it to us for several months before he bulldozed it for about $300 a month. It had last been used as a summer camp for a church group. There was no running water, and, while we were working there, we had to carry our water from a spring down a steep hill, quite a distance away. The house didn't have a suitable basement for filming. So we decided to film our basement scenes on a set built in the basement of the building where The Latent Image was headquartered."

Now that they had their setting, the eager filmmakers rushed headlong into production, ready or not, before their enthusiasm had a chance to wane. While placing Romero in the director's chair was a no-brainer, many of the other assignments were largely improvised. Sound engineer Gary Streiner, younger brother of Russ, recalls: "I wasn't a soundman. I was just a guy who put his hand up and said, 'Okay, I'll do that.'" Gary felt inspired by the troupe's determination. "I saw people who were actually doing things, not just talking about them. So many people don't do things out of fear. I think the beauty of The Latent Image and the beauty of the association with George and the rest of the guys was that there was no fear. It was, 'What did we have to lose? What's the alternative? Nothing!'"

Nearly all The Latent Image/Image Ten principals multitasked during the production. Romero not only directed but worked, uncredited, as both cinematographer and chief film editor; Russ Streiner served as a producer, while Karl Hardman operated as a producer and still photographer, ultimately, compiling some 1,250 publicity snaps. Vince Survinski was the production director; George Kosana handled production manager chores. All of the above also played onscreen roles ranging from key characters (Hardman's Harry Cooper) to iconic cameos (Romero's Washington reporter). Propman Charles O'Dato was a part-time taxidermist, so he contributed the animal heads mounted in the farmhouse, each of whom received its own close-up in a scene later famously quoted (and affectionately spoofed) in Sam Raimi's *Evil Dead 2*.

As John Russo summed it up: "We had the zest and determination to work together as a group to pull our ideas off. We could not have anticipated that the Monster Flick would eventually be called a 'classic.' But we fully expected, every step of the way, that we would make a very good motion picture of its type, better than most other pictures in the genre. We were that cocky."

A *Night* to Remember:
What the *Living Dead* Means to Me
by Frank Henenlotter

I first saw *Night of the Living Dead* at the Valley Stream Drive-In in Valley Stream, Long Island. I think it was maybe the fall of '68 or the spring of '69. *Night* was top of a double bill, so I assume it was first run. I'd been out filming one of my amateur 8mm epics with three friends, Tom, Colleen, and Emma. We'd gotten done filming early, so we figured we'd go to the drive-in, which was the fun place for seeing schlock; and any movie named *Night of the Living Dead must* be schlock, right? How quickly the foolish learn.

We sat in that car feeling as trapped and claustrophobic as the people in that house, blindsided by what was obviously the most potent horror film of the '60s since *Psycho*. At one point, someone heading to the snack bar must have brushed against our car because Emma let out with a scream that I thought would bring the cops. It was also the first time I ever looked away from the screen—mommy getting killed by her little-girl zombie was, at that time, the most shocking thing I'd ever seen on the screen, and it was just too much for me.

I didn't feel like we'd spent an evening at a drive-in; I felt like we'd been assaulted. Of course, it was a far more innocent era back then. A little bit of blood went a loooooong way in that pre-Fulci world, especially when there was no Internet for fans to warn and buzz about films in advance. Funny, but I have no recollection what the co-feature was. We either didn't stay for it, or it was erased from my memory in the wake of *Night*. As it was, long after the film was over, Colleen sat in the car crying.

I didn't catch up with *Night* again until it emerged as a midnight movie in Manhattan where I saw it a number of times more. Nowadays, however, I'm sick of zombie movies and just ignore them. Yes, they're gorier and faster paced and blah, blah, blah, but none of them catch the horrific beauty of George Romero's one-of-a-kind original.

Cult writer/director FRANK HENENLOTTER is the brains behind *Basket Case*, *Brain Damage*, *Frankenhooker*, *Bad Biology* and other outré cult fare. His *Basket Case* would occupy the Waverly Theater weekend midnight slot a decade after *Night of the Living Dead*.

CASTING A CULT CLASSIC

"They're dead. They're . . . all messed up."
—Sheriff McClelland, *Night of the Living Dead*

Before filming could begin, Image Ten looked to cast the core characters caught up in the zombie menace. Most crucial was the lead, Ben, who would have to carry much of the movie on his shoulders. As originally written, the character was a resourceful but rough and crude-talking trucker, a role initially envisioned for Rudy Ricci. Those plans changed when a thirty-one-year-old African-American actor named Duane Jones competed for the part.

"A mutual friend of George's and mine was a woman by the name of Betty Ellen Haughey," Russ Streiner relates. "She grew up in Pittsburgh, but at that time she was living in New York and she knew of Duane Jones. He'd started off in a suburb just outside of Pittsburgh, yet he was off in New York making a living as a teacher and an actor. And she said to us, when *Night of the Living Dead* was really developing in preproduction and building steam, 'You should meet this friend of mine from New York.' Duane happened to be in Pittsburgh visiting his family for one of the holidays, and we auditioned him. And immediately everyone, including Rudy Ricci, said, 'Hey, this is the guy that should be Ben.'"

Romero agrees with that recollection: "Duane Jones was the best actor we met to play Ben. If there was a film with a Black actor in it, it usually had a racial theme, like *The Defiant Ones.*

31

Consciously I resisted writing new dialogue 'cause he happens to be Black. We just shot the script. Perhaps *Night of the Living Dead* is the first film to have a Black man playing the lead role regardless of, rather than because of, his race." (Contrary to that opinion, oft-expressed by Romero and others, Jones was *not* the first black actor to be cast in a non-ethnic-specific starring role; Sidney Poitier earned that distinction in 1965 playing a reporter in James B. Harris's nuclear sub suspenser *The Bedford Incident* and, the following year, portraying an ex-military man turned horse-breaker in Ralph Nelson's western *Duel at Diablo*, doubly ironic given *Duel*'s racial theme, albeit one centering on Native-Americans.)

At that, black actors were no strangers to Latent Image ads. "In looking at some of those old [mid-'60s] commercials," says Russo, "we always had black actors and we always gave a lot of work to people who had a tough time getting it. That was our nature, so we didn't blink at casting a black actor in that role." The slim, handsome Jones was himself quite familiar with aspects of the ad world, having earlier posed as an *Ebony* magazine model in layouts selling everything from liquor to Listerine.

> "We didn't blink at casting a black actor in that role."
> —John Russo

Still, Russo detected an initial uneasiness. "At first he distrusted those of us on the crew, behind the camera. He wondered why we would cast a black man in the lead role of our movie, and he thought we might be out to exploit him in some way." Jones quickly overcame any brief initial reluctance he may have had but did not completely separate his ethnicity from the character: "It never occurred to me that I was hired *because* I was black. But it did occur to me that because I was black, it would give a different historic element to the film."

While still earthy and capable, Ben acquired an at once intense and understated quality that Jones brought to the role. According to the late Karl Hardman: "His [Ben's] dialogue was that of a lower-class/uneducated person. Duane Jones was a very well-educated man. He was fluent in a number of languages." A B.A.

graduate of the University of Pittsburgh, Jones had dabbled in writing, painting, and music, studied in Norway and Paris, and was completing an M.A. in Communications at N.Y.U. between *Night* shoots. "Duane simply refused to do the role as it was written. As I recall, I believe that Duane himself upgraded his own dialogue to reflect how he felt the character should present himself."

A look at the original script (courtesy of Marilyn Eastman, who'd saved the only known existing copy) demonstrates the difference. When white Ben first arrives at the house, he says to Barbara: "Don't you mind the creep outside. I can handle him. There's probably gonna be lots more of 'em. Soons they fin' out about us. Ahm outa gas. Them pumps over there is locked. Is there food here? Ah get us some grub. Then we beat 'em off and skedaddle. Ah guess you putzed with the phone."

As translated by Duane Jones, the same speech goes: "Don't worry about him. I can handle him. Probably be a whole lot more of them when they find out about us. The truck is out of gas. The pump out here is locked—is there a key? We can try to get out of here if we get some gas. Is there a key?" (*Ben tries the phone.*) "'Spose you've tried *this*. I'll see if I can find some food."

Same basic information, but in the original script, *white* Ben is a stereotype. Via Jones's interpretation, black Ben is not.

According to soundman Gary Streiner, "Ben was Duane in most every way. Duane was very intelligent, thorough, and professional. If he wasn't on camera, he was running his lines or just plain reading. Duane was not chatting people up when not working, but you were never waiting on Duane because he didn't know his lines. I think he adopted his interpretation of Ben in the casting session and for evermore was the holder of the character."

Hardman approved of Jones's approach and adjusted his own performance accordingly. "Duane played the character so calmly that it was decided I should play Harry Cooper [Harry "Tinsdale" in the original script] in a frenetic fashion with fist-clenching and that sort of thing, for contrast. There was absolutely no working up into character. Harry Cooper started up with a hardass attitude, and he did not deviate one iota."

Jones also contributed what proved to be an important component in perfect synch with the zeitgeist, an element vital to the film's runaway success: black rage. In that pre-"blaxploitation" era, Jones's Ben emerged as a cross between contemporaneous characters in a Sidney Poitier vein (e.g., *In the Heat of the Night*'s Virgil Tibbs, *Lilies of the Fields*' Homer Smith) and the edgier African-American protags, like Richard Roundtree (*Shaft*) and Ron O'Neal (*Superfly*), who would soon change forever the image of black men on screen. While he earned audience support, Jones's Ben made for an unusually harsh "hero," even shooting an unarmed Harry Cooper in cold blood (though it would be hard to say he didn't deserve it).

But that was a large part of the point: Ben *wasn't* a hero. He was an average guy, an everyman of any ethnic stripe, who simply reacted to an irrational situation with strong survival instincts and a competence that, though far from infallible, surpassed that of his five adult companions trapped in that zombie-besieged farmhouse.

Since Ben's character *was* written sans a specific ethnicity, there's never any overt reference to race in the film—not even in those heated shouting matches between Ben and Harry (though one senses the ever-seething Harry's unvoiced bigotry). Yet the character's black identity undeniably adds another layer of anger to the pair's ferocious battles for alpha-dog status. Ben's blackness also lent greater tension to his relationship with the alternately comatose and hysterical Barbara. As Russ Streiner admits, "We knew that there would probably be a bit of controversy, just from the fact that an African-American man and a white woman are holed up in a farmhouse." When Barbara claws at her clothes, citing the house's unbearable heat, the scene suggests a subtext of sexual repression and fear. John Russo points out: "And then she falls into his arms. And I know that a lot of the bigots in the country are going to be thinking, 'Oh my God, now what's he going to do? He's got this white woman in his arms,' and lays her down on the couch and he unfastens her coat . . . and so I was aware that it might have those kind of vibes."

A panicky Barbara then angrily lashes out. "It was written in the script that Barbara was to smack Ben at least three times," says actress Judith O'Dea. "But this was a very sensitive issue for Duane Jones at that time and he said, 'I can accept being smacked once. But I don't want to play it the way that you've written it.' It was rewritten . . . I gave him a smack. And he gave me the fist—right in the face." When Ben punches Barbara, a white woman—this *before* Poitier's groundbreaking smack of a racist aristocrat (Larry Gates) in *In the Heat of the Night*—that act supplied another envelope-pushing note to the proceedings. Those scenes provoked palpable reactions in audiences of the day.

Jones himself had opposed the punch, rejecting the idea that Ben would behave in so violent a manner. Russo concurs with that evaluation, "It really is out of character for him to hit her, but we needed him to because we had to get her unconscious for the sake of the plot. The truck driver, the other character, would have hit her."

Jones, in general, proved notably nonviolent. Says Romero: "He hated any kind of firearm—he really hated that gun. So we had to have somebody hand it to him. It had to be taken from him right after. He had to take one of the boards off the wall and he hit my camera. He couldn't work for like an hour!"

Jones received on-the-job gun training from jack-of-all-trades Lee Hartman, who did quadruple duty as a background reporter in the newsroom scenes, a funeral-suited zombie, and a posse member: "Duane Jones never shot a rifle before, so I let him have mine. I said, 'Keep it against your shoulder.' It was a 30–30 rifle. 'Aim it at the bottom of that tree there.' He was aiming at the top. 'It's gonna go a mile and a half if you miss it.' He had a real bullet in there; we didn't have any blanks." Despite his antipathy toward weapons, Jones quickly got the hang of it.

One thing the actor consistently did *not* want to back down from was his character's color. "Duane actually thought we *should* take note of it," says Romero. "Now I think we probably should have. Not to make it a big point, but to refer to it at least. We had written this guy as angry for no reason at all. But that automatic rage that comes out, that would have been an interesting overlay. Duane was the only one who knew this." Romero also allowed that if they *had* consciously played the race card, the results might have been heavy-handed, disrupting *Night*'s delicate balance.

At one point, when the filmmakers considered lensing an alternate ending that would permit Ben to survive, it was again Duane Jones who stood firm. "I convinced George that the black community would rather see me dead than saved, after all that had gone on, in a corny and symbolically confusing way." Besides, said Jones, "The heroes never die in American movies. The jolt of that and the double jolt of the hero figure being black seemed like a double-barreled whammy."

Many audiences perceived the parallel between America's increasingly violent civil rights struggles—particularly, the then-recent assassination of Martin Luther King by racist hitman James Earl Ray, with the suspected cooperation of the FBI—and Ben's execution at the guns of the redneck posse at film's end. Without a black actor in the lead, *Night* would still have been an innovative shocker but wouldn't have hit the cultural nerves it did.

In 1987, shortly before his premature death from heart failure the following year, Jones granted *Fangoria* journalist Tim Ferrante an extremely rare, exclusive in-depth interview, wherein the actor—who'd largely shunned his association with the cult hit, adopting something of a "Ben there, done that" attitude—revealed his feelings about working on the then-twenty-year-old film: "Even when I wanted people to leave me alone about it, I never regretted that I did it. I remember it as great fun. We worked very hard. There was a wonderful feeling of camaraderie and good humor and goodwill. They were very considerate people to work for. You never felt that you were being abused or misused. They used to have to drive me back to my parents' home, all the way out to Duquesne, every night. Jack Russo, usually. He never did that begrudgingly. They were wonderful folks to work for. They really were."

Jones owned up to having problems with many critics' perception of the film. "The thing that used to bother me the most was that interviewers just *assumed* that we were a bunch of amateur actors. It was an interesting mix of amateurs and professional actors, which was even more clever on George's part."

Jones also had high praise for the filmmaking approach. "The best storytelling in the world goes on in commercials. So there was that cleanliness and very sharp editorial eye that went into it. Internally, in the film itself, they captured somehow an independent aura. If you really look at it technically, it was most professionally done."

In that same interview, Jones conjured a rare sour moment, a negative incident that had haunted him for two decades. "I guess because everything was so pleasant that one of the things that sticks out in my mind is a moment that was strangely *unpleasant.* There was a point where George and the crew were planning a shot and setting up. It was getting to be late afternoon, evening, and this magnificent butterfly wandered into the house. I remember clearly that it landed on the far wall. And to a person, every single one of us stopped what we were doing and we were just standing around admiring this beautiful, beautiful creature that had just come in as a spirit among us and attached itself to the wall. Soon it was time to get started and someone thought that his idea of a joke would be to come and smash the butterfly. I remember the stunned silence of the group, and the visceral reaction of wanting to regurgitate was just so real that that moment sticks out in my mind that it was out of synch with everything. Nobody could believe that he had done that to us— and to the butterfly. I don't think we ever quite convinced him that it was a horrible thing to do."

Though Jones would go on to appear in several subsequent regional and New York City films—most notably as an academic vampire opposite Marlene Clark in Bill Gunn's 1973 cult fave *Ganja and Hess* ("another underground classic," Jones once stated, "one of the most beautifully shot films of that period")— Hollywood didn't come calling. Nor were any other *Night* players summoned. Jones had his own theory on that subject. "For whatever reasons, the reality of who we were in the first place was never clear. Critics assumed we were all a group of amateurs from Pittsburgh. The so-called 'amateur' they decided to bestow professionalism on was George Romero. I would never for one second begrudge George any of his acclaim and fame. But some of us could have used another kind of boost to our career, whereas nobody ever assumed we were actors or professionals in the first place."

Instead of pursuing a West Coast film avenue, Jones followed his first loves, devoting most of his professional life to the theater and teaching, separated, for the most part, from his Ben persona: "I was teaching at N.Y.U. and I used to walk past the Waverly—I used to get out of the subway there—and it showed at the Waverly at midnight for years. One time I was with a group of acting students after class. We were sitting in a restaurant in Manhattan. And it was getting on into the Halloween season and two of the kids were sitting across the table from me and I looked up at the television and realized that the movie being shown was *Night of the Living Dead*. So I glanced at it for a moment and we went on talking. I kept glancing at it too often because eventually they followed my eyes to see what I was looking at and they looked at the television. And they did not recognize that it was me. Then, when one of the students *did* identify that that was me, the other two argued that it was not. So we left it at that and went on talking. One said, 'What ever happened to him?' I was sitting across the table from him!"

Ferrante fondly recalls his meeting with Duane Jones. "The moment he spoke you just knew he was a special human being. You suddenly forgot he portrayed Ben; he was far too interesting in many other ways. He was gracious, fiercely intelligent, funny, charming, respectful . . . it was impossible not to like him." Jones had zero interest in exploiting his cult rep. "It was his practice to not draw attention to himself," Ferrante explains. "He wasn't going to live in a world that forever identified 'Duane Jones' as the star of *Night of the Living Dead* and nothing else. He wasn't arrogant about it, though. He certainly recognized the power of the movie and his role in it, but he was too gifted an intellectual to permit that kind of societal typecasting. I remember pointing out that millions of people loved him in that role; his withdrawal from it wouldn't make that go away. He appreciated and understood it and was somewhat grateful, but such singular adoration wasn't a necessary ingredient in his life. He expected people to recognize him as a person and not as Ben, which they did because that's how he carried himself. He had class. Besides, he was such an arresting man. *Night* was a mere sliver of his life."

Jones's *Night* cohorts felt the same way. Judith Ridley recalls, "Duane was the only black man on the shoot and perhaps he was feeling a little out of place. He'd always bury his head in a book; he was always reading. But you did really admire him—he was a very classy person." Gary Streiner holds a similar impression. "I really liked Duane but I didn't get to the point of friendship with him as I did as with lots of the others." Says a grateful John Russo, "I doubt that our movie

> "I doubt that our movie would have been a success without Duane Jones."
> —John Russo

would have been a success without him. His screen presence was one of the key ingredients that helped lift that low-budget pipe dream up by its bootstraps and make it into something that it almost had no right to be. The dream became reality, partly because of Duane Jones."

With Ben present and accounted for, other key roles went to a variety of Latent Image cohorts. For Barbara, Romero originally wanted Betty Aberlin—"Lady Aberlin" on the Pittsburgh-based *Mr. Rogers' Neighborhood*, for whom The Latent Image had occasionally labored—but a perhaps overprotective Fred Rogers discouraged her from appearing in a horror film. The part went instead to Judith O'Dea, a twenty-three-year-old actress and voice-over specialist who had been working in regional theater since the age of 15 and had recently returned to the Steel City after a stint in L.A., where she'd been trying to break into the Hollywood acting ranks. "I had been there a short while when Karl called and said we're gonna make a movie. It changed my life. It was exciting. It was where I wanted to be. Anything that came my way, whether it was long hours, whether it was waiting two months to go back and readdress a scene that was already done, didn't bother me. I loved doing it."

O'Dea also enjoyed working with Romero. "George would describe what he was trying to achieve in each scene—plot progression, emotion, and so on—then let me 'go at it.' Barbara evolved every time we shot a scene." And Romero allowed for ad-libbing when the situation called for it. Says O'Dea, "The one section I can recall specifically is when Ben tells Barbara what happened to him, and then she explains what happened to her and her brother. For me, that was all ad-lib. I had read the script, but then we just, basically, went by the seat of our pants." She adds, "That scene was done fine on the first take. I had really gotten into it. I can remember crying like a fiend when they filmed me talking about Johnny. But something went wrong with the sound recorder, or so they had thought. We did shoot it again, but they later found out that the first take was okay."

O'Dea credits the cast and crew's earnest approach with putting the story over. "When we were shooting, we wanted it to be as real as possible. I know that many of us really did go through a lot of that emotion and terror making it. It wasn't done with tongue in cheek. It was done very seriously." And O'Dea had the literal scars to prove it. "[Duane] never made contact with my chin. But he sure put black and blue marks on my arms where he grabbed me during that fight scene. I didn't realize till I got home how black and blue they were." But the filmmakers saved her scariest moments for last. "Barbara's death sequence was an extremely frightening thing to film—being pulled out amongst all those people."

Russo feels fortunate that an actress of O'Dea's caliber was available for the role: "Judy O'Dea brought a tremendous energy to her part in the movie. The way she ran, you really believe her life's in danger, the way she's terrified and so on."

Regarding Barbara's oft-criticized "helpless" behavior, O'Dea maintains, "I believe Barbara exemplifies honesty. How she got through her horror ordeal is probably the way many real people would. . . . When the zombies were breaking into the house, she snapped back into reality. It was time to fight back. And she did, until her death. If Barbara is remembered for her honest behavior in the 'evolution of women in horror' then I'll be thrilled."

Today O'Dea notes: "I believe everyone was too much involved with the 'present' and all its challenges to think that movie magic was being made. I honestly had no idea it would have such lasting impact on our culture. People treat you differently. [I'm] ho-hum Judy O'Dea until they realize [I'm] Barbara from *Night of the Living Dead*. All of a sudden [I'm] not so ho-hum anymore. I've had several decades of families come up to me and say, 'You scared me to death when I was a little kid.' The first thing out of my mouth is, 'Oh, I'm so sorry' . . . And then I stop myself and say, 'Well, I guess that's what we were *supposed* to do.'"

> *"I believe everyone was too much involved with the 'present' and all its challenges to think that movie magic was being made."*
>
> —Judith O'Dea

In addition to working at The Latent Image, Russ Streiner had been an actor at the Pittsburgh Playhouse, so he seemed a natural to play Barbara's bored, mocking brother, Johnny. Besides, as Russo points out, "Russ kind of got pressed into service because we could save money by casting ourselves in various roles."

As for Johnny's trademark gloves, Romero explains, "Since Russ was *not* Robert Redford, we figured that we would need some way to recognize him and that's why we used the driving gloves, to recognize him later when he returns from the dead." Streiner was very conscious of the props and made sure to milk them to the max. "You might remember me putting on the driving glove in the cemetery. I was being very blatant about it. When I burst in through the door, my hand with the glove slapped on the door jamb in direct view of the audience." And the nerdy pens poking from Johnny's shirt pocket? Per Karl Hardman, "We thought he looked like an accountant or CPA and they always have pens in their pockets."

Johnny's teasing relationship with Barbara still strikes a chord with modern audiences. "I think underneath it typifies the kind of sibling relationship that a lot of brothers and sisters have," Russ Streiner interprets the scene's credibility. "Brothers especially get into taunting and tormenting their younger sisters. And I think that comes through to the fans, and a lot of people comment on it. 'Oh, that's how my brother used to treat me,' and so forth. So I wanted to keep it realistic on that level. That plus the fact that we as actors knew what was coming, we knew that this was going to be the very first onset of the living dead things, and I just wanted to set the stage for the gloomy things to come."

In fact, the pair's increasingly juvenile behavior reinforces the film's dark fairy-tale flavor, as the two young adults regress into a veritable Hansel and Gretel, ripe, edible prey for the creatures of the forest—or the graveyard. "Russ and I had a great time doing that scene," O'Dea recalls. "It amazed me how it took me back, warp speed, to when I was a little girl visiting the cemetery with my mother. Those visits always scared me . . . *Death* scared me back then. So being upset with Johnny in our cemetery scene was pretty easy to do."

To portray the quarreling Coopers, Harry and Helen, the filmmakers chose close cohorts Karl Hardman (born Karl Hardman Schon) and Marilyn Eastman. In addition to running Hardman Associates, Karl had performed in commercials like The Latent Image's *The Calgon Story* and, before that, like Judith O'Dea, had tried his luck in Los Angeles. Karl's on- and off-screen daughter, Kyra Schon, remembers, "He did study acting out there. He did some theater. But he didn't get anything permanent, so he moved back to Pittsburgh." Marilyn Eastman had worked extensively in regional theater as well as TV, performing such varied roles as a live commercials model and weather girl to a lady vampire on local horror host Bill "Chilly Billy" Cardille's *Chiller Theater.*

Both Karl and Marilyn were also well-known figures in the Pittsburgh radio orbit, with Hardman logging in several years on a mega-popular comedy show called *Cordic and Company*, for which he wrote skits and voiced some fifteen characters. The two also recorded and sold routines for radio syndication before that market dried up in the mid-'60s. The highly verbal, versatile pair improvised much of their *Night* dialogue, with Eastman coining the oft-quoted line, "We may not enjoy living together, but dying together isn't going to solve anything!"

A receptionist at Hardman Associates, the then-nineteen-year-old Judith Ridley was originally considered for the part of Barbara before being assigned the somewhat less demanding Judy role. Judith O'Dea affirms, "They originally considered Ridley over me because she was a hell of a lot prettier than I was! I have one of those character faces." In fact, on *Night's* iconic original poster, Ridley's face is weirdly superimposed over O'Dea's body. But the ultimate casting choice proved the correct one. "I was dreadful when I read for Barbara," Ridley confesses. "I'd never done any acting. I think they took pity on me. They liked me. They made a little spot for me. But I was not prepared to be Barbara. I couldn't have done that role."

Keith Wayne (born Ronald Keith Hartman), cast as Judy's earnest young beau Tom, was, likewise, completely new to acting, though not to performing—he led the busy local band Ronnie and the Jesters and would later front such musical aggregates as Keith Wayne and the Unyted Brass Works. He spent much of the *Night* shoot commuting between Pittsburgh and a steady weekend gig in Myrtle Beach, South Carolina. Romero, for one, was quite impressed by the lad: "Of all the people in the cast, I thought he was the celebrity. He was the showbiz cat. He was our Frankie Avalon."

> "Of all the people in the cast, I thought he was the celebrity. He was the showbiz cat. He was our Frankie Avalon."
>
> —George Romero, on Keith Wayne

No *Night* performer would go on to enjoy a more devoted cult following than 9-year-old killer kiddie Kyra Schon, who commits the most transgressive acts of all in a movie packed with them—she kills her mom and devours her dad (!). She was literally fed up with him. For many '60s youths and later punks and headbangers who proudly bore her image emblazoned on T-shirts or tattooed on their bodies, Kyra represented the ultimate in rebelliousness. Her only two words of dialogue in the film—"I hurt"—spoke volumes about the failure of her bickering parents and their misguided values—and, by extension, the entire social system—to nurture her.

A schoolteacher today, Kyra looks back fondly at her time as a cannibal kid. "The role had originally been written for a boy but since there was a boy shortage that year, they settled for the nearest young, warm body they could find. That was me. I was already a horror-movie junkie at that point in my life, watching

Chiller Theater every Saturday. *The Crawling Eye* and *The Wasp Woman* were my favorite movies. I just couldn't believe my good fortune that I was gonna get to play a little monster and kill people. What could be better?"

> "I just couldn't believe my good fortune that I was gonna get to play a little monster and kill people. What could be better?"
>
> —Kyra Schon

Kyra certainly made the most of her limited screen time. "I don't do a whole lot in the movie! For most of it, I'm lying there on a table, and that was one night. Then there was the struggle with Duane Jones. That was kind of funny. I was sure he was going to miss the couch completely and throw me through the wall. But he didn't. Then there was the trowel thing. . . . Shooting the scene wasn't nearly as dramatic as watching it. I was stabbing into a pillow with the trowel. And then someone was behind me throwing chocolate syrup against the wall to make it look like the blood was splattering. I had a great time doing it. I didn't feel that way so much when I was really young, because I took a lot of teasing as a result of it. Maybe it was just their way of paying attention. But I never liked being the center of attention."

Today Kyra doesn't shy away from her association with Karen—nor do her students. "[They] always ask me, 'Which one were you in? Oh, you were in that old black-and-white one!' And I say, 'Yeah, the *real* one.'"

Like most of *Night*'s participants, Kyra ended up doing double-duty on the film. "I was used as the upstairs body because they needed someone to drag away. I guess of all of the people there, I was probably the smallest." Still, the most traumatic moment for Kyra occurred watching rather than appearing in the film. "I never liked seeing my father shot and falling down the stairs. It was too much, watching him grapple with that coat rack."

For the most part, though, the experience proved a childhood high point: "It was fascinating to watch ordinary people transformed into flesh-eating ghouls. I loved seeing zombies stand around the barbecue grills waiting for their hot dogs, zombies smoking cigarettes, zombies driving cars. There was a surreal quality to that scene that could only be truly appreciated by the mind of a child."

Another key to Image Ten's successful secondary casting: hiring people to essentially play themselves. William Schallertesque Charles Craig, a radio and TV veteran who'd worked as Alan Freed's newsman on the pioneering rock deejay's *Moondog Show* in Cleveland and served as an actor and writer at Hardman Associates, portrayed the television newscaster who relayed the breaking bad news regarding the ongoing ghoul epidemic.

"It was pure happenstance I was on the scene at that time as an experienced newsman," Craig later related. He even wrote his own news copy *and* added a turn as an intestine-chomping zombie. Craig could also be heard as the eponymous character in the local morning radio comedy series *The Teahouse of Jason Flake*, produced by and featuring Hardman and Eastman.

Similarly, *Chiller Theater* host and all-around WIIC-TV frontman Bill Cardille agreed to play the television field reporter—and had to wait some twelve hours on-set before his turn arrived, after a full night working at the station. "When you see me in that movie, that's after no sleep for about two days."

Local news cameraman Steve Hutsko signed on to appear as Bill's cameraman. His story is typical of *Night*'s naturalistic casting. He'd earlier accompanied Cardille to the set to shoot a local TV story about the filming in progress: "We went to the old farmhouse and they were setting up things. That's how we got involved. Bill Cardille asked me, 'Do you want to be in the film? I'm gonna be a reporter and they need a cameraman.'"

Hutsko took a week's vacation to make sure he could fit the filming into his schedule. "[There] didn't seem like there was a script for anybody," he recalls. "I never saw one. The director said, 'When you go on a news assignment, what do you normally do?' I said, 'If we got an assignment like this, and we're out there half a day, you call into the office and let 'em know what's going on.' So I told Bill, 'What if I tell you I'm gonna call the office?' And he said, 'Go ahead, Steve.'" The moment plays completely smoothly on screen.

Production manager George Kosana contributed a memorable

bit as Sheriff McClelland, ad-libbing his lines, including the deathless, "They're dead. They're . . . all messed up." (Which ranks right up there with Streiner's scripted, "They're coming to get you, Barbara!") Posse member Vince Survinski, meanwhile, became the unwitting villain of the piece—it was his perfect shot that nailed Ben. "I shot the hero without knowing it," he later revealed. "I didn't know what I was shooting at in that scene until I saw the picture. The first time I saw it with an audience of kids at a matinee, I was afraid to leave the theater! I waited until they all left and snuck out a back door!"

Rounding up the requisite zombies posed far less of a challenge than initially anticipated. According to Russo, "We were worried that we did not have enough money to pay a sufficient number of extras. But we got plenty of volunteers, including people from in and around Evans City, who jumped at the chance to be in a movie. We let them be posse members or made them up as ghouls. They were patient and enthusiastic. They gave the movie a 'real people' look that probably added to the believability."

Casting a wide zombie net, Image Ten likewise looked to their immediate peers for assistance. Romero recalls, "We had a company doing commercials and industrial films, so there were a lot of people from the advertising game who all wanted to come out and be zombies."

Sometimes, the filmmakers resorted to more aggressive recruitment tactics. Evans City cabinet shop owner Ella Mae Smith remembers, "We were sitting in our yard and a car pulled up in front. A girl got out and she said, 'Hi, we're from the movie back there that we're making. How would you and your husband like to be in it?' And of course my husband said, 'No.' And I said, 'Yeah, I think that that would be lots of fun.' So I kind of pleaded and begged and he said, 'Okay, I'll go back and see what's going on.' But we had no idea what the film was about. So we went back and they started putting this goop all over our faces and we were ghouls. I was thrilled to death our names were up there! Maybe it was because they paid us $25." In all, some 250 zombies showed up for the shoot.

Naturally, those zombies wouldn't have much impact without a convincing living dead look. Just as she'd once been considered to play Barbara, Judith Ridley had been picked as a possible candidate to apply the greasepaint. "I was asked at Latent Image to take a makeup course," she remembers. "They thought that in the production work, if I could do the makeup, then that would be one less freelancer that they would have to hire." After doing a full makeover, complete with false eyelashes, on volunteer John Russo, Ridley surrendered the assignment to Marilyn Eastman.

With another projected prospect, Tom Savini, serving in Vietnam, Eastman, who had done her own makeup as a regional theater actress, now seemed the logical choice, even though her zombie-making approach proved a work in progress. "You'll see in the beginning everyone looks like a raccoon. Gradually, they got a little more sophisticated." With the help of a mortician's friend called derma wax, Eastman says, "We tried to make variations in the wounds and costumes of the flesh-eaters, to indicate that they must have died in the midst of different normal activities. These were supposed to be the recently dead brought back to life."

Since the zombies had only newly departed this mortal coil, Russo points out, "They, logically, would not be especially decayed or deformed, so this made the makeups easier. I played the part of one of the first zombies we filmed—the Tire Iron Zombie. My idea was that I would have a certain amount of rigor mortis, so I purposely twisted my face out of shape and moved stiffly, albeit with 'deadly intentions.'"

As for that notorious nude pin-up ghoul who would adorn the movie's poster (though often wearing airbrushed bra and panties, presumably to discourage the necrophiliac trade), Eastman says, "I just dusted her down with gray makeup to make her look kind of gray and dead." Russo relates, "We used an artist's model for this scene. We figured that some of the dead bodies in morgues would have risen, and we wanted to illustrate this point. It was another 'believability' factor. We also didn't mind any word of mouth that might accrue regarding one of the few nudes to appear in horror movies at this time."

Word of mouth apparently spread quickly—long before the film was completed. According to Judith Ridley, "The night they filmed the nude ghoul, all of Evans City found out about it. They had their lawn chairs set up around the edges of the property. It was funny to see the rest of the zombies trying to keep their eyes elsewhere instead of looking down at the obvious places on the nude one." Meanwhile, going many of her cohorts one better, Marilyn Eastman did *triple*-duty on the film, also contributing a cameo as the infamous insect-eating zombie.

> "It was funny to see the rest of the zombies trying to keep their eyes elsewhere instead of looking down at the obvious places on the nude one."
>
> —Judith Ridley

What may be most remarkable, in a pre-reality TV/YouTube/and generally camera-savvy culture, is how *Night*'s zombies are never caught looking at the lens or deviating from their living-dead personas. Gary Streiner attests to the undead extras' extraordinary discipline: "The acting experience level of our cast was limited, to say the least, but still everyone was always totally in character. I don't remember there being abnormal amounts of retakes being done."

From the get-go, the filmmakers took care to establish fairly strict guidelines to set the parameters for appropriate zombie behavior. Says Russo, "We reasoned that they would move slowly; in fact, they had to move slowly, or else the script would not have worked; it would not have been believable that our hero Ben could elude them after the failed escape attempt."

The iconic role of the opening cemetery zombie was originally reserved for Russo. "I was going to be the cemetery zombie because nobody else was around to do it. I got into makeup and then Hinzman showed up. We said, 'Oh good, he can be the zombie because I can still load the magazines and work the clap sticks.' So there I was all day in zombie makeup working clap sticks and Bill became the famous cemetery ghoul."

Hinzman worked as a snapper at Latent Image by day and moonlighted as a part-time police forensics photographer. His terrifying performance in *Night* still sends chills down contemporary spines. "I pretty much picked that up from a film with Boris Karloff," he reveals. "It was the one where he got electrocuted and he came back to life [*The Walking Dead*]. He had one arm that was sort of dangling and he was dragging his leg. I think that's where I got that from, subconsciously." Marilyn Eastman's adroit makeup reinforced that resemblance, as did Hinzman's own hairstyle and coloring. Hinzman later recounted, "I sprayed my hair white and put some black on my cheeks. I was really surprised by how scary it turned out. I've been told several times how I scared the hell out of people as the lead ghoul."

Hinzman had a major fan in Kyra Schon: "Bill Hinzman, the graveyard ghoul (or, as he prefers to be called, '#1 Zombie'), was, in my opinion, the scariest looking zombie and my personal favorite. He was my zombie role model. I compare all others to him, and everyone else pales (no pun intended) in comparison."

That assessment passed a real-life test when Hinzman neglected to get out of character after leaving the set. "I remember coming home one night in makeup, returning to my little four-room hovel apartment, and I walked into the hall where the next-door neighbor was standing. Well, I damned near scared the shit outta her!"

Observant *Dead*heads have noted that Hinzman's zombie exhibits a bit more pep than most of his living dead peers. Hinzman explains, "Russell (Streiner) comes to her (Barbara's) rescue and attacks me. At that point George said, 'Okay, he's attacking you, you have to kill Russell.' I said, 'How am I supposed to kill this guy when throughout the film you were always telling us that we have no power except in tandem with each other and could only rely on each other for strength.' And he thought about it for a while and the famous line, in my memory, is, 'Oh fuck it, just kill him.'" Those were, in fact, the final scenes shot, so Romero might be forgiven for his zombie-empowering impatience.

Many of the volunteers went above and beyond the call of living-dead duty. Romero cites local TV personality Dave James's drop-dead fall as one of the zombies popped by Sheriff McClelland's posse as a prime example. "People get up in front of the camera," he says with wonder, "and all of a sudden someone who's never done anything like that before does something spectacular like that—that's a stuntman fall!"

Assembling the zombie-hunting posse proved a relatively

easy task. "We were able to drum up lots of cooperation," says Russo. "David Craig, the actual Safety Director of the City of Pittsburgh, appeared in the film. So did four Pittsburgh policemen with their police dogs." Adds Hinzman, "The scene with the dogs was a very scary scene for the number one zombie. Because the direction was, 'Don't turn around and look.' And you knew those dogs were right on your butt. And you were hoping they wouldn't get loose." Russo also earns props for his participation in that particular sequence: "I was lying down with a 16mm camera right in front of them, with them barking in my face. I thought if they ever break the leash, I'm finished."

Filling out the posse's civilian ranks were Evans City citizens who supplied their own firepower. "They were all happy to have guns in their hands," says Romero. "We had quite an arsenal." It was George Kosana's job to keep the posse in line, making sure those guns *weren't* loaded. But the extras' amateur status didn't earn them any breaks from Romero. Judith O'Dea recalls, "I'll never forget when George was filming, he had all those men a quarter of a mile, way out into the field, and he yelled, 'Action!' These guys, the first take, are intense, walking along there with their guns, and they get a quarter-mile in and George says, 'Cut! Let's do it again.' They must have walked back and forth and back and forth I don't know how many times—it was hysterical at the end. These guys were practically dragging their rifles, they were so tired."

While the posse's all-white, redneck makeup made the film more powerful, especially to midnight moviegoers and African-American audiences, the filmmakers did not go out of their way to achieve that ethnic composition. "We would probably have used anybody and everybody who showed up," Russo states today, "because we had put out desperate calls for extras, many of whom were friends and friends of friends from Claireton, Pennsylvania, my old home town, where George Kosana and I were living at that time. American society was much more stratified at that time, and so most of the people we closely associated with happened to be white in that small town, although most of us who worked on *Night of the Living Dead* were not prejudiced in that regard." Though they would have been accepted, no hippies applied for the gig either. Says Russo, "That fashion wasn't so big right in the narrow spectrum of time in which *Night of the Living Dead* was filmed, so it is pure accident that no longhairs showed up."

Not even the police—or their dogs—were immune to the zombies' menace. "We were having lunch and it was a posse day," Bill Hinzman looks back. "I was dressed in a zombie outfit, of course. I was having lunch with one of the girls at a picnic table. One of the cops was sitting there with a German shepherd police dog. And this cop was trying to impress the young lady sitting across the table, saying he was a great dog, he wasn't scared of anything. One of the girls playing a zombie [Paula Richards] came around the corner; she had on a long white gown and black hair and zombie makeup on. That dog took one look at her and took off in the opposite direction!"

A *Night* to Remember:
What the *Living Dead* Means to Me
by Allan Arkush

It always struck me as a movie that wasn't made so much as found moldering in the cellar of an abandoned house. And I do mean that as a compliment. Yes, that's how convincing I find the movie to be. It looks like it must have *really* happened!!!

In the early '80s, when I was directing rock videos, I once met with Motley Crue and presented them with a concept for their next video. I wanted to recreate *Night of the Living Dead* with them playing the living dead. In the style of the movie, they would be chasing down hot video girls in scratchy 16mm black and white. Sadly, the only part they liked was chasing down hot video girls. Oh, well, a lost opportunity.

A graduate of the unofficial Roger Corman Filmmaking School, ALLAN ARKUSH earned his cult-movie stripes directing the 1979 fave *Rock'n'Roll High School*, which had its New York City premiere at *Night*'s perennial venue, the Waverly Theater. He has since gone on to a prolific career in TV movies (*Elvis Meets Nixon*) and episodic television, executive producing and frequently directing the hit series *Heroes*.

5 SHOOTING *THE* DEAD

The rock hit George and the camera.
Luckily, it didn't hurt the camera.
—Bill Hinzman

Even with the cast in place, the production got off to a less than flying start, due to daunting climatic conditions. Recalls Russo, "One of the problems was that, the script having been written, we found ourselves in the midst of a bitterly cold, late winter . . . far too cold to be out filming. George Romero and I went out one weekend with a camera to see what it would be like, and not only did we freeze, but the camera motor froze, too, and the gears stopped turning. The only logical thing to do was wait till spring, even though George and I were champing at the bit, afraid something would happen to make the dream evaporate if we stood still for too long."

The eager filmmakers managed to maintain their enthusiasm, though, and shooting finally commenced in early June. "The first burst of shooting was nineteen days at that house," Russo remembers, "and we had to get back to commercial work." The film would be completed in thirty shooting days (some of said days going the full twenty-four hours), mostly on weekends, spread out over seven months.

One faithful, time-tested 35mm Arriflex camera shouldered most of the shoot. "When we were shooting dialogue, the camera was housed in a blimp, a gizmo designed to dampen the sound of the camera, which was as loud as a Sherman tank," Romero laughs. "The blimp weighed as much as a human and was roughly the size of a Volkswagen. This largely explains why the dialogue sequences are so static. When the camera was out of the blimp, it was a twelve-pound wonder. It could be held one-handed, with your thumb on a red 'Shoot' button—only slightly more cumbersome than today's camcorders. The only thing about it was the film load, but you didn't have to load 440-foot reels; you could load 100-footers and feel as free as the breeze."

The veteran Arriflex contributed mightily to the film's documentary feel. "I was able to shoot only MOS [without sound] sequences handheld," Romero resumes, "that's why they look like newsreels. I was able to shoot non-dialogue action sequences the same way; that's why I was able to make so many shots. I always used to say that I'd rather have 100 bad shots than ten that are beautiful. You can edit 100 shots in a million different configurations, until you come up with something that's close to what you intended. A single shot, no matter how perfect, leaves you no options."

The filmmakers had decided early on to lens their picture in black and white and "full frame" Academy aspect ratio (1:33), one of the last films to utilize that format. While increasingly rare on the big screen, black and white was still being used by directors like Richard Brooks (*In Cold Blood*) and John Frankenheimer (*Seconds*), to cite two contemporaneous examples, looking to achieve a stark verite atmosphere. "Most televisions were black and white, color TV was sort of just beginning to happen," Romero reasoned. "We would never have been able to get the texture in color. The final scenes in the film, which were all hand-held, I was trying intentionally to make that look like the news that we were seeing, from Watts, from 'Nam."

The process also helped mask budgetary deficiencies. "One advantage of shooting in black and white," Russo asserts, "was that our makeups and effects didn't have to be sweated so much. Sometimes we used red ink for blood, and other times we used

> "Sometimes we used red ink for blood, and other times we used chocolate syrup, depending on whether we wanted it to streak or splatter."
>
> —*John Russo*

chocolate syrup, depending on whether we wanted it to streak or splatter. Either substance was dark enough to register well for the camera." When the group received a fiscal infusion a week or so into filming, there was some discussion about shifting to color, but cooler heads, citing the necessity to switch from 35mm to 16mm and reshoot several scenes that were already in the can, ultimately prevailed.

Once the decision to lens in black and white was locked in, Romero opted for a Val Lewton look, using "gobos"—black paper with shapes cut out—to light the interior scenes, lending them a '40s feel, a la Lewton's 1943 classic *I Walked with a Zombie*. Lighting supervisor Joseph Unitas comments, "We spent a lot of time lighting Judy O'Dea and Duane Jones nailing the doors shut." Exterior work required equal care. According to Unitas, "That lighting was very dramatic because we could only use so many lights on that set outside—with the mammoth field the ghouls were all coming up, approaching the farmhouse. I would put lights on the right side, lights on the left side and cross-light them, with maybe one light as a frontal light. Big color tran lights, 1000 watts."

One of *Night*'s most striking lighting effects occurs at the Evans City Cemetery, when lightning frames zombie Hinzman's snarling, feral face in extreme close-up. "It started to drizzle," Russo remembers, "so we figured if we could see the drizzle, maybe we better throw in some lightning. And so we brought in a color tran light and flashed it on and off."

The actual Evans City Cemetery served as the set of the film's classic opening sequence. "We for the most part were on private property," says Gary Streiner, "including the cemetery, but we didn't need permits, just permission. We sure didn't have any for the opening road shots." The filmmakers were mindful to take some precautions, though. "We were afraid to show any names [on the tombstones]," Russo points out. "We thought somebody might sue us."

Life—and death—would later imitate art when nature struck the location. "A tornado uprooted the cemetery," Russo relates, "and about 200 bodies were lifted up out of the earth. They had to reinter them, and I'm not sure if they're reinterred in that same cemetery." A similar catastrophe would befall The Latent Image basement when a flood hit Pittsburgh in the 1980s. "The *Night of the Living Dead* workprint and a lot of the elements that went into the movie and a lot of the early films were destroyed."

Barbara's frantic flight from the cemetery was not only the first scene shot but very nearly caused the first on-set mishap. When Judith O'Dea streaked into the farmhouse yard, she remembers, "that gas pump wasn't bolted down. I ran into it full steam—nearly killed George."

Before Barbara made her way into that farmhouse, followed by a surviving George Romero and his hand-held Arriflex, set designer Vince Survinski spent some two months dressing the decaying house, mostly with furnishings purchased from Goodwill for a grand total of $50. Marilyn Eastman and other Image Ten members contributed additional items to fill closets and junk drawers, lending the site a greater lived-in/died-in look. Russo, for one, was impressed: "There are a lot of little touches in that farmhouse that are just so natural," he notes. "That was sort of our forte. Between Latent Image and Hardman Studios, all of us have that grounding in commercial/industrial production of TV commercials, where every detail has to be right or some agency person was gonna not buy it. And we brought that attention to detail to the movie."

Some items have acquired special significance, for the filmmakers and their fans alike. Two examples are the coat rack Harry Cooper grabs before he staggers, mortally wounded, down the cellar stairs, and the table from which Ben tears off a leg to wield as a zombie-clobbering club. Scenes in the house leading up to that critical moment had to be shot in sequence, another instance of the pervasive budgetary crunch—the filmmakers couldn't find or afford a matching stunt table!

Typical of the touches that, like *Carnival of Souls* before it, elevated *Night* above the usual run of the era's drive-in horror fare is the music box that mesmerizes a bewildered Barbara with its delicate design and tinkling tune, a whimsical vestige of an abruptly vanished gentility in that farmhouse turned charnel house. Credit for the prop goes to production designer Survinski, who requisitioned the item from his sister's home and added it to the living room décor. Lighting supervisor Unitas came up with the idea for the shot itself. "I said, 'George, go in for a close-up on that.' I was kind of happy about that, that he thought enough to put it in there. I put the light through that little music box. We had the music come up on it." The actual sound emanated from a separate, less photogenic box, now in Kyra Schon's possession. The onscreen box mysteriously disappeared during the final day of filming.

As a director, Romero looks to foster a mood that encourages that sort of happy accident to happen. "My sets are very open," he's pleased to note, "and anybody's allowed to say whatever they want . . . I think that if you're confident in what you're doing, you accept ideas that fit, and you reject ideas that don't . . . I'll buy anybody's suggestion if it works." This was one case

Keepsakes of *The Living Dead*

Kyra Schon: "I still have the bandage that I wore on my arm (it covered the wound I'd sustained from the zombie bite that eventually led to my demise) and some makeup left over from the shoot. I also have the music box that my dad recorded for the movie."

Judith O'Dea: "I kept my costumes and the blonde hair piece. They were tucked away for many years in my closet. Then, as I moved from place to place, they got lost along the way. As you can well imagine, I sure wish I had them now."

Judith Ridley, on her burgundy pants: "I painted in the pants—the pants became my paint pants. I didn't want to part with them. I think the shirt became a dust rag."

Russ Streiner, on Johnny's cemetery tie: "I still have it. It's one of my favorites."

John Russo: "I did not save any of the props I contributed to the movie, because I did not know any better at that time. I wish I had saved the tire iron that pierced my head—or even my army uniform, which I wore when I played the 'general's driver' in the Washington, D.C., scene."

where it most definitely did, supplying a sustained celluloid nightmare with a rare poignant moment. "Everyone seemed to get along well," says Judith O'Dea, echoing Romero's intent. "We all chipped in to help wherever and whenever it was necessary. It was a great learning experience."

Interior scenes were usually lensed during the day, exteriors at night. The frequent shooting interruptions posed major continuity challenges, with the pivotal props having to be in the same spots when the camera was ready to roll again. To avoid confusion, the boards were labeled; one such label is clearly visible when Ben and Tom tear it off the front door during their planned truck escape. Just as important, Duane Jones was not "handy," so holes had to be pre-drilled into the boards before he could hammer the nails into them. And not unlike the living dead themselves, vandals would frequently raid the house during prolonged filming intervals, breaking windows and molesting stored dummies slated for use as distant extras in the zombie crowd scenes.

Judith O'Dea recalls one production dummy with particular dread. "I remember we had a store mannequin in the hall upstairs in the farmhouse. It was made up to look like a really creepy ghoul with horrific bloody facial wounds. Those wounds were made from derma wax—the stuff funeral people use on dead people to prepare them for public viewing. It freaked me out so much that I couldn't walk by it and had to go to a different room to put on my makeup."

Another dummy—the corpse at the top of the stairs that Barbara discovers soon after entering the farmhouse—received more decomposed face time. That image still sends shivers, even though it consisted of a simple store-bought plastic "Living Skull" model, which Romero himself tricked out with modeling clay, fake hair, and ping-pong ball eyes.

During periods of intensive filming, several of the principals camped out in the house, with few amenities but high resolve. Russo recalls, none too fondly, "There were no showers. George, Vince, Gary [Streiner], and I slept in the house and took cat baths in the morning." Water had to be hauled from a nearby well to flush the toilets. Romero became the only reported casualty of the rugged conditions when the canvas cot he'd been sleeping on collapsed under him.

Most participants, though, including the cast, chose to commute, however arduous that daily round trip. "It was thirty miles to my parents' front door," says Judith Ridley. "On more than one occasion, they found me on the glider asleep on the front porch—that's as far as I got. Then I would shower and off we'd go again for another marathon." As Marilyn Eastman remembers the scene, "We were either very hot or very cold, very tired or very hungry, very dirty. It was primitive, but fun!"

Since the farmhouse cellar was too small and dilapidated to allow for filming, The Latent Image basement subbed for that important location. To sell the illusion, Vince Survinski built a false doorway through which the actors could enter and exit.

The Hardman Associates offices were conveniently converted into the television newsroom, where announcer Charles Craig dispensed the latest dire developments in the outbreaks of mass murder plaguing the area and later flashed the names of local rescue stations where citizens were urged to report.

"We put real towns and city names on the screen," says Russo, "because we figured if we have to carry our own picture from drive-in to drive-in to get it on screens, maybe people would recognize McKeesport and Claireton and all these different towns and that would motivate them to come out and see the picture." That tack presented a bit of a problem once *Night of the Living Dead* entered its own broadcast phase. Russo explains, "The TV stations were afraid that people would actually start calling these emergency numbers. They were afraid something like Orson Welles's *War of the Worlds* phenomenon might set in."

Equally improvised was *Night*'s sound recording—a mix of the primitive and, in post-production, the elaborate. During the shoot, soundman Gary Streiner states, "There wasn't a boom man. Everything we shot you had to watch the blocking, watch where the action was gonna go, and put a microphone in the most common spot, which is just a barbaric way of doing sound. The fact that you can actually hear what people are saying in *Night of the Living Dead* is actually a bit of a miracle." Incredibly enough, nearly all the dialogue was captured "live." "I can't say we didn't do *any* looping, but I can say we did very, very little."

While voice dubbing may have been minimal, Romero frequently used sound to mask imperfections, a technique he would carry over into his subsequent guerrilla-style films, *There's Always Vanilla* and *Jack's Wife*. "I've done things where if I don't like the timing or if there's a pause in dialogue that I don't like, I'll throw a dog barking in the background or something in there that just keeps the ear occupied."

For the sound effects, Romero and crew went the homemade route. Audio experts Karl Hardman and helpers excelled at utilizing sound to heighten the fear factor. The smashed melon that subbed for the sound of Johnny's head hitting the cement cemetery marker stands (or, more accurately, falls) as a prime example. "That sound really got to my grandmother at the premiere," Russ Streiner recalls. "She was very upset. She was having a hard time with the suspension of disbelief. She thought that her grandson was really injured!"

Ditto for when ghoul girl Karen takes a trowel to mom Helen. It's a sequence clearly designed to conjure overt associations with Hitchcock's classic *Psycho* shower scene, from the rapid-fire close-ups of the terrified victim's face to the frenzied violin strings on the soundtrack. "Of all the sound effects that we created," sound technician Richard Lococo says, "the one that still gives me goosebumps when I hear it is Marilyn's screaming as [Helen] is killed by her daughter. Judy O'Dea's screaming is a close second. Both were looped in and out of echo over and over again." The fact that the Image Ten filmmakers, like *Carnival of Souls'* Herk Harvey before them, had unlimited, relatively unhurried access to their own equipment put them several steps ahead of indie auteurs who had to pay out of pocket and watch the clock while completing post-production.

Contributions came from many quarters, some unexpected. As related in the informative 2009 feature documentary *Autopsy of the Dead*, an otherwise innocent bystander named Lee Hollihan earned a micro-niche in horror-film history simply by holding the tape for the nocturnal crickets loop. "I like to tell the story that I worked on *Night of the Living Dead* for ten minutes." Hollihan was looking for his friend Jack Givens, Hardman Associates' chief audio engineer, and found him in the cutting room. "He was in there making this loop and he had it going from one tape machine, up around a nail that he had in the wall, over across the doorway, down another nail, and into another tape machine. So basically it kept going around and around. He didn't want the loop to be too short because it would be too repetitive. It was just crickets—that's repetitive to begin with. So I helped him get the tape working. I was over there holding one piece, so it wouldn't get jammed up. That was my part. It was about a twenty-second loop of crickets that kept going around while he added other bugs from the sound effects library. And that's what was used in the movie. And if you watch the movie, all you hear are those cricket sound effects. I kept telling him, 'Those crickets are too loud!' Around Halloween time, if they're running that movie on TV and it's in the next room or something, as soon as I hear the crickets, I know that's what it is: *Night of the Living Dead*'s on!"

The production met with many emergencies that called for instant improvisation. The cemetery scene was shot over two days. In the interim, someone had put a visible dent in Johnny and Barbara's car, which belonged to Russ Streiner's mother. Romero rescripted the sequence so that the car would crash into a tree, thus explaining the damage for observant viewers and, as a fortuitous byproduct, actually adding to the chaos of the scene. The unlucky auto took a further beating when zombie Hinzman shattered the windows with a heavy rock. "Russ's mother had given us permission," Russo recalls. Even that act proved more perilous than anticipated. "I expected that rock to break the window the first time," says Hinzman, "and it did not. When it finally did break, it came out of my hand and George was laying on the seat with the camera. The rock hit George and the camera. Luckily, it didn't hurt the camera."

More cars, indeed a veritable convoy, were put into play to facilitate location shooting in the nation's capital, a brainstorm that hit the filmmakers midway through the shoot. Russ Streiner relates the event: "We all piled into some cars, drove to Washington, D.C. on a Sunday, had no permits, had no anything. We put military flags on the front of Karl Hardman's Continental to make it look like an official car, we thought. Just to show that, yeah, we do have some budget connected with this picture." Said flags were designed by Marilyn Eastman, the ersatz Betsy Ross of the group: "We had red flags with white stars—nobody complained."

Eastman does recall one tense moment from the important scene. "We were parked in front of the Capitol, we'd already been parked there for maybe fifteen or twenty minutes. Pretty soon a guard came down, sticks his head in and says, 'I'm sorry, I have to ask you to move because if we let one general park here, they'll all want to park here.'"

Russ Streiner assumed camera chores so Romero could cameo onscreen as an inquiring reporter quizzing a trio of authority figures. The two scientists and a military official fail to inspire confidence as they squabble among themselves while ducking the media and hustling to Karl Hardman's Lincoln, where none other than John Russo, clad in his old army uniform, waits to open the door for the harried dignitaries.

The sequence may have been a last-minute improv, but Romero now sees it as a crucial component not only of *Night* but his subsequent *Dead* films as well. "As far as the people on television not really answering questions and making it more confusing, that's been a conscious part of the zombie films. That's generally what it's about—'Ladies and gentlemen, there was just a plane crash that took out a small piece of Manhattan, more later.' It's never reassuring; it's always alarming, and that's been a kind of conscious through-line." It's another tribute to *Night*'s sheer scare quotient that audiences rarely noticed actors appearing, albeit briefly, in multiple roles or the many goofs and gaffes that riddle the film. For most viewers, then and now, surviving the *Night* took precedence over nit-picking.

While the D.C. excursion added welcome gravitas and scope without incurring a significant outlay, the budget crunch was severely felt in many other areas of production. Says Russo, "We couldn't afford cranes, dollies, booms, sound stages, and many other niceties that are taken for granted on major productions and which enhance any movie's overall look. We *were* able to work in some helicopter shots when the chopper owned by KQV, a local radio station, showed up to cover us for a news report and the pilot was nice enough to help us out. We were constantly on the lookout for 'frills' like this." Russ Streiner volunteered to board the chopper and film those panoramic overhead shots of the zombies staggering across the immense field with the trigger-happy posse in leisurely but deadly pursuit.

On an even more basic level, says Russo, "We could not afford to buy and process ample filmstock. The Monster Flick was shot on a ratio of six-to-one. There came a point about halfway through our shooting when George was just winging it—getting only two or even *one* good take and then going on to the next shot. If he had missed anything critical, we would have been hit hard."

Romero agrees that performing first-time feature-film directorial chores, shouldering responsibilities ranging far beyond basic budgetary restrictions, proved the most difficult part for him. "I was this nonconfrontational guy who didn't want to have to hassle with anything. That was the hardest thing for me—making decisions."

Gary Streiner supports Romero's self-description but gives the novice helmer high marks. "I don't think the film that came out would've been the same if George wasn't the person he was or at the professional level he was. And that's a compliment because he wasn't a film director at that point; he'd never directed anything over sixty seconds prior to that. He did a few other longer-format films, maybe ten minutes long, travelogues, and things like that for Pennsylvania, but never had to carry dialogue, or carry a scene for a long period of time. So, sometimes he took a lot longer to figure it out, like a lot of young directors I've worked with since then. They never know whether it's really right or wrong until they see it. They end up doing things a bunch more times than they have to, just to have the ability to see it more times and figure it out. So, I think George fell into that category as much as any real first-time director would."

According to brother Russ, however, Romero's keen filmic judgment would, ultimately, carry the day. "I think that one of George's biggest assets is his creative mind, his ability to think conceptually and in mental pictures . . . George could see things artistically, which the rest of us didn't necessarily have the ability to do."

Romero typically adopts a more modest view of his abilities and accomplishments, once telling *Cinefantastique* Online interviewer Steve Biodrowski: "I did what I could trying to make the starkness seem deliberate, stealing what I could remember from [Orson] Welles's *Othello* and *Macbeth*. Only backhanded credit, if any, is deserved—the sort of credit awarded to a cat burglar. The images that most resemble reality were shot in daylight— most notably, the scenes of a posse arriving with their dogs to scour the countryside." He further insisted, "When I made the film, I wasn't an auteur in command; I was a student, an apprentice, learning every day . . . I had a gut feeling for what worked and what didn't work. I stole what worked, for me, and used it, in some cases shot for shot, wherever I could." On the upside, says Romero, "There were things we were able to do here because it *was* just us guys that I haven't been able to do on much bigger-budget things."

Russo affirms, "Our big advantage was that we had no shortage of talent, ability, and 'sweat equity.' A big piece of all of us went into that movie. People with drive, guts, determination, and loyalty made it possible for us to pull off the phenomenon that *Night of the Living Dead* has become."

Russ Streiner elaborates: "One of the things it does, it puts a tremendous amount of human energy on the screen. You care about these people. You may not like Harry Cooper, but you certainly do care about what happens to him simply because he's in this predicament that is not of his making, and no one even knows exactly what it is they're dealing with."

Seconds Romero, "None of the actors quit on us. There were no protections going either way. We just lucked out that everybody stayed with it, and we managed to pull it off."

Night's filmmakers are rightly credited with creating a new breed of movie monster, a combination of the menacing (they want to eat you) and the pathetic (they're dead . . . they're all messed up). *Night* was also the first film to depict zombiism as a contagious condition akin to the vampirism in Romero's beloved literary model, Richard Matheson's *I Am Legend*, and its first screen adaptation, *The Last Man on Earth*. As Russo points out, "These were probably the first flesh-eating ghouls ever in a movie. Before that, zombies didn't eat flesh. That really struck a chord with people. It was a big part of the movie's success."

Judith O'Dea cites another factor in accounting for the living dead's appeal. "I think because before they became zombies, these were feeling, caring, loving human beings—for the most part. And to all of sudden turn on their families, their fellow man, without any care and become so vicious is a frightening concept." As for the horror genre in general, she reflects: "I think it's just like wanting to get on a roller coaster and be scared to death. I think it's a part of the human psyche to get a rush, to get the endorphins going. I think so many of us need that. That's a part of it. And being able to sit and watch other people die and go home and have a beer is nice!"

Night, likewise, significantly deviated from most—if not all—previous horror films by omitting a precise explanation for the dire situation, namely, the rise of the hungry dead. "I didn't think it did [need an explanation]," says Russo. "I thought we could simply show scientists and authority figures arguing, scrambling, and struggling to get at the cause of it and find a solution—the way they would be doing in real life . . . and our movie would end with them still struggling."

As filming progressed, however, that lack of rationale began gnawing, not unlike flesh-starved zombies, at some members of the team. Bill Hinzman remembers: "While we were looking at the dailies, someone said, 'Why is this happening? Why are people coming back to life?' And we all had a big roundtable discussion about it. I'm pretty sure I was the one who suggested that the Russians had just launched a Venus satellite. And I said, 'What if one of those things comes back and causes radiation.' I guess that was thought about and we used it."

Romero recalls that a number of explanatory moments were shot but excised from the final cut. "There were three proposed causes, and we cut two of them out because the scenes were boring and the scenes around them were boring, and that one we left in because it was part of that newscast and it made it seem a little bigger. People said, 'Oh, that's what happened.' You know, some Venus probe came back and brought some kind of bug. I don't want there to be a cause, it's just something that's happening, it's just a different deal, it's a different way of life."

Russo agrees. "We never said it was *definitely* the cause of the 'ghoul disease'—it was merely suspected." When Romero moved on to shoot his subsequent *Dead* films, he did away with explanations, though he did retain, in *Dawn of the Dead*, scenes of media "pundits" spreading confusing conjecture regarding the zombie plague's possible origins.

Few filmgoers seemed bothered by the filmmakers' nonchalance in this area; if anything, in keeping with Romero and Russo's original intent, that mystery *heightened* the movie's nightmare quality: How do you fight a disease with no known cause or cure?

They did, however, see the need to establish firm ghoul rules. Says Russo, "About the recently dead, that was another point that was brought up in the script discussions: If the dead are coming back to life, why aren't they *all* coming back to life? Why aren't they coming up out of their graves? We couldn't afford special effects like people coming out of their graves en masse, so we came up with the idea that it would only be the recently dead that came back and the others couldn't."

Romero and crew realized too that, however relentless and numerous the zombies might be, they couldn't be entirely unstoppable because that would rob the film of potential suspense. After some consideration, they decided to pinpoint the brain as the lone area of vulnerability, a lesson the characters and audience learn at the same time. "Richard Ricci played the first ghoul Ben shoots," Russo points out. "He gets shot twice in the chest, but he only dies when he is drilled through the head. People begin to get the idea that you have to destroy a ghoul's brain. That's one of the good things about this film—the revelations are carefully paced. The first guy in the cemetery could be just a deranged man, for all you know. Then he's joined by another one. Are they two deranged men? Later you find out they can be killed when I get it with the tire iron, and so on. When Judy's on the couch, you start to find out they're flesh eaters. By that time, you're totally hooked."

"Once you get past the admittedly hokey premise," says Russ Streiner, "we tried to do it in the most scary way we could. If time is the test, we apparently did a pretty good job of that."

The Image Ten team spent considerable time debating other means of zombie disposal. "Back during our scripting sessions," Russo recalls, "we discussed various methods. Karl and Marilyn joked that maybe at the climax of the film when the ghouls swarm into the house, Ben could discover that they die when they're hit in the face with a Boston cream pie. Then, at the wrap-up, a pie truck could arrive and save the day." As *Dead*-heads well know, Romero would pick up on that unlikely riff in the infamous sequence wherein raucous bikers pie hapless zombies in *Dawn of the Dead*.

And on the subject of eats, the filmmakers also had to address another all-important matter: zombie cuisine. The guts for what became known on set as "The Last Supper," when the zombies chow down on Tom's and Judy's scrumptious remains, were supplied by a local meat-market chain owner and investor. "We knew that we needed intestines, livers, hearts, and stuff like that," says Hardman. "So he arranged to get those things from the slaughterhouse from which he purchased meat. They were all goodies belonging to lambs, which are, supposedly, somewhat similar to human organs."

Vince Survinksi filled the innards with water to give them that appetizingly squishy, squirmy look. As for the ravenous zombies who consumed them *con mucho gusto* (to say nothing of relish), Russo remarks, "They were all commercial clients of ours that we considered rather staid people ordinarily, and they just stunned us that they chomped into those organs!"

When the moment came for little Karen to tuck into dad's arm, Kyra Schon says, "They were trying to figure out how to pull it off. Earlier in the day, we were eating hamburgers or meatball sandwiches, so they just smeared chocolate syrup all over it and that's what I was biting into."

Professional fireworks experts Regis (brother of Vince)

Survinski and partner Tony Pantanello rigged the realistic-looking bullet squibs—small explosive charges triggering blood bags—attached to the zombies, this at a time when that technique was still rare in major Hollywood films, let alone low-budget indies. Arthur Penn was among the first to employ them in spectacular fashion for the climactic execution of *Bonnie and Clyde* (not yet released when *Night* began filming), while Sam Peckinpah further popularized them with more pervasive use in

> *"Earlier in the day, we were eating hamburgers or meatball sandwiches, so they just smeared chocolate syrup all over it and that's what I was biting into."*
>
> —Kyra Schon

1969's *The Wild Bunch*. Fortunately, no zombie extras were harmed in the making of this motion picture, as the squibs detonated with flawless precision.

The critical truck explosion posed a thornier challenge for the pair. According to Regis, "Tony and I went out to a real old, abandoned strip mine. To our luck, there was an abandoned truck out there, a panel truck. We practiced on that panel truck till we got what we liked. We put the charge in the bed of the truck. We got pieces of old carpet, plywood, pieces of timber, anything that could fly through the air with the fire as it exploded. I made a special bomb three inches wide and three inches long with my special flash composition. We had two one-liter bottles with a mixture of gasoline and oil. And when the bomb went off, it broke the plastic bottles, it caught the material on fire, it threw the pieces into the air, and it made one hell of a flame! One take." The duo's work habits made Romero more than a bit nervous, though. "They're working with two tons of explosives and they have cigars hanging out of their mouths!"

Romero employed three cameras in a bid to get the max out of the one-time stunt. "Russ and I were nearly hit by some of the shrapnel," says Russo. All in all, though, the ghoul gods must have been smiling on the scene, since no one received so much as a scratch. And the cost of the truck? Forty-five bucks. Only

Kyra Schon copped a negative attitude regarding the stunt. "I recall being extremely disappointed when I wasn't allowed to see the truck explode because it was past my bedtime."

Another, potentially more dangerous sequence played out when the besieged farmhouse characters were called upon to toss Molotov cocktails at the zombies milling outside. Gary Streiner remembers, "We're throwing mason jars of

> *"I recall being extremely disappointed when I wasn't allowed to see the truck explode because it was past my bedtime."*
>
> *—Kyra Schon*

gasoline with wicks on them. And nobody said, 'You think it's okay to have Karl Hardman light a Molotov cocktail and throw it into a crowd of people? What might happen?'"

Something *did* happen to John Russo—fortunately, by design. "I said to George, '*Somebody* has to catch fire in this sequence, because it won't be believable to have so many Molotov cocktails bursting all around and none of the slow-moving ghouls get hit.' So I volunteered. When I felt myself getting hot, I'd fall to the ground, and people were ready with blankets to smother the flames."

Bill Hinzman was the next to step up—in this case, to feel the fiery fury of Ben's blazing torch. "He was lashing out with that torch that everyone was supposed to be scared of. I thought, 'Why don't you just hit me with the torch. I'll back up, put some lighter fluid on my suit and I'll duck out of the way and get it put out right away.' And George said, 'Okay.' 'Cause no one *suggested* I set myself on fire."

Neither Russo nor Hinzman wore safety clothing, just extra layers of regular apparel. Both were a lot luckier than soundman and impromptu prop worker Gary Streiner, who agreed to prepare the chair that Ben sets aflame to distract the zombies.

"I am, to the best of my knowledge, the only victim," he recalls today. "I set myself on fire—a case of pressing your expertise to a place where you probably shouldn't. I shouldn't have been allowed to be carrying around a gallon jug of gasoline, pouring it on a chair that was going to be set aflame that had already been set aflame. We did a take. The chair went up. It was out

> **"I jumped back and all of a sudden I'm on fire!"**
> —Gary Streiner

probably at least a half hour . . . I just went over and started to pour the gas on and the liquid found a hot ember somewhere and a flame just came up into this container I'm holding in my hand. I jumped back and all of a sudden I'm on fire!" Fortunately, quick-thinking, fast-moving zombie Hinzman tackled Gary and got the fire out.

All scary things must come to an end, at least in the movies. In *Night*'s case, contemporaneous TV atrocity news footage and Sidney Lumet's famous freeze-frames climax for his 1964 doomsday thriller *Fail-Safe* combined to inspire Romero to conclude his film with a somber photo montage that sees dispassionate posse members hook, drag, and burn Ben's lifeless body. That climax was unprecedented in horror-film history—the hero whose emotions we'd intensely shared for ninety minutes abruptly destroyed and discarded, an anonymous piece of meat.

The sequence succeeded in both sobering (despite the ambient midnight-movie marijuana smoke) and angering young audiences who couldn't fail to note the parallel between Ben's cold disposal and the body-bagged U.S. soldiers and mangled Viet Cong and civilian corpses shown on the nightly news reports, a parallel earlier pounded home verbally when Sheriff McClelland blandly notes, "We killed nineteen of 'em today, right in this area." According to Russo, though, the montage approach also had a more practical side. "We were trying to come up with an effective ending that would also save some shooting days, so we shot those stills, and they were printed through cheesecloth to give them that grainy look. A group called The Animators, who were downstairs from Latent Image, added the titles." Those no-frills end credits accompanying the vérité-looking stills added immensely to the overall chill.

> **Much of Night's power lies in its complex editing, incredibly rigorous for a low-budget indie.**

To further raise the fear level, the filmmakers searched for an appropriate musical score and quickly realized they lacked the bucks to commission an original. "One of our big stumbling blocks was music," Russo recalls, "where to get it and how to get it cheaply. Over a period of a couple of weeks during the rough-cut stage, we had some pretty wild and zany sessions, trying to create our own weird music, even though none of us were musicians. But we had The Latent Image's recording studio available, with Gary Streiner on drums, we plucked guitar strings, banged cymbals, and made eerie noises with our own voices—and even with things like ratchets and drills—while Gary experimented with reverb, or tried running some of the sounds backwards after they were recorded. Some of this crazy stuff actually got used in bits and pieces on the effects tracks.

"Karl and Marilyn created some sounds that were used more extensively. We went through all this trouble because we really didn't want to use library music—we wanted an original score. We didn't think we could find enough good library selections to score an entire horror movie. Finally, we ended up using the Capitol Hi-Q library. Karl Hardman and George Romero made such great selections that our movie track ended up being quite successful—in fact, most fans and critics consider it a tremendous boon to the film."

Bill Hinzman, for one, was impressed by Hardman's efforts. "He cut the music to match the scenes. Sometimes you can get lucky that way. You go, 'Oh, look at that, the beat fell right over on the cut.'" Sound technician Richard Lococo adds, "We chose a selection of music for each of the various scenes and then George made the final selections. We then took those selections and augmented them electronically."

In the final edit, attentive listeners can discern cues from such genre-film forebears as *The Hideous Sun Demon, Teenagers from Outer Space* (both 1959), and *The Devil's Messenger* (1961), as well as the TV nature series *Wild Kingdom*. The recycled music angle pleased Romero, who wrote in his liner notes for the Varese Sarabande *Night of the Living Dead* soundtrack LP, "This was the real article. The scoring heard in nightmares conjured by yesterday's matinees. For a nonmusician, the closest thing to composing a score is working a good set of library tracks into your picture."

With his footage complete, Romero settled in for a long but

rewarding stretch in post-production stir. Much of *Night*'s power lies in its complex editing, incredibly rigorous for a low-budget indie. The final film boasts nearly 1,100 cuts, far more than your average high-end Hollywood movie of the time. Judith O'Dea's roughly three-minute flight from her crashed car to the farmhouse alone has some 55 cuts.

As Romero explains his approach, "I'd shoot a *lot* of coverage. Very often I'd cover my ass and shoot conversations, I'd shoot masters here and there, but then I'd do coverage on, basically, everybody that was in the scene . . . if I wanted to make dialogue edits or whatever, I'd have the ability to do it, and I wasn't locked into master shots where you either cut the whole scene out or you're stuck with it."

Since Romero didn't have studio bigwigs breathing down his neck, he was able to lavish a full five months on post-production, allowing the necessary time for that painstaking edit, even with frequent interruptions for pressing Latent Image commercial work.

Russo pretty much spoke for the whole crew when he viewed the result of Romero's labors. "I remember when the first edit was finished. That's when we really started to get excited. We had seen little bits and pieces of the first edit, but when we saw a relatively complete edit, it just smacked us in the eyes. Karl jumped up and said, 'Damnit! We've got it! We have a movie!'

> **"When we saw a relatively complete edit, it just smacked us in the eyes."**
> —*John Russo*

We knew then that it was a good horror film. All of us felt that way, and we knew it was capable of making some sort of splash, at least with horror-film fans."

A legendary but true incident helped *Night* make it to its final print stage, when Russ Streiner challenged Jack Napor, head of Pittsburgh's WRS Motion Picture Laboratories, to a chess game. The stakes: Napor would eat Image Ten's lab bill if he lost. He did, saving the filmmakers from a *Night of the Living Debt* situation.

Despite the considerable TLC lavished on the film, some slip ups went undetected right through the final cut. A few actually work to *Night*'s advantage, reinforcing its surreal nightmare quality. Barbara's opening line about daylight savings time, for starters, is in stark contrast to the obviously barren autumnal setting. Later, when she looks out the window after reaching the farmhouse in daylight, it's night. Both "gaffes" up the eerie ante. Ditto for when Ben assures Barbara the house is boarded up tight, and there's an unprotected window in full view behind them. In fact, beyond that aperture was a sheer fifteen-foot zombie-proof drop, but its existence hadn't been clearly established in the film.

Other goofs were caught and corrected, more or less, in post. The synch was lost during Tom and Judy's big "smile" scene—itself hastily written on set only the night before when it was felt such a sentimental speech was needed. The fix resulted in a slight change of voice pitch, one hardly noticeable to the untrained naked ear. Characters occasionally faced in opposite directions during dialogue cutaways, but only the rare unscared onlooker would care. Tom tells his fellow farmhouse inhabitants, "We were on our way up to the lake to go swimming"—this, despite the stark fall setting apparent in the opening cemetery scene.

A bit more glaring was the end credit typo listing Bill Hinzman as "Heinzman," though the man himself claims the "mistake" was deliberate. "I told George to misspell my name on purpose because people would continually mispronounce my name. They would say '*Hins*man,' so in the film, we spelled it Heinzman just to get the pronunciation right. I never heard the end of it from my relatives!"

But all those errors, actual or intended, pale beside a far greater goof whose unending consequences would cause serious grief down the road.

A *Night* to Remember:
What the *Living Dead* Means to Me
by William Lustig

I first became aware of *Night of the Living Dead* when it was playing on the bottom of a double bill with a quickly forgotten, if ever remembered, film entitled *Slaves* starring believe-it-or-not Dionne Warwick. The then-*New York Daily News* première movie critic Rex Reed devoted his entire column raving about the ultra-frightening experience of seeing *Night of the Living Dead*. But before I could run to 42nd Street (then called the Deuce), the film had already been pulled a week after it opened, which was common in those days, thus becoming a holy-grail film for me to watch out for its resurface.

I didn't have to wait so long when the West Village Walter Reade Waverly Theater (now the revamped IFC Center) announced the first-ever midnight showing of *Night of the Living Dead* using the Reed review as its ad. Needless to say, I was there at the very first showing, standing on a long line along with other horror fanatics waiting with anticipation of this promised ultimate horror experience. I remember sitting near the front off to the side in the jam-packed theater. Not since *Psycho* had I experienced a more nightmarish film. Just the opening notes of the main titles stock music let you know that you are about to enter a world of unbelievable horror, and, boy, did it deliver.

I was around fifteen at the time, living in Englewood Cliffs, New Jersey. After that screening, I remember the 3 A.M. mile walk home from the bus stop through desolate suburban streets punctuated with wooded areas, scared out of my mind. Since that Waverly midnight show, I saw *Night of the Living Dead* no less than a dozen more times wherever it played over the years. No other film had been able to capture *Night*'s unrelenting terror until *The Texas Chainsaw Massacre*.

WILLIAM LUSTIG earned cult director status at an early age when his graphic slasher classic *Maniac* terrified early-'80s viewers. He continued scaring audiences with shockers like *Maniac Cop* and *Uncle Sam* and later founded the pioneering DVD label Blue Underground, which he continues to run today.

6 MARCH TO MIDNIGHT

Being able to sit and watch other people die, and go home
and have a beer is nice!
—Judith O'Dea

Now that the hard work was finally complete, finding a distributor for the finished film posed a fresh problem. Image Ten aimed high from the
get-go. "Columbia [Pictures] came very close to offering a deal,"
Russo relates. "After numerous screenings for their sales staff
and promotions people, the picture got turned down mostly because it was in black and white." Russo explains, "Putting
widescreen color in the theaters was a way of competing with
the little black-and-white tubes in most people's homes. Also,
the drive-in market was more important than ever, and we were
told that black-and-white pictures didn't have enough resolution
over the long distance from projector to screen in the huge drive-
ins, and so could not be shown in the hours of dusk, before the
sun was completely down."

The group next turned to the most prominent among the
second-tier usual suspects but were met with a friendly rebuff.
According to Russo, "Sam Arkoff, president of American International Pictures, explained that AIP couldn't distribute every picture that came along; they only had a budget for a certain
number of pictures." AIP execs erected another hurdle: They
wanted the filmmakers to change the ending, allowing Ben to
survive. But Romero and crew wouldn't budge on that point. To

them, the redneck posse led by Sheriff McClelland represented *not* the cavalry riding to the last-reel rescue but yet another force of chaos and destruction.

As Romero sums it up, "We didn't *want* to restore order. The whole reason for doing the piece is to kick 'normal' in the butt. I've never understood why you'd want to bring things back to normal after you've upset the apple cart that much." Romero and cohorts felt that far too many so-called fright films suffered from Happy Ending Syndrome. "My biggest complaint about horror, about fantasy cinema, usually is that you do it to upset the ways of the world. And then, traditionally, in the end you sort of restore it all. And you say, 'Well, why the hell did we go through it in the first place?' And so I thought, 'I have to leave the world a mess, first of all.' It's when daylight comes and here comes the posse and here come all these rednecks. And, to me, those are the real zombies, you know? We were '60s guys. We really thought that we had an honest chance at having changed the world in that time. And then you turn around and not only has it not changed for the better but probably, to some extent, for the worse. Things were actually starting to get worse right then. That was sort of the beginning of that down hill. And so that's the anger that, I think, created those final scenes. If we'd ended it any other way, it would have been hard for us to hold our heads up."

Grim and violent reality would soon reinforce Romero's feelings. As Russ Streiner relates, "The night that George and I were driving on the Pennsylvania Turnpike to New York with the answer print to try to arrange a distributor is the night that Martin Luther King was assassinated. That's when we heard the news."

When they did arrive in New York City, Romero and friends finally found a more simpatico partner in Continental Releasing, a subdivision of the Walter Reade Organization. Russo was buoyed by the prospect. "We were impressed that the people who had

> "We were impressed that the people who had distributed such great 'art house' product as David and Lisa, Lord of the Flies, and Every Bastard a King would want to acquire our picture."
>
> —Russ Streiner

distributed such great 'art house' product as *David and Lisa,* *Lord of the Flies,* and *Every Bastard a King* would want to acquire our picture. With *Night,* Continental was, for the first time, taking on an exploitation picture, and we thought that said something for the quality of our work."

In fact, rather than seeking to soften the product, the accommodating distributor desired even *more* gore. "Continental wanted more cannibalism scenes put in, if possible," Russo recalls. "We didn't have many shots of the ghouls feasting that we had not already used, but we were able to scrape up a couple." At the same time, Continental excised

> *"Continental wanted more cannibalism scenes put in, if possible."*
>
> —John Russo

some ten minutes of finished footage, mostly of expository dialogue and character development, with much of the Coopers's quarreling ending up on the cutting-room floor.

Romero relives that sometimes painful process. "The biggest, widest shot of the zombies out in the field got cut out. Instead of putting it in somewhere else, it just got cut out. That's the shot I wish we had back. I remember it being a great-looking shot. We stood some mannequins up way off in the distance. There was some dialogue that came out; I can't even remember what it was. I remember Russ was in New York at the distributor and he said, 'I figured out this place where I can get these few lines out of here.' And they didn't even have moviolas or anything. He was just looking at it against a lightbox. And they took it out."

With a distributor at last in place, and determined to make a splash on their home turf, the Image Ten crew commandeered the Fulton Theater, a downtown Pittsburgh picture palace. On October 1, 1968, complete with limos, tuxes and rotating klieg lights, *Night of the Living Dead* had its gala world premiere. With personalities like horror host Bill Cardille hyping it on his *Chiller Theater* program and local news shows offering periodic progress reports, the community had been rallying around the work-in-progress for months. Russ Streiner put Image Ten's achievement in perspective. "This was the first modern picture that had been done in Pittsburgh. There had been scenes from

Perils of Pauline and various other silent movies that had been made in Pittsburgh, but this was the first modern picture."

With a house packed with *Night* cast, crew, family, and friends, the evening proved a rousing success. "I remember waiting for the lights to go down and thinking, 'My God, we're going to see *our* film in *our* local theater, and I'll be up there on the screen about twelve feet tall!'" Judith O'Dea recreates the thrill. "It was exciting to think I had participated in something like that, something that had been completed and would be distributed." As Russo happily remembers, "We got a standing ovation at the end." But would the pic play in Peoria? Or even the Pittsburgh 'burbs?

To learn the answer, Image Ten and Continental booked the movie in some fourteen area drive-ins and neighboring *bijous*. Says Russo, "Over the next few days, we started to drive around to the various theaters where our picture was playing. Every theater we checked out had a big crowd. All the reactions appeared to be very good." Romero conjures a personal turning point: "I went to see *Night of the Living Dead* in a drive-in with Karl Hardman, Marilyn Eastman, and Russ Streiner. It was like a picnic for us. The very fact that our film was playing there suddenly made it a real movie."

The weekends drew even larger numbers and the *Living Dead*, under Continental's supervision (in-house publicity promoted the pic as "the most realistic and frightening horror film to be produced in the last six years"), began shambling from city to city, attracting healthy crowds and mostly positive, if occasionally cautionary, reviews. Things did not go so smoothly at the film's New York City premiere, though. Recalls Russo, "While coffee and donuts were being served in the theater lobby—which Russ and I thought were pretty shabby refreshments for a movie premiere—the reviewer from *Variety* charged over to [distributors] Harold Marenstein and Jerry Pickman and gave them a nasty tongue-lashing" for, according to him, not treating the press with proper respect in the past and not readily making their pictures available for previewing.

This particular reviewer ended up writing one of the most devastating reviews *Night of the Living Dead* has ever gotten:

"This film casts serious aspersions on the integrity of its makers, distrib[utor] Walter Reade, the film industry as a whole, and exhib[itor]s who book the pic[ture], as well as raising doubts about the future of the regional cinema movement and the moral health of filmgoers who cheerfully opt for unrelieved sadism."

The *Variety* scribe wasn't the only naysayer. "We were just slammed!" Romero told a *VideoScope* interviewer decades after the fact. "The MPAA didn't exist yet, so we were taking all kinds of heat for being brutal. Roger Ebert did a big piece about kids running crying from the theater."

Today, Ebert's review, erroneously dated January 5, 1967, on his Web site (1969 was the more probable annum, which was when *Reader's Digest* reprinted the gut-munching movie review, opposite, apparently sans irony, a yummy ad for Roy Rogers Roast Beef Restaurant), may be more interesting for its many gaffes than for its frothing rhetoric. To wit: "The opening scene was set in a cemetery . . . where a teenage couple [?] are [sic] placing a wreath on a grave." Later, Rog gets to the good parts: "When the fire died down, the ghouls approached the truck and ripped apart the bodies and ate them. One ghoul ate a shoulder joint with great delight, occasionally stopping to wipe his face. Another dug into a nice mess of intestines." Still later:

> "This was ghouls eating people up—and you could actually see what they were eating."
> —Roger Ebert's review, 1969

The Negro has to kill the little girl-ghoul, and then her father.

The kids in the audience were stunned. There was almost complete silence. . . . This was ghouls eating people up—and you could actually see what they were eating. This was little girls killing their mothers. This was being set on fire. Worst of all, even the hero got killed.

Night of the Living Dead was passed for general audiences by the Chicago Police Censor Board. Since it had no nudity in it [Rog must have been shielding his eyes by the time the naked zombie gal surfaced], it was all right for kids, I guess.

In Ebert's defense, he ends his somewhat inattentive jeremiad with the recognition that the newly established but not yet implemented MPAA code would have properly placed *Night* off-limits to the kiddie crowd. (In a revisionist intro to his Web site-posted review, he cites that he admires the movie itself.) The code would go into effect a month later.

As Romero points out, "We didn't make the movie for kids! It's not *The Beast from 20,000 Fathoms* [a film itself considered a bit strong in its day (1953) for a scene showing the titular titan swallowing a cop]. *We* didn't put it on a double-bill with whatever kids' show was on. They were booking it on double-bills with very benign little horror things or fantasy things, but we didn't do the bookings, and that's not what the movie was for. We really got dropped!" Ironically, but perhaps not surprisingly, Ebert's warning only succeeded in drawing more attention and business to the film.

Romero remained unapologetic re *Night*'s purpose. "The intention of this movie was to scare you, yes, and to push the envelope beyond where other scare movies had gone, with the gut-eating and all of that stuff."

Some influential critics were less harsh in their appraisal. In *The New York Times* Vincent Canby categorized the film as "spare, uncluttered, but really silly"—not exactly a ringing endorsement but at least a step in the right direction.

Despite the occasional drubbing, there was still plenty of life left in the *Living Dead*, which, ultimately, played in thousands of theaters, often held over for weeks, even months at a stretch. For a time, it was paired with the fairly innocuous British sci-fi TV spinoff *Dr. Who and the Daleks* and later with Mario Bava's far stronger *giallo Blood and Black Lace*, usually complete with schlocky ad campaigns promising "IF 'NIGHT OF THE LIVING DEAD' FRIGHTENS YOU TO DEATH You Are Insured for $50,000" or proffering a "Death Certificate" to sign. At one point, the National Association of Theater Owners named *Night* "exploitation picture of the month."

In 1970, *Night* shared a double-bill (on the bottom, no less) with the black-themed *Slaves*, an overheated antebellum pot-boiler starring Stephen Boyd, Dionne Warwick, and Ossie Davis.

Continental further emphasized *Night*'s racial angle via lobby cards depicting Ben slugging Harry. Later, in its seemingly endless run, *Night* often split bills with outright "blaxploitation" films. At the time, African-American audiences reportedly comprised a disproportionately large (some 30 percent) portion of moviegoers, particularly for horror films. Soon-to-be-fellow-cult-movie-king John (*Pink Flamingos*) Waters remembers catching *Night* during this period. "I saw *Night of the Living Dead*'s first-run at a drive-in. *Night of the Living Dead* was scary, not fun." In a true double bill to die for, Manhattan's Bijou Theater briefly married *Night* with *Freaks* ("One of us! One of us!").

And early in 1971, over two years after the film's initial roll-out, a Washington, D.C. theater began running it at midnight, kick-starting a trend that reached its zenith soon after at New York City's Waverly Theater. "It stayed there for about two years," Russo remembers, "and kept on attracting huge crowds. During the early part of that run, in the spring and summer of 1971, it got glowing reviews from Rex Reed and Howard Smith, and also an article in the *New York Daily News* that stuck it with the 'cult' label."

Reviews for *Night of the Living Dead* had definitely enjoyed an uptick since *Variety*'s screed first saw the light of day. Wrote Reed: "If you want to see what turns a B movie into a classic, don't miss *Night of the Living Dead*. It is unthinkable for anyone seriously interested in horror movies not to see it." The influential Pauline Kael stressed the film's intense sincerity, labeling it "one of the most gruesomely terrifying movies ever made—and when you leave the theater you may wish you could forget the whole horrible experience. . . . The film's grainy, banal seriousness works for it—gives it a crude realism."

> "If you want to see what turns a B movie into a classic, don't miss **Night of the Living Dead.**"
> —*Rex Reed's review, 1971*

That oft-cited grainy quality was not intended by the filmmakers nor was it evident in all prints. "We didn't have enough savvy to specify what kind of film stock the original prints were made on," a sadder but wiser Russ Streiner later explained, "and the original distributor took the easy way out, printed the release prints of the movie on out-of-date, and in some cases, mismatched stock and that sort of thing, and so consequently when the picture showed up on a movie screen or a television screen, it never looked like that rich black-and-white picture that we knew we had in the can."

Bill Quigley, a buyer at Walter Reade, recalls, "It was a different kind of age, because all the movie theaters just had single screens. We had eleven screens in Manhattan, that's where it really found its audience and really took off."

Meantime, the kudos kept on coming. A reviewer for *Film Daily* opined, "This is a pearl of a horror picture, which exhibits all the earmarks of a sleeper." Which, as time would tell, proved to be a serious understatement.

Hip critics stressed *Night*'s subversive elements. Film historian Sumiko Higashi pointed to the film's black-and-white newsreel-style footage, search-and-destroy missions complete with whirring helicopters (well, one anyway), and, of course, the grisly violence. *Midnight Movies* co-author and film critic J. Hoberman noted, "The movie was made in 1968. It was made in the most violent year in American history since the Civil War. It's shot like cinema vérité, as though it were the evening news. It never wavered from its desire to terrorize the audience and offer no hope at the end. . . . *Night of the Living Dead* could only be understood as a movie about the Vietnam War." *The Village Voice*'s Elliot Stein, likewise emphasized *Night*'s Vietnam parallels, pointing out that the action "was not set in Transylvania, but Pennsylvania—this was Middle America at war, and the zombie carnage seemed a grotesque echo of the conflict then raging in Vietnam."

It was Stein who coaxed Museum of Modern Art curators Larry Kardish and Adrienne Mancia to a 42nd Street grindhouse to see the film, leading to a prestigious MoMA screening, part of a "Cineprobe" series devoted to new directors like Romero, who fielded audience questions after the show. No one was more shocked by these fortuitous turns of events than *Night*'s novice helmer: "When we were making *Night of the Living Dead*, we thought it was going to be playing in a few drive-in theaters and maybe return our investment," said Romero. "And maybe if it did that, we'd be able to make something else. That's really as far as it went." Future *Document of the Dead* director Roy Frumkes, who attended the MoMA event, recalls: "He [Romero] seemed to be distancing himself from the film, assuring the audience that he had other, nonhorror projects in mind. Which he did, but horror reclaimed him before long."

Romero was well aware of *Night*'s highly extolled subversive subtexts, which, in 1968, were still unusual in horror. They certainly flourished in other genres, however, even westerns, where traditional themes were being treated with an often violently revisionist irony, spurred in part by the success of the postmodern spaghetti oaters of Sergio Leone and his Italo cronies. "I thought it had all gone unnoticed in *Night*," Romero said. "It took about three years before anyone said anything about it like that, that it might have some merits in that regard."

The film, meanwhile, received even more serious critical consideration—and commercial success—in Europe, scoring rave reviews from Britain's *Sight and Sound* (even though England's censors had drastically cut the film) and France's influential *Cahiers du Cinema*. *Night* attracted especially large crowds in France, Spain, where it unspooled at Madrid's largest theater for eighteen months, and Italy.

Above all else, the timing was right. Romero puts the film in cultural context: "All the big Japanese monster movies are anti-nuke movies. You could say a lot of the stuff in the '50s and '60s, the stuff that immediately preceded *Night of the Living Dead*, was about the fear of science. But nothing really went deeply into the societal whole. Nothing was really very much of a sociopolitical satire, if you will. So I think that's partly why the film got recognized."

Beyond its sociopolitical ramifications, the film hit home on a purely visceral level, making it one of those rare outings that scored with drive-in, midnight-movie, *and* art-house crowds. Critic George Abagnalo noted that normally jaded and notoriously vocal 42nd Street patrons often departed those grindhouse theaters in a state of shock. "Some people laugh when the film ends," he observed, "but not because it is funny or badly done.

They laugh because they can't believe what they have seen. Some leave silently, looking like they're about to vomit."

Says Romero, "I think the fact that it didn't flinch and pushed the envelope a little bit rather than cut away when someone is bitten by a zombie or torn apart by a zombie, that sort of opened the doors, as well. I wouldn't have been able to do it if there was an MPAA at the time."

Russo agrees. "The little girl, Karen, cannibalizes her mother and father. At that time, I don't think it would have gotten an R rating, neither would many of the other scenes."

As for the film's enduring appeal, Russo posits, "It is clear that all of us must have a deep-seated fear of being set upon, attacked, by unfeeling, uncaring personages who do not take the time to know and respect, but only to hate us. We all dread the witch hunters, the lynch mob, the terrorists who plant bombs to kill those they have never met. The existence of this primal fear, this dread, within our psyches, and its vivid evocation, is the truly basic reason for the success of *Night of the Living Dead*."

Romero elaborates, "I think there are several underlying themes in *Night of the Living Dead*: People's inability to communicate—the protagonists are in a situation that they could probably easily solve if they would stop fighting among themselves. They cause their own downfall. They don't really address the problem because everyone has a different perspective on it, and they can't bring their views together. Tribalism keeps people from the end goal. The thing that I was working with foremost in my mind was the idea of a revolutionary society taking over, and, in this case, literally swallowing the outgoing civilization that doesn't even realize it's being overcome. That's really the theme of the zombie films I did, on a sociopolitical level." Besides, "It was 1968, man. *Everybody* had a 'message.' I was just making a horror film, and I think the anger, and the attitude, and all that's there is just there because it was 1968."

Russ Streiner reflects, "*Night of the Living Dead* has taken on a life of its own, so to speak. How that happened is new audiences are constantly being introduced to it. And that has perpetuated this film, and, apparently, enough people think it's a good picture, they find different things they like about it. But this common creative effort that we all put together as a team, people are still sensing that there's something good and valuable in the story itself."

Above all, says Romero, "One thing it had is an absolute goal. We were all pushing toward that goal. It doesn't lie to you." Russo agrees, "One of the key ingredients is that we were always true to our concept, and we did not try to snooker the audience; instead, we tried to pay them off, to give them the kind of movie they always hoped to see."

Judith O'Dea chimes in, "In regular horror films, it took you at least forty-five minutes before you got to see the monster. Here, the terror begins from the very beginning. It was no-holds-barred. You saw everything and nobody survives."

> *"The terror begins from the very beginning."*
> —Judith O'Dea

"We had no idea what we were making," says Gary Streiner. "George had a better idea than most of us, but even George had little clue. We were much more concerned that whatever we did, we were 100 percent behind it. I don't think *I* knew how big it is until I started the [*Living Dead*] fest and started communicating with the fans. They are a big part of its magic."

Brother Russ sums it up even more succinctly: "We made it a good film. The fans made it a classic."

A *Night* to Remember:
What the *Living Dead* Means to Me
by Larry Fessenden

I am often asked to name my favorite horror movie. I have been giving the same answer for years, even though it is an impossible question, because the genre is filled with so many outstanding films that stretch the gamut from monster movies to slasher; ghost stories to zombie pictures. But I always answer *Night of the Living Dead*. For me, the film is at the fulcrum between the old black-and-white horror films from Universal Studios that I loved as a kid—*Frankenstein*, *The Wolf Man*, *The Creature from the Black Lagoon*—and the harsher films that were made in the '60s and beyond, like *The Texas Chainsaw Massacre*, *The Thing*, or *The Shining*.

Night of the Living Dead ushered in a new era on several fronts. It is the first film I know of that acknowledges its own genre while changing it: Barbara and her brother are in a graveyard and a shadowy figure approaches from a distance. Teasingly the brother utters, "They're coming to get you, Barbara" in a Boris Karloff voice, a reference to a half century of horror tropes that had come before. The distant figure approaches and kills the brother, and the film veers into a modern existential nightmare—the quaint horror of the past becomes a shocking reality.

Beyond its genre resonance, *Night of the Living Dead* has an effortless cultural significance, in portraying a black man as the stable and rational hero of the film, while the zombie hunters on TV, the petty family in the house, and the broken heroine, Barbara, all evoke some aspect of the white racism of the time. While none of these evocations are even remotely telegraphed by the film, they give the movie an indelible tension, and Ben an added dignity.

The zombies that director Romero created for *Night of the Living Dead* are relentless, mindless, and determined; they seem to represent all that is despicable and terrifying about the masses in modern life—destructive and stupid; this archetype still resonates today. What I like

---

Since his 1991 feature-film debut, *No Telling*, filmmaker (and frequent actor) LARRY FESSENDEN has become synonymous with thoughtful, independent horror films, from *Habit* (1997) through *Wendigo* (2001) and *The Last Winter* (2006).

about *Night of the Living Dead* is that, while it may be inspired by the cultural upheaval of its time—the chaotic late 1960s—it is first and foremost a fantasy film, a product of the imagination. A zombie movie, however scary, remains metaphorical and not literal, which provides the viewer the pleasure of artifice. By contrast, the slasher movies that have come to define horror today seem to wallow in the depravity of real violence without offering the poetry of the fantastic.

Finally, it is the utter hopelessness of *Night of the Living Dead* that makes it striking, and a stark departure from the movies that preceded it, where the monster was destroyed and order restored. Throughout the movie, the humans battle each other, even as the monsters beating at the doors are the perceived enemy. When victory over the night seems to signal a new beginning, our hero is gunned down arbitrarily, mistaken for just another zombie, tossed on a heap and burned. The bleakness of the film is its greatest resonance and what keeps it relevant.

Night of the Living Dead stands as a testament to independent film-making; it was created outside of the system through sheer ingenuity and spawned an entire subgenre in cinema: the zombie movie. Its story takes place in one unified time and place, giving it a classic Aristotelian structure, and while its themes and violence and expressive stark film style make it modern, its depiction of life's futility makes it timeless.

7 AFTERLIFE OF *THE LIVING DEAD*

When you're making films in Pittsburgh, you look at
all the other movies out there and you start thinking,
"I can do that."
—George Romero, on *There's Always Vanilla*

By the time the tally was in, five years following its initial release, *Night of the Living Dead*, with a total final cost of $114,000 (including deferrals), earned the title of the "most profitable horror film ever produced outside the walls of a major studio." After a decade, the take would climb to between $12 and $15 million in domestic box office alone. The film had been translated into more than twenty languages and distributed across Europe (where, according to the *Wall Street Journal*, it was the top-grossing film of 1969), Canada and Australia, raking in an additional $30 million internationally.

Karl Hardman and Marilyn Eastman experienced *Night*'s international popularity firsthand. Explains Eastman, "We were in Spain doing a show, and blocks away we could see a marquee with huge cutouts of ourselves and other cast members. The line to get into the theater was two or three blocks long. We simply couldn't believe it was our movie playing there until we got up real close and, yup, there it was." The reality of the pic's global impact became even more up close and personal during a French sojourn. "Karl and I were in the Paris airport," she said, "and people were coming up to us and recognizing us and asking for autographs!"

Even the early domestic returns were not lost on the Image Ten crew. "That left us chomping at the bit to make another feature," Russo recalls. But obstacles again loomed. "Even though *Night* was earning plenty of money, none of it was immediately finding its way back into our pockets. It was taking the Walter Reade Organization months and months to collect from the theaters in which the picture had already played." And there was another sticking point. "Even if money *had* come back to us quickly, we would've had a problem using it, since Image Ten had been set up to produce only one picture.

"We believed that our second time out of the gate we would make a real stunner and, perhaps, sell it to a major studio for a ton of money. At first, the leading candidate was something we referred to as the *Horror Anthology*, which we envisioned as a compendium of perhaps five vignettes that would be the most suspenseful, terrifying pieces ever committed to film."

Later, Russo concocted an alternate thriller concept, "about a group of people shipwrecked on an island. . . . One day they find some evidence that some other people are on this island. They're attacked by wild, crazy people, wearing three-corner hats, and they have rusty old guns. It turns out that the island is populated by descendents of French soldiers that were on their way to America to fight in the Revolution and got shipwrecked. It was going to be the conflict of the eighteenth century with the twentieth."

Romero, however, as per his Museum of Modern Art address, resisted these ideas. Nor did he wish to revisit the *Dead* so quickly. "I didn't want to rush into that. I didn't want to get typecast or go right back out and do something that would have been pretty much the same as *Night of the Living Dead*. I didn't really have a good idea for extending the story. I had the germ of an idea, but we really wouldn't have had the money to make something like *Dawn of the Dead* out of it. I couldn't really get a lot bigger with the concept."

After contemplating *Horror Anthology* for a spell, several

> *"We envisioned . . . a compendium of perhaps five vignettes that would be the most suspenseful, terrifying pieces ever committed to film."*
>
> —John Russo

of the *Night* cohorts, including Russo, fell into line with Romero's thinking and decided to spurn the fright field, at least for their sophomore movie. The group's first proposed project, Rudy Ricci's script *Beauty Sleeping*, was a drama about a woman who feels trapped in a loveless marriage. When that failed to land backing, they decided to chase *The Graduate*'s tail, which led to the wannabe hip and happening "youth" drama *There's Always Vanilla* (a.k.a. *The Affair*), a feature-length expansion of a half-hour black-and-white film called *At Play with the Angels*, starring Ray Laine and written and directed by Rudy Ricci.

At the time, Romero was convinced that jumping on the '60s youth-movie bandwagon would be the way to go, despite a glaring absence of finances and the star power needed to drive a non-genre film. The director felt sure the goal was within the group's grasp. "When you're making films in Pittsburgh," he explains, "you look at all the other movies out there and you start thinking, 'I can do that.' *There's Always Vanilla* was really an imitation of a Hollywood film."

From the get-go, not all the original *Night* movers and shakers were thrilled by the prospect. "We gave Karl Hardman and Marilyn Eastman an opportunity to be part of the enterprise," says Russo, "but they did not see the merit. So Russ Streiner and I were going to coproduce it, with George directing from a screenplay by Rudy."

In the film, Laine stars as Chris, a typically smug, perpetually amused '60s musician and slacker (with a rich dad) and a chronic sufferer of what used to be known as Elliot Gould Syndrome (a thankfully since-cured malaise). He's the only one who, with his built-in BS detector and psychological X-ray vision, can clearly perceive modern life's myriad hypocrisies and absurdities (you know, or probably once knew, the type.

Romero opens the film with a lyrical, if clichéd image of two colorful balloons free-floating against an azure sky, set to the strains of "Wild Mountain Thyme." We almost immediately crash to Earth, zeroing in on urban gawkers surrounding an outdoor device called the Ultimate Machine, an elaborate, expensive Rube Goldberg-style contraption that appears to serve no useful purpose, a metaphor for encroaching corporate culture and its manufactured consumerism. Chris then addresses the camera, as he will at arbitrary intervals throughout the film, to share his faux-hippie, free-spirit observations.

The movie morphs into sort of a Pittsburgh-set *Darling* with the introduction of foxy commercial model Lynn (*Night*'s Judith Ridley, using her married name Judith Streiner), first seen on the hectic set of a fantasy-heavy beer ad. Chris and Lynn, who radiates a bit of a homegrown Brigitte Bardot vibe, quickly connect for a fling that runs the gamut from groovy romantic montages to a harrowing sequence in an illicit abortionist's office (complete with a cameo by erstwhile Sheriff McClelland, George Kosana, as a scary medical henchman).

Along the way, Romero displays his considerable cinematic skills with imaginative shots and ironic touches but, overall, seems to be borrowing, liberally and ill-advisedly, from John Cassavetes' muse. Today, *Vanilla* succeeds more as a regional time-capsule—for starters, it's the only pic to proffer a whirlwind inside tour of the Steel City advertising world—than a compelling film in its own right. It rates a look for armchair counterculture historians, as well as Romero completists.

The enthusiasm that had fueled *Night*'s creation dissipated dramatically as the *Vanilla* shoot dragged on, sowing seeds of dissension among the band. "Things immediately began falling apart," Russo remembers. "Our previously tight little group started to come unglued. There were internal arguments over the script, the concept, the cast, the production schedule, and the functions of key production personnel. Whereas with *Night* we had pulled together as one, now we were pulling in separate directions. A movie eventually got made, but it was far from our best work. Our picture needed to have timeliness and innocent charm, and those qualities had been smothered and lost in the production squabbles and hassles."

Romero doesn't disagree. "I don't think any of us were very happy with the way it turned out. It was an awful experience, and I care very little about it." Judith Ridley echoes a similar, if somewhat softer sentiment. "It was a difficult film to get through," she said. "I was underqualified. I wanted to do my best on the picture, but I never saw myself as an actress. I never felt that there was much in the way of talent as far as I was concerned. It was not as pleasant shooting that movie as it was Living Dead; there was a lot of tension."

> "It was not as pleasant shooting that movie as it was Living Dead; there was a lot of tension."
> —Judith Ridley, on making There's Always Vanilla

Distributors weren't any happier with the end result. Says Romero, "I think a lot of people turned it down just because it wasn't a horror film—it didn't have any other kind of obvious hooks." In fact, *There's Always Vanilla* didn't receive a sporadic release until 1972, via Lee Hessel's Cambist Films. The $100,000 film tanked with critics and audiences, even in its native Pittsburgh.

Meantime, Image Ten investors were growing impatient regarding *Night*'s invisible returns. Russ Streiner explains, "We received a letter of estimate from our producer's representative that went into some detail describing to us how, by the end of 1969, from just the United States and Canada, we would have accrued a quarter of a million dollars."

The actual payback fell far short of that figure. Image Ten filed a lawsuit against Walter Reade to regain rights to the picture along with $1.5 million in damages for allegedly being shortchanged on the grosses. The case dragged on interminably. Not until 1975 did the Pennsylvania Supreme Court even get around to deciding that the case should be tried there rather than New York; by that time the lawsuit had doubled to $3 million. The distribution rights reverted to Image Ten when Walter Reade went bankrupt in 1978.

To this day, neither Russo nor Romero hide their disappointment. "We never got any money from them," Russo states flatly.

"Some of the things that did happen with judges along the way were pretty strange." Adds Romero, "We got knocked off amazingly by them. We did everything right, the American way, and all that bullshit. We were going to beat them in court, and, all of a sudden, the cats from Walter Reade stopped showing up. It reached a point where they were held in contempt. We went through every judicial avenue we could go through and were left with nothing that we could do short of physical violence. What do you do in that situation? You walk away and you say, 'I learned something.'"

"It's very unfair that the distributor took advantage," Judith Ridley choruses. "They worked so very hard, struggled, and did without. They really deserved the rewards that *Night of the Living Dead* could have brought them." Echoed Karl Hardman, "Words can't describe the magnitude of frustration and distress we all felt. We *knew* the picture was making lots and lots of money." Putting the issue in personal perspective, Romero adds, "The bottom line of it all is that of all the people involved with *Night of the Living Dead*, I have the least to complain about, because I'm the one that got the reputation and all out of it."

Around the same time, the Image Ten crew absorbed an even greater shock: Their picture didn't have a legal copyright. "Our first finished 35-millimeter print bore the title *Night of the Flesh Eaters*," Russo explains, "but we had to change it when we got threatened by a lawyer whose clients had already made a picture by that name" [1964's *The Flesh Eaters*, which has since acquired its own small but loyal cult following]. Romero picks up the sad story. "When Walter Reade put the film out, they changed the title. They titled it *Night of the Living Dead*. They didn't include the copyright on the titles when they did the new overprints. We had put our title copyright notice, the C with the circle around it, on the titles. We should

> "It remains to this day in public domain. It's a technicality we argued for fifteen years. . . . It's very hard to fight off the pirates unless you've got the bucks."
> —George Romero

have put the copyright notice at the end of the film, which is where it belongs. Nobody noticed that the copyright notice had come off. Three or four years into the film's release, a lot of people noticed that the film had no copyright on it. And it remains, to this day, in public domain. It's a technicality we argued for fifteen years. In 1983, we won a copyright in federal court. The company, Image Ten, has no money and never made a lot of money off the movie. It's very hard to fight off the pirates unless you've got the bucks."

"Curiously, since *Night of the Living Dead*, they've changed the copyright laws so the same kind of thing could not happen to a picture today," Russ Streiner notes. The United States' Berne Convention Implementation Act and Copyright Term Extension Act provided for automatic copyright on any work once it assumed a "fixed form" and automatic copyright term renewal on all copyrighted works, whether or not the copyright notice appeared on the work. "So that's the underpinning as to why we believe that our position is, ultimately, right. And we just have to keep pursuing it, because it is rightfully our property, and there's no other argument to be made."

Tensions were running high at The Latent Image headquarters. These were due not only to *Vanilla*'s nonperformance, the *Night* copyright snafu, and the above cash-flow problems but because personality conflicts were intensifying, too. Romero's unpopular decision to bring outside ad exec Al Croft into the fold to handle the agency's commercial side further exacerbated the volatile situation. Richard Ricci recalls, "By the end, people wouldn't talk to each other, and best friends for a lifetime split apart and began talking to their lawyers."

Romero, for one, felt it was time to fly solo, an ambition he'd been harboring even before starting *Vanilla*. "By the time we finished [*Night*], I was lusting for control. I was frustrated by the compromises, both creative and social, that were forced by our democratic process. . . . I came out of it wanting all the controls, wanting to be the auteur, yet appreciating the need for cooperative effort in this medium with all its technical and creative specialties, many of which are far better served by others than by me. I longed for the day when I could pay for services, and, there-fore, be the boss man."

While crafting commercials by day, Romero soldiered on with several still-friendly Latent Image alums (production super-visor, Vince Survinski; coproducer, Gary Streiner; and cemetery zombie, Bill Hinzman, the last signed to handle lighting and ad-ditional photography chores) to embark on a new feature film, *Jack's Wife* (1972), lensed in 16mm and later blown up to 35mm. A raw but frequently effective fable, dealing with the mental meltdown of Joan, an upper-class, early middle-aged woman (soap opera actress Jan White in a bravura performance). Alien-ated from her husband (Bill Thunhurst) and prattling female friends, the character is deserted by her runaway college-age daughter (Joedda McClain) and engaged in an ill-advised affair with the latter's snarky, head-games playing, sometime boyfriend Greg (*Vanilla*'s Ray Laine). Joan seeks release by drifting into am-ateur witchcraft.

Driven by simultaneously harrowing and ironic (and alto-gether brilliant) symbol-laden dream sequences, frequent ex-treme close-ups, and intense confrontational acting, the picture is, like *Vanilla*, more reminiscent of John Cassavetes' *Faces*—with a dash of Bergman-style depression and a pinch of Felliniesque surrealism—than *Rosemary's Baby*. That Roman Polanski chiller, then (and still) the yardstick for witchcraft films, even receives an onscreen reference, as does *The Graduate*, with Laine's Greg calling White's Joan "Mrs. Robinson."

Powerful, even profound images abound. Greg tricks Joan's loud, tipsy friend Shirley (Ann Muffly) into believing she's smok-ing her first joint; the humiliation is almost too uncomfortably real to endure. Two nightmare segments likewise stand out. One is the film's opening sequence, when Joan is led Svengali-like by a casually callous Jack through autumnal woods, where sharp, bare branches slap and slash her face, leading to their ultimate destination: Joan's outdoor kennel (!). Another heart-racing dream sees Joan pursued through her house by a hideously masked killer (*Dead*'s cemetery zombie Bill Hinzman, again in a menacing mode). In an earlier fantasy scene, a slick salesman leads her on a tour of her own barren existence, including a mirror that reflects the image of Joan as an old woman. This is simultaneously heady and horrific material, if partially undermined by some uneven acting and persistent pacing problems.

Although far more of an artistic success than *Vanilla*, *Jack's Wife* experienced similar budgetary woes. Says Romero, "Not only did it suffer from being a $250,000 movie, but it suffered from being a $250,000 movie that had to get made for a hundred grand! The differences between this and *Rosemary's Baby* are vast in terms of just execution. But, thematically, it's there. *Jack's Wife* was really sort of a feminist picture—the beginning days of women's liberation, and so forth. Even though I wrote it, I wrote it based on the feelings and observations of some female friends of mine."

Romero incorporated the sinister, semi-supernatural elements as a secondary thread. "I wanted to sort of touch back on the horror roots using witchcraft. Even though this is not a horror film, there are a couple of scary sequences." In the end, Romero discovered his eyes were bigger than his budget. "This was a script I liked very much, but due to the financial muddle, my first time in the driver's seat was a woeful experience that all but destroyed me financially."

> **"I wanted to sort of touch back on the horror roots using witchcraft."**
> —George Romero
> on Jack's Wife

With its paucity of true horror overtones (although the filmmaker incorporates a neat *Night* nod with a comic "zombie" moment in Jack and Joan's bedroom), the movie, like *Vanilla*, presented a major marketing problem. "This is the kind of film," Romero later realized, "that needs a name cast in order to get good distribution." With that key ingredient absent, distributor Jack H. (*The Blob*) Harris reedited the film with radical cuts and tried to disguise it as an erotic exploitation venture under the dubious moniker *Hungry Wives*, but that likewise failed to fly. The film eventually surfaced on VHS in 1985 as *Season of the Witch* (with Donovan's titular tune on the soundtrack); that misleading title disappointed fright fans looking for a jolt of expected Romero madness à la *Night of the Living Dead*.

Romero still regrets the missed opportunity. "The only one I'd like to remake is _Jack's Wife_. Of my first four films, it's one of the best ideas and the least successfully executed."

Meantime, the many Latent Image lawsuits, an unpaid bank loan to finance _Jack's Wife_ and commercial cash-flow problems left the cult filmmaker in serious debt. It was enough to drive one . . . well, crazy.

A *Night* to Dismember
or, "They're Coming to Get You . . . Toxie!"
by Lloyd Kaufman

Greetings from Tromaville! George A. Romero's *Night of the Living Dead* brings me back to a very, very special time in my life. Yes, I remember it well: a brisk fall evening at Yale University in 1968. My Friday night date and I were walking across the old campus. Thomas and I had just left the Gay Power Sock Hop and were coming down off a pretty reckless afternoon of binging on, as Bob Dylan allegedly described it to Andy Warhol, "that faggy speed shit." As we were walking, we noticed a poster for an event hosted by the Yale Film Society.

On this particular evening, they were screening a virtually unknown film by a virtually unknown group of filmmakers from, of all places, Pittsburgh, Pennsylvania. Naturally, my interest was piqued. After convincing Thomas that we could spoon later, we entered the theater. The lights dimmed and the projectionist ran a grainy, 16mm print of *Night of the Living Dead*.

Because the movies that the Yale Film Society usually screened were by directors like Stan Brakhage or Sam Fuller, I thought *Night of the Living Dead* might be of the same ilk. Accordingly, I was at first a bit disinterested; I was also distracted by Thomas's hand inching towards my throbbing, two-inch member. Just as his hand finally made contact, I looked up at the screen to see the Graveyard Zombie grab Barbara. While Barbara's brother Johnny struggled with the zombie, Thomas struggled into my pants. I let out a gasp—but not a gasp of delight, a gasp of shock as Johnny's head was smashed against a tombstone. From that point on, I could not take my eyes off that movie!

Freaked out by the images on the screen—and jealous that I was paying too much attention to the Graveyard Zombie—Thomas left the theater in a panicked huff. I spent the next hour and a half engrossed in what ended up being one of the most politically poignant films I had

LLOYD KAUFMAN, president of Troma Entertainment, is no stranger to the cult-movie biz, having created such enduring outré icons as *The Toxic Avenger*, mop-wielding mutant star of stage, screen and television, and distributing *South Park* duo Trey Parker and Matthew Stone's celluloid debut *Cannibal! The Musical*.

ever seen. Immediately, I could see that this was both a masterpiece of art, as well as social commentary, and I marveled at George Romero's courage to address an issue which I was, and still am, very passionate about: Gay rights.

Many have made the case that *Night of the Living Dead* confronts Cold War fears and Civil Rights issues. Yes, the film may have had something to do with Capitalism versus Communism and white vs. black. I, however, knew immediately that the infighting between Ben and Harry Cooper, over whether to stay in or out of the basement, was representative of a homosexual couple struggling with their gay identity and debating whether or not to bring their relationship out of the closet! Also, since this was twenty years before CNN would be showing body parts during prime-time television, I was totally blown away by how graphic Romero's movie was.

Today, I believe George Romero is America's most underrated director and his films have been a major influence on my filmmaking career. You can clearly see Romero's influence on my satire-cum-gore in *The Toxic Avenger*, *Terror Firmer*, and *Tromeo and Juliet*, to name a few. My latest film, *Poultrygeist: Night of the Chicken Dead*, not only takes a cue from Romero in its title but also touches on the issue that Romero had the nerve to confront in 1968: Gay rights!

GOING *CRAZIES*

Jesus Christ, this is so random!
—Richard France, *The Crazies*

After two strikeouts, Romero finally resolved to return to his horror roots with *The Crazies*, a *Night of the Living Dead*-like tale about a town overrun by toxic citizens, trigger-happy soldiers, and typically inept, deceitful authorities—an ideal recipe for pure Romeran terror. The project took shape when Latent Image cohort and frequent composer Paul McCullough wrote a cerebral screenplay entitled *The Mad People*. In that scenario, the government and the military try to contain a bio-weapons spill that contaminates the Evans City water supply, spreading death and dementia among the locals.

Romero interested Cambist Releasing honcho Lee Hessel—who'd earlier handled *There's Always Vanilla* and had a cult hit with John G. Avildsen's raunchy romp *Cry Uncle* (1971)—in backing the project. Hessel was ready to take the plunge but only with a major script overhaul calling for less meditation and more action. "Paul tried to write a couple of drafts but didn't like the way it was going," Romero recalls, "so he sold the property to Latent Image." Romero agreed to rewrite the script, later admitting, "It's nothing like Paul wanted it to be, but I hope he's okay with the result."

Night of the Living Dead continued to enjoy a growing reputation and receipts via an extended rollout (including many inferior, pirated prints) and expanded midnight bookings. But it hadn't yet fully penetrated the zeitgeist when Romero began filming *The Crazies*. He did have a somewhat bigger budget—$270,000—to play with and had reason to hope for a better outcome than he'd had with *Vanilla* and *Jack's Wife*. While *The Crazies* marked the filmmaker's first SAG production, Romero again indulged his preference to mix professional thespians, cast out of New York in this instance, with local part-time actors and, for smaller roles, outright amateurs.

For the first time, Romero relinquished the camera, the same 35mm Arriflex used to film *Night*, entrusting erstwhile cemetery zombie Bill Hinzman with cinematography chores. "I sort of wanted to take a break and be able to talk to the actors a little more," Romero explains. "It was the first time I had my hands off the camera and free to do some other stuff. I knew Bill was really good, so he did it." Says Hinzman, "From the very first, working with George, I learned his style of camerawork and I still have the same style. When someone asks him why I was shooting instead of him, he said because Bill can read my mind, which I took as a compliment."

Romero returned to the *Living Dead*'s old stomping grounds, Evans City, along with nearby Zelienople, where he would spend some forty days in the field directing the film. The basic message remains the same as *Night*'s: "In crisis, you can't tell who's crazy and who isn't."

Crises virtually grow on trees in *The Crazies*. While it doesn't have quite the same nightmare intensity as *Night*—what *does?*— *The Crazies* creates an atmosphere of unrelenting anxiety and chaos. As in *Night*, much of the mood is achieved via Romero's signature kinetic cutting, a technique acquired from years of shaping complex, info-packed thirty- to sixty-second ad spots; Romero also cites being influenced by Jean-Luc Godard's cubist approach in *Breathless* and Sam Peckinpah's squibfest *The Wild Bunch*. A pulse-racing martial drumbeat score à la *Dr. Strangelove*—we're even treated to a few bars of "When Johnny Comes Marching Home"—further propels the nonstop action; later in the film, the soundtrack occasionally gives way to more conventional, less effective library music.

The Crazies opens at full-tilt. In a home not unlike *Night*'s fabled farmhouse, a young brother and sister, portrayed by Bill Hinzman's offspring, play a familiar game. The brother does his darnedest to unnerve Sis by staggering up the cellar stairs, arms

"Billy, you're trying to scare me!"

—Sis, in The Crazies

outstretched, in his best zombie impersonation. Screams Sis, "Billy, you're trying to scare me!" Suddenly, Billy's face goes rigid as he spies Dad putting the pop in apoplexy, destroying furniture, and generally freaking out. Sis discovers Mom's bloody body, an apparent victim of her spouse's unexplained rage, and we're off to the races, George Romero style.

"I guess there are some similarities to the opening sequence," the director concedes in a DVD commentary shared with fellow fright filmmaker William (*Maniac*) Lustig. "A brother and sister in sort of a normal situation that, suddenly, goes south. It also starts in the cellar. There's the similarity of the family unit cracking up, too. I guess, except for a couple of direct references—the kids playing zombie on the stairs—they were probably unconscious or subconscious connections."

Soon Dad is busily dousing the house with gasoline and tossing his flaming Zippo into the lethal liquid, causing a spectacular—and seemingly budget-challenging—conflagration. Luck and timing played vital roles in the scene's success. "The fire department was practicing on an old house," Romero explains. "Their guys were gonna do a practice run. We said, 'If you're gonna do that, let us come and shoot.' That's how we got the fire trucks and everything else."

We're next introduced to a nice, normal couple, fireman David (W.G. McMillan) and pregnant nurse fiancée Judy (Lane Carroll). They've been roused from their blissful premarital bed by separate emergency phone calls—for David, there's that fire to deal with; for Judy, two badly burned kids. At the hospital, Judy learns of a quarantine and a mysterious virus that may be spreading throughout Evans City. A couple of hundred hazmat-suited, machine gun-toting soldiers show up to protect the perimeters and contain the population, operating under the direction of typically clueless military and civilian officials; they're poised to call in a nuclear strike to blow the burg off the map, if need be. Operation leader Colonel Peckem (Lloyd Hollar)—who, in another *Night* parallel, is revealed as an African-American when he removes his gas mask—and an indignant scientist, Dr. Watts (played, in Wellesian fashion, by

Richard France, who off-camera happened to be a professional film critic and Orson Welles scholar) are equally frustrated by their helplessness in the face of the escalating threat. As Dr. Watts expresses it, "Jesus Christ, this is so random!"

Meantime, David aligns with fellow firefighter, Vietnam combat vet and emotional wild card Clank (Harold Wayne Jones). The anonymous, zombie-like, white-suited soldiers (whose gear and mechanical demeanor anticipate *Star Wars'* battle droids) turn increasingly trigger-happy when they're met with mad (in both senses of the word) resistance by many armed, infected locals. David and Clank eventually join with Judy and father-daughter duo, Artie (Richard Liberty) and teenage Kathy (Lynn Lowry), in a bid to escape the escalating mayhem.

Like *Night*'s besieged farmhouse defenders, the fleeing band disintegrates as anarchy again triumphs. "I guess I always prefer to have a group of people fighting for a way out or a way through the situation," comments Romero. "It just gives you an opportunity to have different perspectives and also to show the lack of communication even within the group rather than have a single strong-willed person who's either always right or always wrong."

In this case, David is the character closest to fulfilling the hero function. Unlike Ben, David makes it through the night. Fiancée Judy and their unborn child are the ones who pay the ultimate price in a scene, set amidst a mock fortress of cinderblocks, notably downbeat even by Romero's normal standards.

The director initially had an even bleaker climax planned. "We were going to end it with the two lovers, after having been separated, running toward each other, and just before they reach each other,

> **"I think the monsters are us. I play with that"**
> —George Romero,
> on The Crazies

the screen was gonna go white and they were gonna destroy the town with the bomb. But we didn't do that."

While Evans City seems safe from an imminent nuking at film's end, the situation is far from resolved as Colonel Peckem prepares to depart for a new locale under identical threat. In a bizarre turn of events, a harmless scene depicting the colonel taking a discreetly lensed decontamination shower aroused unexpected controversy. Romero explains, "When you shoot in a place like Evans City, everyone comes around to watch. Some people were outraged because Lloyd [Hollar] took his clothes off during filming. They didn't feature the idea of an African-American man taking his clothes off. Our lawyers had to come out. We had a big meeting in that high school. We had to promise you don't see anything. We actually had to show them the film!"

Unlike *There's Always Vanilla* and *Jack's Wife*, *The Crazies* is clearly of a piece with *Night of the Living Dead*. Here, *most* of the characters, following unthinking instincts or unchallenged orders, are zombies—and they've got guns! Romero remarks, "I love the Jekyll and Hyde idea, and I think the monsters *are* us. I play with that a lot. In the zombie films, I sympathize a lot more with the zombies than with anyone who's going up against them because they're just doing what comes naturally. I like to juxtapose as many of those ironies as possible."

Like *Night*, *The Crazies* teems with indelible images, horror-movie money shots, and cleverly disturbing touches:

- A soldier cautiously ascends an eerie *Night*-like stairway—"a wink at *Night of the Living Dead*," Romero acknowledges—and discovers a kindly looking, archetypal granny knitting in a rocking chair, who silently rises and smilingly jabs a needle into his white-suited heart.

- A crazed priest self-immolates in protest, Buddhist monk-style, outside his church while horrified women and children parishioners look on.

- A female tot plays with a toy machine gun, her innocent giggles turning to screams as she helplessly witnesses her family being roughly "evacuated" by the monstrous-looking military men.

- Soldiers, à la *Night*'s posse, mow down deranged citizens in cold blood, then feel the fatal return fire of more mad insurgents; an entranced woman calmly sweeps the bloody field with a broom.

- In a truly transgressive scene, a going-gonzo Artie makes love to his willing daughter, a deflowering as shocking as any of *Night*'s cannibal tableaux. This is followed by a shot of hymenal blood on Kathy's leg and a close-up of Artie's contorted, bloated face after he's hung himself in the closet.

● In an explicit reference to the then-recent Kent State Massacre, a quietly crazed Kathy attempts to make peace with a group of panicked soldiers who shoot her for her troubles. An earlier speech by David regarding the soldiers makes that connection perfectly clear. "They can turn a campus protest into a shooting war." (He holds the local civilians in equally low regard, adding, "Some of the rednecks that live in this area may be shooting each other and not even care why.") Actress Lowry sells the scene by assuming a suddenly rhapsodic expression and uttering a surprised, gentle murmur of "Oh," as if giving voice to the bliss of exiting this hell on earth. At that very moment, a herd of sheep scampers by. "The sheep add so much to that scene," an equally rapturous Romero remarks. "That's what I think I learned when I was making the film. By delegating other jobs—like *shooting* the film—I was able to think about stuff like that."

Lynn Lowry described the role in an interview with *Video-Scope* magazine: "*The Crazies* was very difficult because I had to be crazy . . . from the very first moment you saw her. But I didn't want the audience to know that yet. So I was on a fine line, trying to keep that from them as long as I could, so it would be a surprise when they really saw she was crazy."

Lowry also attests to the chaos of the shoot. "I always really liked a lot of physicality in theater and films. I love getting in staged fights and getting slapped around, to do all kinds of stuff like that. For me it was a lot of fun and challenging because you had to hit certain marks or you could get blown up. I think I actually slip and fall at one point and my dad picks me up and hustles me on. That wasn't supposed to take place. There were spontaneous moments that happened just because you can't really, definitely, make something like that totally what you want it to be. But I think George knew what he wanted and he planned the whole film out, and it had that chaotic look because he wanted that."

"For me it was a lot of fun and challenging because you had to hit certain marks or you could get blown up."

—Lynn Lowry, on making The Crazies

Other *Night* homages, meanwhile, include a sequence where soldiers burn infected bodies in a human bonfire; Clank examines a cuckoo clock in a scene that recalls Barbara's encounter with the music box; at another point, Clank issues a threat to Artie to "throw her [Kathy] out there and you with her," echoing Ben's warning to Harry Cooper ("I ought to feed you to those things"); and those crickets are back again, incessantly chirping on the soundtrack to increase the craziness quotient. As was already becoming *de rigueur*, Romero contributed not one but two Hitchcockian cameos—one as a full-body walk-on during a high-school scene. In another instance, the back of his head stands in for the U.S. president, a mock patriotic touch reminiscent of *Night*'s opening credits, where the director's name appears next to the cemetery's American flag, flapping in a stiff autumn breeze.

Overall, Romero felt pleased with the process of creating *The Crazies*. "We were able to go off with the money," he says. "And the way we earned that privilege was by delivering. There *are* a lot of filmmakers who would, I think, run amok or who wouldn't know how to tweak the money and spend it here, and don't spend it there, and just constantly be on the phone asking for more, instead of working within the limits of what you've got to work with. Sometimes that pans out. Sometimes they've got the money in a drawer and expect to spend it anyway. But all of that dishonesty running both ways leads to suspicion and rivalries instead of true collaborations. It's nuts. The way we earned our freedom was by delivering. We just came through. They knew the movie was gonna get done. And they left us alone."

The Crazies has its flaws, as Romero freely admits. "Its scale was too big for its budget, it was rushed, the cast was weak in part, and yet it came close to representing, for the first time, my filmmaking personality. It's the first film a viewer might be able to identify as mine based on its style."

In hindsight, though, *The Crazies*, along with 1972's *Rage*—a film directed by and starring George C. Scott, about a previously straight-arrow rancher seeking revenge for the death of his son, and subsequent coverup, in a government-caused toxic mishap— arrived as one of the last of the 1960s' great protest films clad in genre garb. The decade officially died not at Altamont in late 1969, as a clueless contemporaneous mainstream media oft insisted, but with Richard Nixon's reelection in 1972, as those present at the metaphorical funeral will still attest. True to his politics and vision, Romero says today, "I'm satisfied to put *The Crazies* out there just the way it is and let it stand there as part of the body of work."

Yours truly, editing the terror-film tabloid *The Monster Times* in New York at the time, was fortunate enough to catch *The Crazies* at one of its few, possibly only, press screenings, where it exerted a powerfully disturbing influence on most of the assembled critics. But when it came to getting the film in front of a paying public, Cambist head Lee Hessel adopted an ill-advised tack.

"Instead of doing a good campaign for putting it out in neighborhood theaters and releasing it wide," Romero says, "he decided to throw everything he had into a big opening at two theaters in New York City." While that opening came complete with a huge Times Square billboard featuring a white hazmat-suited soldier, the pic failed to draw a crowd when it debuted in March, 1973. It played other venues under the uninspired title *Code Name: Trixie* with similarly dismal results. Romero shoulders some of the blame: "It's frenzied, and I think it was really inaccessible to a lot of people because of that frenzy. I think it may have driven people away from the film."

The Crazies has been scarcely forgotten, though, least of all by rival filmmakers, being ripped off in Wolfgang Petersen's 1995 *Outbreak*, paid homage to in the opening scene of Zack Snyder's 2004 *Dawn of the Dead* remake, and remade in Breck Eisner's 2010 *The Crazies*, with Romero serving as an executive producer.

More important at the time, *The Crazies* led, however circuitously, to a new partnership and eventual greater glories. Romero elaborates, "I was in New York doing an interview about this film with a guy who was writing for a filmmakers' newsletter named Richard Rubinstein. That's how he and I met and became partners. Richard said, 'Let's take a little breather.' I was ready to take a breather. After *Night*, *Vanilla*, *Jack's Wife*, and this [*The Crazies*] were frustrating experiences. Not from the filmmaking standpoint but from the release. So Richard and I did television for three years. We did a series of sports docs"—including a portrait of a pre-notorious O.J. Simpson entitled *O.J. Simpson: Juice on the Loose*—"and documentaries and tried to learn the ins and outs of the 'real biz' instead of trunk-of-the-car garage filmmaking in Pittsburgh."

While these transitory gigs may strike Romero fans as a mundane, if not downright wasteful use of the filmmaker's talents, they served their purpose, providing a beneficial regimen of cinematic stretch exercises. Romero and Rubinstein formed a partnership, the Laurel Group, with plans for several feature films.

"Then he and I did *Martin* together," Romero says. "Not that *Martin* was a big commercial success, but it got me back in the saddle, and it still is my favorite film. I think I learned a lot from those years off and working on the docs."

In *Martin*, filmed in Pittsburgh in the summer of '76, John Amplas excels as a confused youth who's fallen victim to the fanatical religious superstitions of his aged cousin and guardian, Tada Cuda (Lincoln Maazel), who believes the family lineage has been tainted with vampirism. Tada is further convinced that Martin is the latest manifestation of that genetic curse, addressing him as "Nosferatu," stringing garlic outside his door, and generally giving him a hard time (to put it mildly). Tada's daughter Christina (Christine Forrest, a.k.a. wife Chris Romero) tries to help, but our tortured, sexually repressed young protag takes his assigned affliction to heart, preying on vulnerable young women with the aid of his blood-extracting hypodermic needle and ready razor blade.

> "Not that **Martin** *was a big commercial success, but it got me back in the saddle, and it still is my favorite film.*"
>
> —George Romero

While neither as scary as *Night* nor as disorienting as *The Crazies*, *Martin* emerges as an extremely unsettling experience. "There is no magic" is a recurring mantra repeated throughout the film, most vociferously by Martin himself, who becomes something of a local radio show celeb. His call-in phone confessions regarding his sanguinary crimes are treated as morbid flights of fancy and earn him the sobriquet, "The Count." As the film amply demonstrates, there may be no magic but there's also scant protection against sociopaths like Martin. The Catholic Church—represented by Romero himself in a fully developed role as Father Howard, a pleasantly dismissive, wine-sipping "progressive" priest—proves useless, even when Tada secures an elderly hard-line cleric to perform an unsuccessful exorcism. As in John McNaughton's 1986 cult hit *Henry: Portrait of a Serial Killer* (which owes a bit of a debt to *Martin*), police presence is virtually nonexistent. And "therapy" takes the form of that exploitive radio freak show.

Also in the McNaughton mold, Romero stages his kill scenes for max shock value. The first one we witness, during the opening sequence, unfolds within the cramped confines of a train compartment. Romero masterfully employs that limited space to create an atmosphere of almost unbearable claustrophobia and terror. Like wild sex acts, the frenzied murders are followed by periods of post-coital calm, when Martin acts tenderly toward his now-late "lovers."

A house invasion scene, where Martin bursts in to find not only his intended victim but her secret beau, operates at a pitch feverish enough to rival *The Crazies'* sustained hysteria. Romero intermittently counterpoints his deliberately mundane Pittsburgh *mise en scène* with stylish, gothic, Universal-style, black-and-white fantasy tableaux where Martin imagines himself stalking beautiful, candle-bearing women and being pursued by torch-wielding mobs.

While *Martin* doesn't register as strongly as *Night*, it easily surpasses *There's Always Vanilla* and *Jack's Wife*, setting the stage for the director's triumphant return to Living Dead Land. As Romero points out, "That's when we met Dario [Argento]. The Italian money was the first money in for *Dawn*. So this was a very important film that way."

With *Martin*, a solid new genre film under his belt, Romero was ready to again tackle the *Dead* head-on.

Fest of the Living Dead
Gary Streiner on the Annual Living Dead Festival

"I was one of the original Image Ten gang that moved on and had a career away from Pittsburgh. Russ [Streiner], Jack [Russo], and all those guys got onto the convention circuit and stayed much closer to the *Night* fan base than I did. After I ended my career in advertising and filmmaking, I returned to the farm I've owned for thirty-eight years here in Evans City. Not being in a position to completely retire, I was glad to get a call from Rick Reifenstine, a member of the Evans City Historical Society. At one of their meetings, Rick came up with the idea that something needed to be done to celebrate *Night*'s fortieth. He called to ask if I would be interested in helping out. In most ways it's a perfect project for me. I love meeting new fans each year and digging deeper into *Night*'s history." For the full story see: thelivingdeadfest.com.

DAWN OF THE DEAD

When there's no more room in hell, the dead will
walk the earth.
—Ken Foree, in *Dawn of the Dead*

After the artistic and critical, if not financial, success of *Martin*, which rebooted the traditional vampire concept as radically as *Night* had altered longstanding celluloid zombie lore, Romero seriously entertained thoughts of revisiting the Living Dead. "For years I'd been reluctant about doing a sequel to *Night of the Living Dead*," he admits. "Part of me was paranoid about being pigeonholed as a horror guy. I've always loved the genre and I grew up on it; I grew up on EC comic books. But when you want to be a filmmaker, you don't say, 'Hey, I want to be a horror filmmaker, or I wanna make jungle movies, or I wanna make war movies.' Back in those days, I thought I might be able to resist the genre by doing other kinds of things." But with *Martin* rekindling his interest, Romero decided the time was right to return to his roots.

The idea for *Dawn of the Dead* had first occurred three years earlier, in 1974, when Romero was invited by friend and potential investor Mark Mason, of Oxford Development Company, to visit the Monroeville Mall, an immense indoor shopping center that Mason's company managed. Romero recalls:

> When they first showed us around, they took us to where they had sealed-off rooms upstairs packed with civil defense stuff, which they had put there in the event of some disaster—and that's what gave me the idea. I mean, my God, here's this cathedral to consumerism, and it's also a bomb shelter, just in

case society crumbles. I said, "Wow, this is perfect!" People are on the run, the world is in chaos, and they happen to land on the roof of this shopping mall. They find these little rooms up top and decide, "Man, we got everything we want" and just fall into the trap of the possessions and that life.

> "People are on the run, the world is in chaos, and they happen to land on the roof of this shopping mall!"
>
> —George Romero, on Dawn of the Dead

Not unlike *Night*'s screenplay, Romero's early, incomplete draft adopted a dark, bitter tone, but he later decided to lighten it to reflect a new era: "I think a lot of the sequences in *Night of the Living Dead* with the posse [and] the rednecks played into the zeitgeist of that particular time. I thought, 'What is there about the '70s? How can I do a caricature of the '70s and set the next zombie film in that?' I decided it was all about rock'n'roll, splashy colors, and consumerism, shopping malls where kids were starting to hang out. I didn't start with a story (Who's it gonna be? Who are the characters gonna be?), I started with *that*."

While some local investors came onboard, the final figure fell far short of the projected $1.5 million needed to make the film. The Laurel Group's foreign rights agent, Irvin Shapiro, submitted Romero's script to Italian interests; it eventually wound up in the hands of fright maestro Dario (*Suspiria*) Argento, a huge *Night* and *Martin* fan who convinced his friends, Romans, and countrymen to participate in the project. Romero would retain final domestic cut, while Argento received the right to re-edit the film for European release. "It was a really strange deal," Romero marvels. "I've never seen another one like it. But Dario is such a very nice guy."

Argento even put the "Rome" in Romero, temporarily ensconcing George and Chris in a Rome apartment, where the director completed his final draft in a relaxed environment, far from the rigors of Pittsburgh. Unlike a typical Hollywood producer, Argento had no desire to tinker with Romero's vision, at least for the

American version. Romero recalls, "He said, 'You make the film you want to make.'" A fast friendship and profitable union formed.

Shooting commenced on November 13, 1977 under the title *Dawn of the Living Dead*. The mall and its natural sets (130 of 143 stores were made available to the filmmakers) came at a nominal fee of $40,000, but certain restrictions applied. Says Romero: "The main problem was we could only shoot at night. There were taverns in there, they didn't close till 2:00 in the morning." And the Muzak came on at 7:00 A.M. sharp. "So we had 2:00 to 7:00 every morning. And that was it. We would get all set up in the big conference rooms that they had and make the zombies up so that we were ready to roll right at 2:00 A.M."

As its title implies, *Dawn of the Dead* picks up right where *Night* left off, albeit with an entirely new cast of characters (logically so, since none of the major players made it through the *Night*). The film opens on Fran (Gaylen Ross), a local TV station worker, asleep on a blood-red office carpet, momentarily oblivious to the bustle around her. She wakes to learn the nightmare hasn't ended, as a contentious scientist and hectoring talk-show host loudly, and uselessly, debate the growing zombie epidemic, while the director and his assistant (George and Chris Romero in dual cameos) try in vain to control the situation. As some panicked station employees furtively begin to bail, Fran's beau, TV traffic helicopter pilot Steven (David Emge), urges her to meet him on the roof for an airborne escape. Says Steven: "*Someone has to survive.*"

Cut to the chaos across town, where a SWAT team and National Guardsmen are raiding an ethnic housing project. Just as *Night* closed with a black man's execution, so *Dawn* presents us with a bullet-flying attack by (integrated) authorities on minorities (African-Americans, Hispanics, with a few impoverished Anglos tossed in). It's during said raid that *Dawn* firmly establishes itself as one mean mother of a movie: a racist cop (Jim Baffico) shotgun-blasts a black inhabitant flush in the face, resulting in the screen's very first graphic exploding head. When audiences witnessed that unprecedented shock, they knew all traditional bets were off, and they were in for a wild ride.

After more extravagant violence claims zombies, their victims, and unlucky assault team members alike, Romero puts the basement in debasement, taking us down to hell's cellar. Here, residents have stashed their deceased, many of whom are now zombies chowing down on found prey. It is a truly sickening sight, so much so that Guardsman Peter (Ken Foree) relishes head-shooting the simultaneously dangerous and pathetic creatures. Peter and pal Roger (Scott Reiniger) then join Steven and Fran in the waiting helicopter and lift off for parts unknown.

At a refueling stop at a local airfield, several memorable monster-movie money shots stand out. First, a Frankenstein-domed zombie (Jim Krut) has the top of his head sheared off by a chopper blade. Then Peter is forced to execute two little zombie tykes. Having upped the zombie body count, the four land atop the massive indoor mall that serves as the film's main set and metaphor. Despite the presence of hundreds of milling zombie ex-consumers—as Steven points out, "This was an important place in their lives"—they set up house in the upstairs civil defense rooms.

Here, Romero boldly mixes horror with black comedy, signaling his intentions by cross-cutting between mall store mannequins and their reanimated human counterparts. Zombies heedlessly stagger and stumble through their erstwhile consumer paradise, now shopping solely for living flesh (to the vapid strains of a still-active Muzak). Later scenes played for laughs depict the deaders attempting to negotiate intricate escalators and a formerly festive ice rink.

The human survivors have their own comic montages as they help themselves to an abandoned bank's money, now utterly meaningless (despite Peter's winking aside, "You never know"). They also conduct a spirited dead-zombie cleanup while brisk martial music blares from the loudspeakers (whence automated shopping announcements still emanate as well). Romero also injects a masterful suspense sequence when Steven is stalked in a boiler room by an unseen zombie (played by future Broadway director Warner Shook); his bullets eerily ricochet about the heavily shadowed enclosure.

Though not a director given to littering his films with references to other movies (a habit more common in younger, film-schooled helmers), Romero does incorporate nods to his own earlier works. *The Crazies'* gas masks make a return appearance, while *Night's* mounted animal head trophies cameo in a gun shop scene. And, though sporting a different name and an unexplained eye patch here, film scholar-turned-actor Richard France virtually reprises his scientist role from *The Crazies*, this time as an impatient television pundit who explains that the zombies are not cannibals in the strict sense. "They do not prey on each other. These creatures cannot be considered human." His pronouncement that there are "reports of these creatures using tools" represents a sly reference to Jane Goodall's pioneering chimpanzee research, much in the news at the time.

Meanwhile, ambition and meaning inexorably begin to fade from the lives of our four survivors as they surrender to the mall's myriad temptations. After gorging themselves on free goodies—from gourmet foods to fancy clothes to expensive toys—our protagonists reach that dreaded destination achieved by candy-stuffed children, clueless lottery winners, and the idle rich the world over—spoiled resentment and stultifying boredom. Now that they have it all, they discover all is not worth having. What's the point, if there's no one left to envy them?

Larger concerns soon kick in. Roger suffers a slow-acting zombie bite partially caused by his overly macho showoff behavior, and, at his request, Peter plants a bullet in his skull as soon as he "turns." Then, in an inspired twist, a biker gang invades the mall, and Steven resolves to defend his domain. Romero gives free reign to biker mayhem as the gang launches a cream-pie attack against the initially hapless zombies. Stanley Kubrick had envisioned a similar pie-driven sequence for the conclusion of *Dr. Strangelove* but scrapped the idea when he couldn't make it work. By previously inserting some slapstick zombie bits, Romero effectively prepared his audience for the risky scene and, against all odds, it succeeds brilliantly, another instance of the auteur creating cinematic alchemy, as he had in *Night*.

Almost immediately *Dawn* switches gears as Romero revs up the action for a three-way melee among our armed protags, acting as snipers; the zooming, wildly firing bikers; and the perpetually flesh-famished zombies, ever ready to descend on unwary prey. Several bikers become zombie lunch in gory, gut-munching scenes, while Steven, slowed by a biker-inflicted gunshot wound, gets bitten and joins the living dead ranks. The film ends with Peter and Fran flirting with suicide before opting instead for another rooftop escape—destination, and future, unknown. Boldly blending seemingly impossibly disparate tonal and emotional elements, Romero succeeds in fashioning a cult classic that, while not as purely terrifying, proved every bit as influential as *Night of the Living Dead*.

For budgetary reasons and personal preference, when it came to casting *Dawn of the Dead*, Romero again chose to shun L.A. "I like the idea of not using stars," he says, "because then you don't know what's gonna happen to who. I would try to call up people that I knew, if they could do it. I always preferred to work that way, with friends."

But instead of casting out of Pittsburgh, Romero and New York City-based partner Richard Rubinstein looked east to the Big Apple. Rubinstein and assistant producer Donna Siegal conducted the initial auditions, while Chris Romero made the final decisions. At the time Scott Reiniger and Pittsburgh Playhouse veteran David Emge (the lone Steel City actor among the principal cast) were working in the same Manhattan restaurant, Lady Astor's. A Duane Jones connection surfaced in the casting of Ken Foree, who recalls, "There was a point when I became involved with a group calling themselves the National Black Theater—it was more of a '60s revolutionary thing. Duane Jones was in this company. I had known him for about a year when, one day, I walked by a theater in the community and spotted his picture. It was *Night of the Living Dead*, and I asked him about it later. He said, 'Please! Don't mention that!' "

Through a friend of a friend, Foree heard about the *Dawn* casting sessions, showed up and made the cut. "It wasn't until we went into the hallway for coffee that I spotted a *Night of the Living Dead* poster on the wall and mentioned it was one of my favorites. That's when I realized who these people were. I had no idea who I was meeting!"

Casting the female lead loomed as an especially crucial

challenge. By this time Romero had taken some serious heat concerning his portrayal of women in *Night of the Living Dead*. Several revisionist critics characterized Barbara as the typically helpless distressed damsel, shocked into a state of near-catatonia and unable to function on her own. Although Judith O'Dea doesn't see it that way, viewing her character more as a transitional horror-film figure, one who, ultimately, comes to Helen's rescue (though it's open to debate whether Barbara's looking to save Helen or join Johnny— she succeeds in doing both). Judith Ridley's Judy, on the other hand, seemed the standard-issue innocent ingénue who stands by her man, Keith Wayne's Tom (himself a less than dynamic character, ever the conciliator between violent competitors Ben and Harry). But Judy does insist on following Tom into the zombie fray, though her "clumsiness" contributes to the couple's fiery demise. Marilyn Eastman's Helen arguably (and arguingly) holds her own against bullying hubby Harry, at least in the early going. And, certainly, no one could accuse Kyra Schon's little cannibal Karen of being anyone's idea of a pushover.

"Usually in horror films it's women in underwear running around screaming and crying and being chased by the monster."
—*Gaylen Ross*

Still, the stigma persisted, and when Chris Romero cast Gaylen Ross, an acting student who had never previously performed professionally (she later admitted to having enhanced her résumé), George Romero quickly found he had a feistier femme onboard. When asked to scream during the early airfield scene, Ross refused, determined to take her character in a tougher direction. "I liked it when Franny got strong," she says. "Usually in horror films it's women in underwear running around screaming and crying and being chased by the monster."

Romero approved of the move. "Gaylen sort of woke me up to the idea that that's [helpless women] not the sort of way it should go." So, while she doesn't quite measure up to Sigourney Weaver's Ripley in the same year's trendsetting *Alien*, Fran proves as resilient as her male counterparts.

As was the case with his previous films, Romero relied on the kindness of strangers to fill many of the secondary roles. Most of the bikers—who were not in the original script but added during filming—were members of the real-life Pittsburgh motorcycle club, The Paragons. The gang, Romero remembers, made a dramatic entrance: "For these guys to ride their bikes through a mall must've been a charge. It was one of those stunning moments where you think, 'What have I wrought'?"

Tom Savini had been selected as the movie's makeup guru but, along with his assistant and best bud Taso Stavrikis, volunteered to join the onscreen fray. Says Savini, "We saw everybody dressing up in costumes and stuff, so when it came time for the bikers to come in, Taso and I said, 'Hey! We can do that!' So we dressed ourselves up with bandoliers and swords. I had all kinds of props with me. I became Blades and I had this rubber sledgehammer, so Taso grabbed it, and he became Sledge."

To act as the police and National Guardsmen, Romero received permission to deploy actual National Guard volunteers, who, by all accounts, relished the fun assignment. As with *Night of the Living Dead*, the filmmakers also had little trouble recruiting zombies to the cause. While the "specialty" zombies— Sweater Zombie (off-screen weapons coordinator Clayton Hill, who could walk the wrong way on an escalator while remaining in living dead character and who later became a regular on the horror-film convention circuit), Nun Zombie, Nurse Zombie, Hare Krishna Zombie, Fat Guy in Bathing Suit Zombie—were played by local actors and friends, the majority of dead extras were area thrill-seekers who'd heard about the shoot. "People would come and stay all night!" an exultant Romero told author Paul R. Gagne. "It was something to do—instead of going to a midnight showing of *Rocky Horror*, they'd come to the mall and be zombies!"

Martin star John Amplas, who has an onscreen cameo during the opening raid sequence, as a doomed National Guardsman, was put in charge of recruitment, overseeing some 1,500 volunteer zombies in all, including several amputees eager to serve as limb-severed Living Dead. Chris Romero remains amazed to this day.

"I couldn't believe everybody wanted to get shot or bitten." According to Savini, zombie extras would even vie for the privilege of devouring actual pig intestines onscreen.

Much of the zombie mayhem was improvised on the spot, from the decision to let the poignant nun "live" to the grand-scale zombie pie attack (which claimed *Document of the Dead* filmmaker Roy Frumkes as one of its victims) staged by the marauding bikers. Some zombies had greatness thrust upon them: The baldheaded ghoul who became the film's literal poster boy was a last-minute recruit. Says Savini, "This guy"—a musician with a shaved head—"was just floating around. George said, 'We need a zombie to walk through the door [at the airfield]. And he became the logo!' "

As he had in *Night of the Living Dead*, Romero tried not to stifle his zombies' style. "You just have to say, 'Be dead. Be your own kind of Frankenstein.'" When the violence became too rough, a dummy, nicknamed Boris, bore the brunt of the humans' aggression.

Beyond breathing life into Roger and Steven, actors Reiniger and Emge also had to perfect zombie personas. The latter, after being shot and mangled in an elevator, faced the more arduous chore. Emge tailored his Living Dead moves to the injuries his character had received, further adopting an elaborately twisted gait inspired, he says, by Lon Chaney, Jr. in his *Mummy* films.

Some zombies' sense of brio occasionally crossed the line, resulting in Ghouls Gone Wild antics. A few undead extras took to killing their off-time at the mall's Brown Derby saloon. According to Savini, "I heard a story where drunken zombies stole a golf cart and went driving around the mall and crashed into a pillar or something." Romero insists, "That was the only one that did any real damage."

Other zombies liked to take pictures in full makeup and paste them on the mall photo booth. Still others enjoyed throwing a scare into the senior citizens who would gather at the mall for their early-morning walks. Fortunately, no reported cardiac arrests ensued among either faction.

As noted, makeup artist Savini had been pegged to perform

identical chores on *Night* before being called to serve in Vietnam as a combat photographer. That sometimes grisly experience helped him fashion accurate effects in a fictional context. "I did see a lot of first-hand anatomically correct gore," he states, "and I think the most important part of that was if we create a dead body or situation there's a certain feeling you get from seeing the real thing. If I'm creating a gory effect and I don't get the same feeling when I saw the real stuff, I'm not satisfied."

For the majority of zombie extras, Savini and his team of eight assistants—one of whom, part-time actor Joseph Pilato, would double onscreen as a police captain and later portray Rhodes, the fascistic lead military officer, in Romero's *Day of the Dead*—followed predecessor Marilyn Eastman's basic approach, applying blue or gray facial shading to emulate a deathly pallor. Savini explains, "Some zombies were just people who looked like they were fresh from a funeral parlor, made up real pretty like a mortician would do. We tried to make them look like they were people who had died in great ways." For the specialty ghouls slated to receive more face time, like Sweater Zombie, the makeup was more elaborate, often involving foam latex wounds.

With *Dawn* being shot in bright, almost carousel colors, particularly in the mall sequences, the blood substitute had to be more vivid than *Night*'s chocolate syrup. The fake plasma ultimately used in *Dawn* had a nearly flourescent hue. Savini initially opposed the substance, citing its artificiality ("melted red crayons," in his words), but was overruled by Romero, who thought it helped capture the comic book look he was going for.

The violent effects posed a greater challenge than the makeup. Since Romero couldn't equal *Night*'s pure terror quotient—and never intended to try—he chose to go further over the top with the kills, beginning with that opening-scene exploding head (three years before David Cronenberg's *Scanners* would make exploding heads hip). The head was a plaster cast of Gaylen Ross, originally earmarked for use at film's end, filled with food scraps. "It was really spectacular," Romero says. "We needed that kind of sucker punch just to say, 'This is real horror.'"

Even the actors fell under the sets' gruesome spell. Upon first spying the zombies in the tenement basement, Scott Reiniger remarked, "Oh my God, this is disgusting!" His grandmother would have a similar response when he reluctantly brought her to the film's New York City premiere, only to quickly escort her out, much like Russ Streiner had done with his granny at the original *Night of the Living Dead* opening a decade before.

Other special effects highlights include the screwdriver thrust into zombie (and future director) John Harrison's ear, the female neck flesh and gristle torn out and chewed by a hungry zombie in the opening raid, and the unfortunate bikers who have their guts clawed out and devoured by the ravenous zombies, among other indelible "gags." While these and many other *Dawn* effects surely shocked audiences of the day, Savini remains modest re his *Grand Guignol* accomplishments: "You can sit and think for *months* of how to do something like that, but sometimes you come up with your best ideas when you're under pressure."

Case in point: A fan favorite scene sees a zombie's head cleaved nearly in half by a machete-wielding biker. Explains Savini, "I cut a groove out of the machete in the shape of the guy's head and we ran blood tubing into his hair. We shot that in reverse—I placed the machete on his head and actually pulled it *off*. When you see the scene played forward, it looks like it's going into his head, and you can't see the groove in the blade because it happens so fast."

The mall became a virtual isolation tank for cast and crew during the four months of filming, necessitating, according to Chris Romero, a "total immersion in this world." Romero tried to lighten the burden by creating a playground atmosphere, likening the set to a "tailgate party." (That sporting feeling grew when Pittsburgh Steelers star Franco Harris dropped in one night and stayed to do the slates for a scene!) "I tried to make it as much fun as I could for people," says Romero. "You know, we're not doing surgery."

> *"I tried to make it as much fun as I could for people. You know, we're not doing surgery."*
> —George Romero, on Dawn of the Dead

As with all his films, Romero encouraged a participatory situation. "I love working collaboratively," he admits. "I think it breeds cooperation, it breeds a spirit. Everyone just gets more involved." Adds Savini, "You *want* to do something for someone who treats you so well and respects your ideas. And makes you feel part of it. Life was so boring compared with being on the set of *Dawn of the Dead*."

Romero became the leader of a pack of hyperactive kids loose in a candy store. Aided by the expanded budget, he took full advantage of the visual feast before him, shooting at a ratio of 15–20:1, more than three times the raw footage lensed for *Night of the Living Dead*.

In December, when the mall's busy Christmas season hit, Romero decided to suspend production rather than commit to the time-consuming daily tasks of taking down and putting up the plethora of holiday decorations festooning the site. The break lasted three weeks; Romero used the time to begin editing the footage he already had in the can.

"I shoot a lot," Romero explains his approach, "because I know that I can make the decisions later on the cutting table. I wind up shooting a lot of material that I fall in love with and there's just economically no room for it in the final piece. So it's hard. When I sit down and say, 'Okay, here are ten scenes that I love, which two are least needed?'—that's a very difficult process for me. I think that's where all your bias comes in and all your emotions. It's a lot easier to edit up front while you're writing."

When filming resumed, the fun continued to be contagious throughout the shoot. Ken Foree recalled his personal highlights in a 1992 *Fangoria* interview. "Throwing all that money in the air was great. I never gave it much thought till I actually did it. And the raid on the gun shop was fun. I always wanted to be in a western, and that's probably as close as I'll ever get." And on the subject of guns, Scott Reiniger points out, "The strange thing was that David had to play this bumbling idiot with the weapons, but he had served in Vietnam and was around this stuff constantly. It had to be tough for him to pick these things up like they were lobsters and not know what to do with them, when in reality he had all the knowledge in the world."

Not even the enormous Monroeville Mall could supply all the necessary locations for *Dawn*, though. The site's actual civil defense rooms were too cramped to allow for filming, so a set built at The Latent Image offices filled in, much as Hardman Associates' cellar subbed for the farmhouse basement in *Night*. The mall, likewise, lacked a gun store, so those scenes were shot at Pittsburgh's Firearms Unlimited, while the flight sequences took place at a nearby airfield; an empty downtown tenement served as the site for the opening raid.

Before production ended in February, 1978, the film required one final but major tweak. As Romero detailed in a *VideoScope* interview: "The original script had them [Fran and Peter] dying. They kill themselves. Him with the gun and her with the helicopter. I had done it that way because even though it's not a sequel by Writers Guild terms, I was thinking of it as revisiting *Night of the Living Dead*. Texturally a sequel, but then I realized that it's just a completely different personality. As I was shooting it, I was trying to make it more comic book and more of a reflection of the different decade. I decided that it just wouldn't be right to do that because it's not as dark a film, so I switched gears and decided not to kill them. I didn't remember we had shot it. It was base footage. We never finished it. We just shot a take of her [Gaylen Ross] standing up into the helicopter blades. It was just a close-up and she stood up out of frame. That's all we ever shot. We never did the effects work, the blood work, anything like that. We had shot that stuff earlier in the schedule and, after I changed my mind, we just never came back to it."

For his score, Romero employed an unusual mix of stock cues selected from the DeWolfe Music Library, like the African-flavored "Safari" heard during the gun shop montage. There are also instrumental operatic rock cuts by Argento's musical collaborators Goblin, heavy on dramatic keyboards and shrieking guitar riffs; these dominate Dario's slightly shorter (119 minutes) Italo version of *Dawn*, issued overseas as *Zombi*. (Shortly afterward, the score would accompany the ziti zombie *Dawn* rip-off *Hell of the Living Dead*, directed by Dario paisano Bruno Mattei.) In addition to the sarcastically deployed "Safari," Romero licensed the Pretty Things' mock macho ditty "Cause I'm a Man" from the group's *Electric Banana* LP to poke fun at the redneck posse and chose the comic polka "The Gonk," backed by discordant zombie moans, to play over the end credits. The music matches—or creatively mismatches—the movie's wildly schizy tone, from somber apocalypse to merry splatstick set pieces, and, like *Dawn* itself, defies the odds by achieving a skewed cohesion.

As he had with *Night of the Living Dead*, Romero showed the completed *Dawn* to AIP execs, who, perhaps predictably, requested that he clean it up and whittle it down to an "R." Ditto for Warner Brothers. Though the financial benefits might have saved Romero and Rubinstein from encroaching ruin—not only had they spent their entire budget but were rapidly running out of basic rent money—the pair fiercely resisted that idea. According to Romero, "Richard said, 'I'm just gonna *prove* that there's an audience for this [as is]. And he rented a theater [New York City's uptown Olympia] to show it. He took out a little one-inch ad in *The New York Times*. One screening. We showed up there that night and the mob was all the way up the street. We showed the film and it blew the roof off. It was incredible. It was the best audience experience I think I'd ever had." The filmmakers made a deal with United Film Distribution head Salah Hassanein in the theater that very night—and on their own artistic terms.

Says Romero, "When the distributor took his stance to put the picture out unrated, it's not that he wasn't accepting the restrictions of an X, because he's putting a flag on it that says that no one under seventeen will be admitted, forget with a parent, not at all. He's accepting those restrictions. What he's not accepting is the symbol itself, the X, because the X does automatically say to most people in America that this picture is obscene."

Though some newspapers declined to print *Dawn* ads (themselves relatively discreet—a simple but eloquent image of the disfigured chrome-domed airfield zombie) and the General Cinema circuit wouldn't book the film, Romero and his partners' approach otherwise proved a rousing success. "When the film opened at the Rivoli," Romero recalls, "we saw this crowd down Times Square. I'm going, 'Gee, what movie is that for?' It was for us!"

With the rigors of production a retreating memory, Ken Foree later experienced a similar pleasant shock. "I was working out of a small theater across from Lincoln Center, making $63 a week," he said. "We had finished rehearsing for a play down on 42nd Street and started walking up Broadway. We came upon the Rivoli Theater, and there was my picture plastered everywhere!"

> "When the film opened at the Rivoli, we saw this crowd down Times Square. I'm going, 'Gee, what movie is that for?' It was for us!"
> —George Romero

Indeed, *Dawn* raked in some $900,000 at 68 New York City area theaters in its first week in April 1979, this, against a total advertising outlay of $125,000, resulting in instant profits for the filmmakers. Like *Night* before it, the picture exhibited extraordinary legs, experiencing only a 10 percent attendance drop-off during its second week and holding strong on into the summer, not only in New York City but across the country.

Critical reception was generally positive, often downright ecstatic. Original *Night*-basher Roger Ebert gave the film a top four-star rating, hailing it as "one of the best horror films ever made." *Village Voice* critic Tom Allen tagged it as "a comic apocalypse that has come to maul the becalmed seventies." *Dallas Times-Herald* reviewer C.W. Smith raved, "*Dawn of the Dead* is without a doubt the most horrific, brutal, nightmarish descent into hell (literally) ever put on screen, and its power can be gauged by the peels of maniacal laughter bursting forth from many of us who survived the movie's first few moments." Jay Robert Nash's and Stanley Ralph Ross's *Motion Picture Guide* judged it "one of the most important American films of the last decade.... Romero has created the ultimate American nightmare."

Not that the film didn't attract its share of naysayers. The *New York Times'* Janet Maslin, perhaps the culturally grayest of the Gray Lady's contemporaneous cadre of frequently dismissive critical snobs, departed after fifteen minutes, citing a "pet peeve about flesh-eating zombies who never stop snacking." *NBC Today* reviewer Gene Shalit's amazing colossal wit gave birth to the putdown "Yawn of the Living." And *Variety*, apparently not yet over its *Night* premiere nightmare a decade before, plunged an eviscerating blade into the picture's exposed innards: "*Dawn* pummels the viewer with a series of ever-more-grisly events—decapitations, shootings, knifings, flesh tearing—that make Romero's special effects man, Tom Savini, the real 'star' of the film—the actors are as woodenly uninteresting as the characters they play. Romero's script is banal when not incoherent—those who haven't seen *Night of the Living Dead* may have some difficulty deciphering exactly what's going on at the outset of *Dawn*." The United States Conference of Catholic Bishops Office for Film and Broadcasting didn't dig it, either, labeling the movie morally offensive: "George Romero's camp pulp yarn has metaphorical pretensions as social satire but essentially what's on the screen, peppered with rough language, is a relentless exploitation of gore and violence and the repulsive effects of violence." In short: *Success!*

Dawn would go on to gross some $55 million worldwide, nearly $200 million in 2010 terms. UFD's Hassanein was so pleased that he inked Romero and Rubinstein's Laurel Entertainment to a three-picture deal—*Knightriders*, *Day of the Dead* and the never-realized *Invasion of the Spaghetti Monsters*, a broad sci-fi spoof that harkened back to the concept Romero and Russo had been set to tackle prior to *Night of the Living Dead*.

In Italy, *Dawn* spawned a veritable zombie cottage industry, with scores of imitators, from Umberto Lenzi's *City of the Walking Dead* to Joe D'Amato's *Zombie Holocaust* (both 1980) infesting international screens. Tom Savini, for one, didn't resent the blatant thievery, feeling that the many rip-offs helped generate new projects for Romero and crew. Savini also proved correct in his early assertion that *Dawn* is "*the* zombie movie." *Dawn*'s flamboyant Living Dead supplanted *Night*'s more somber zombies as the models for most subsequent zombie flicks, not only in Italy but Stateside and worldwide as well.

Tasting success, Romero could offer a positive assessment. "This is a romp. When we set about doing it, we felt unrestricted. We knew we had distribution in Italy, Germany, Japan, and places where we weren't going to be censored. We were really able to just do what we wanted to do with it. I was satisfied that we made a film that pays off on several levels. Horror fans dig it, people who want a message or satire dig it. It's a fun ride. And I knew that if we'd done anything at all, we'd made a crowd-pleaser." Anyone who's ever watched the film with an audience that didn't know what was coming next can attest to that contention. To this day, fans from around the globe make pilgrimages to the still-standing Monroeville Mall.

Romero also savored his own overdue recognition, deservedly so. "The controversy surrounding *Dawn*, and its success worldwide, made me 'hot' again, though on a small scale. I was happy. It looked like I was going to be able to keep working for a while."

Living Dead al Dente: 5 Fave Ziti Zombies

The Beyond (a.k.a. *Seven Doors of Death*) (1981), Anchor Bay Entertainment)

The late, great Lucio Fulci's Louisiana-set gruefest, resurrected for a successful midnight theatrical run in 1998 by Quentin Tarantino's Rolling Thunder Pictures, involves a hotel erected on the site of a gateway to hell. The simple setup serves as a sturdy frame for Fulci and makeup effects genius Giannetto De Rossi to fashion some truly stunning over-the-top terror tableaux, including an impressive climactic zombie assault.

Cemetery Man (Dellamore Dellamorte) (1993), (20th Century-Fox Home Entertainment)

Lensed by Dario Argento disciple Michele Soavi and based on the Italo *Dylan Dog* comic book by Tiziano Sclavi, *Cemetery Man* stars Brit thespian Rupert Everett as graveyard watchman Francesco Dellamore, whose buried charges, dubbed "returners," won't stay dead, compelling our hero to dispatch them with bullets in the head. The film takes a night of the living head turn when Francesco falls for the reanimated dome of the local mayor's decapitated daughter (the fetching Anna Falchi). Loosely plotted but determinedly bizarre, *Cemetery Man* is rich in gallows humor, disgusto zombie makeup effects and a deadpan tone all its own.

Cannibal Apocalypse (1980)

Dawn of the Dead meets *The Deer Hunter* in Antonio Margheriti's (operating under his frequent Anglo alias Anthony Dawson) literally gutsy, Atlanta-lensed zombie splatterfest featuring freed American POWs who return Stateside to feast on their fellow citizens. John Saxon gives a strong performance as an ex-Green Beret infected with the zombie virus. In the pic's undisputed highlight, zombie GI John Morghen has his stomach drilled through with a hole so large you can see a close-up of the cops on the other side. A seriously gutted version surfaced on Vestron VHS as *Invasion of the Flesh Hunters* in the '80s, but Image Entertainment delivered the real uncut digital deal in 2002.

Zombie (a.k.a. *Zombi*) (1979, Blue Underground)

Fulci's first foray into zombie territory is less imaginative than *The Beyond* and more overtly imitative of *Dawn of the Dead*, but it manages to pack a lot of legit zombie mayhem into its running time. The fan highlight of this island-based battle between desperate survivors, including Tisa (sister of Mia) Farrow, and rotting zombie hordes is the infamous splinter-in-the-eye shot. A chilling finale also adds to the atmosphere.

City of the Walking Dead (1980, Anchor Bay Entertainment, as *Nightmare City*)

Stronger on gore (the eye-gouging scene recalling *Zombie* demonstrates that the Italians were already imitating *each other*) and action than sense, this heavily Romero-influenced Umberto Lenzi shocker sees military man Mel ("Aim for the Brain") Ferrer lead his troops against rampaging radiation-spawned zombies, while journalist Hugo Stiglitz delivers the unctuous we-brought-it-on-ourselves messages. Highlights include a zombie priest and an undead-infested roller coaster, a scene later homaged in *Zombieland* (2009). Lenzi lifts his it's-all-a-nightmare-but-now-it's-starting-for-real ending from *Dead of Night* (1945) and *Invaders from Mars* (1953).

Zombie Movie Milestones:
Roy Frumkes, *Document of the Dead*

The first feature-length documentary to detail the step-by-step formation of an independent horror film, Roy Frumkes's *Document of the Dead* (1985) brings to vivid life the creation of George Romero's *Dawn of the Dead*. Both directors were venturing into uncharted territory with their disparate films. Romero was attempting to replicate the quality of what, in a mere decade's time, had already been anointed not only a cult classic but one of the most influential titles in horror-film history. Frumkes faced the formidable challenge of capturing that process in a project designed as a film-school teaching tool. At it turned out, both succeeded admirably in achieving their goals.

Document not only works on an instructional level for students but as a richly entertaining spectacle for fright-film fans. After a brief intro recapping Romero's barrier-breaking debut, *Night of the Living Dead*, and his then-recent meta-chiller *Martin*, Part 1 of *Document* follows each phase of *Dawn*'s production, from script through shooting and on into post-production and release. Along the way, we get to meet the core cast of characters: a disarmingly loose, gracious, yet deceptively industrious, Romero; enthusiastic makeup master and actor Tom Savini; pragmatic producer Richard P. Rubinstein; earnest, affable director of photography, Michael Gornick; most of the principal thespians; and others on the crew.

In Part 2, filmed some ten years later, Frumkes rejoins Romero on the set of his Dario Argento collaboration *Two Evil Eyes*. Here he catches up with the filmmaker's interim efforts, most notably *Creepshow*, *Day of the Dead* and *Monkey Shines*. The longer *Dawn* section depicts Romero and crew in a mostly upbeat mood as they sometimes exhaustingly, but always cheerfully, overcome logistical problems and impromptu obstacles. The briefer *Two Evil Eyes* segment offers a valuable lesson regarding working through a patience-testing snafu with a pivotal prop malfunction: When it comes to film, maintaining equilibrium is as important as mastering the medium's technical aspects.

More recently, Frumkes returned yet again to chronicle Romero's *Survival of the Dead* shoot for the newly revised *The Definitive*

Document of the Dead (2010), which transforms *Document* into the zombie-movie equivalent of Michael Apted's *Up* series.

> Joe Kane: *What was your initial experience with and reaction to* Night of the Living Dead?
>
> Roy Frumkes: I saw it in a 42nd Street theater under unusual circumstances. Director Harry Hurwitz and I were going to make a horror film in order to raise more money to finish *The Projectionist,* and we wanted to see what our competition was like. Seeing the film's title on the marquee, Harry snickered and said, haughtily, "Let's see what we're going to 'take'!" When we exited an hour and a half later, he looked at me crestfallen and said, "We can't 'take' that . . ."
>
> JK: Document *was the first documentary feature about the actual production of a horror film. How did you settle on* Dawn of the Dead? *Did you think then it would become the popular classic it has?*
>
> RF: I was teaching film production and screenwriting at The School of Visual Arts in Manhattan and was perturbed, as I had been for years, that there were no teaching films about independent filmmaking. The only "making of" films out there were about films like *Star Wars, Butch Cassidy and the Sundance Kid, Bonnie and Clyde,* and so on. Nothing students could really relate to. The indies would be where all but a rare few would toil for a decade or more after graduation. So I sent a letter to Silas Rhodes, the owner of the school, pitching the idea of making a series of teaching films about indie filmmaking that would go to every high school in the country, listing SVA as one of the producers in the titles and on promotional materials. I had tried this at SUNY Purchase the year before and had received no response. Shockingly, within a week, I got a letter back from Silas, with a check for $7,000. He saw the promotional value for his school and just went for it.
>
> Then I had to look around for a film on whose set I could shoot. New York back then was a "union" state. So was California. All the others were "right to work" states: Meaning union and nonunion films could be shot in those states—

even on occasion films that mixed union and non-union crews. But in New York, the union would station men outside all the camera rental houses each morning to see if nonunion crew members were renting equipment. If so, they would follow them to their sets and . . . well, something like *Dawn of the Dead* would ensue. So I had to look outside of New York for our indie film to document.

Earl Owensby was getting ready to produce and star in Wolfman down in North Carolina. I'd interviewed him a few years earlier, and he was a friendly, sporting guy, who said sure, I could come down. Then I came across Dawn of the Dead, shooting in Pittsburgh, and there really was no difficult decision-making process involved in choosing which film I would cover. I'd known Richard Rubinstein, George's producer, socially, and he saw the value of a doc being made about Dawn, so, with the provisos that I couldn't come within a hundred feet of George—and that I would only get one interview with him—we were invited to the set.

JK: Document *presents a picture of a busy but harmonious set. Were there any difficult moments you caught on film but decided not to include?*

RF: Not really. We covered Savini doing his amazing dive off the mall mezzanine into the mattresses below. He did it several times, and, on one of those dives, he bounced off the edge and broke all the blood vessels in the soles of both feet. For insurance-related reasons, Richard insisted I not mention that. Understandable.

JK: *Had the first version of* Document *already appeared on video before you went back for a revisit with Romero on the* Two Evil Eyes *set?*

RF: No. When the original *Document of the Dead* was finished in '79, the video market was such that I got no offers worthy of making a deal. So I just held onto the film for ten years, and the only way to see it was in my classes, or at the occasional public screening, in which case I would bring the film there and take it back with me after it was shown. There weren't even any bootlegs, as I recall. But rumors spread as *Dawn's* reputation grew, and ten years later, a former student of mine, Len Anthony, having formed a video distribution company called Off Hollywood, approached me with a good offer. He also asked if I would update the film and threw fifty thousand dollars at me. With which I landed on the set of George's half of *Two Evil Eyes*. With both of them combined, and the first section trimmed slightly, the film finally found its way onto home video.

JK: *The* Two Evil Eyes *shoot captured a tense sequence with a special effects malfunction. George looked miserable, with gum and a yo-yo replacing his ubiquitous cigarettes, but he seemed to do a great job of keeping his obvious frustration under wraps. What's your impression of him?*

RF: He gets riled but never rattled. He's a calm presence that spreads out and infects his cast and crew. People love to work with him, and he loves a family environment on his films, so crew members tend to crop up over and over on his shoots. All this warmth is a rarity in the biz, and so *Document* serves more as a work model than as a statement of fact regarding industry working conditions.

JK: *Were you happy with the choice of Susan Tyrrell to do the limited voice-over narration?*

RF: It struck us that there were no female voices in the film. The female lead [Gaylen Ross] wouldn't consent to an interview (method acting, as I recall), and so we felt a female narrator would lend a sense of balance. Angela Lansbury was appearing on Broadway in *Sweeney Todd*, and she'd been in a few horror flicks, such as *The Picture of Dorian Gray* and *The Manchurian Candidate*, so we sent her a letter, and she considered it for a month before refusing, claiming she'd never done a documentary voice-over before and was afraid of trying. Then we went back to a male choice, José Ferrer, but he also declined. Susan Tyrrell was in a play off-Broadway at the time. I loved her dissipated voice-over, as if she'd been through the night of the living dead. She was a great pleasure to work with, although she was also a sybaritic creature and often arrived—how shall I say it— affected by her previous night's activities. Our editor, Dennis Werner, ended up splicing portions of her takes together, often using words from different sentences, to make the voice-over coherent and intelligible. She had to come back several times more than we'd planned because of her penchant for enjoying life, but she never complained. One of the nicest and most stimulating people I've had the pleasure to work with. In the second chapter, the *Two Evil Eyes* section, Susan was long gone to the West Coast, so I asked Nicole Potter, who played the Winette in *Street Trash*, to do her best impression of Ms. Tyrrell in her narration and she kindly obliged us. The second chapter is more of a straight documentary than the first, so there was very little voice-over.

JK: *Do you think, in its educational aspect,* Document *played a role in encouraging the proliferation of the zombie movies that have been flooding the market and film fests?*

RF: I know fans love *Document*. And nowadays when *Dawn* gets released internationally, the companies licensing it always want Document as well. But encouraging young filmmakers? Maybe.

JK: *You mention on your commentary that you felt* Day of the Dead *missed the mark in terms of defining an era the way* Night *and* Dawn *had. How do you feel about* Land of the Dead *[2005] and* Diary of the Dead *[2008]?*

RF: I think the latter films were dealing with current issues and metaphors, certainly, but didn't define the eras in which they were made as successfully. I mean, *Dawn* today is considered one of the key films of the '70s for its use of the mall as a metaphor of zombie living. However, *Land* was elegiac in a way none of the others were, which I found absolutely lovely (its mood is one of my favorites among all of George's films), and *Diary*, of course, dealt with modern technology's zombification of the current generation. Good theme, just not era defining . . . yet. Let's see how history regards it.

JK: *Another* Document *update is on the way. Can you tell us a bit about that and what you cover in it?*

RF: It'll be more in tone and style like my previous doc, The Meltdown Memoirs (which concerned my film *Street Trash*), than it will be like the preceding chapters of *Document*. I've just grown more personal in my old age, and I intrude myself into the film beyond just walking with George. I also put people into the film who I care about, and leave the others out. Also, when I first started, back in '78, no one was doing these films about horror films except me. I was the only one on the set of *Dawn* except for a German TV crew. But today, every time I visit one of George's sets, there are three or four other crews shooting documentary footage that day. So I really had to get creative to make sure *The Definitive Document of the Dead* had exclusive material. I have George's daughter, Tina, in the film, as well as her home movies, featuring her father, which are wonderful, and a number of other fun surprises.

JK: *This is a tough, maybe impossible one: If you had to pick one film to take with you to an underground bunker during a zombie apocalypse, would it be* Night *or* Dawn?

RF: Possibly *Dawn*, because I'm in it, as is Sukey Raphael, my co-producer. Also it's the longest of the zombie franchise and would use up the most time keeping me from getting bored. But truthfully, I might have to go outside the franchise and pick *Martin*, which I feel more warmly about, and think is George's best film, despite how much I love the celluloid zombie parade.

JK: *Another toughie: Why zombies? Why now? What's their perennial appeal?*

RF: I feel that vampires are sexual, werewolves are manic-depressives, and zombies, the way George redefined them, are slackers. Richard Linklater missed his calling. He should have jumped on the bandwagon. These creatures don't bathe, don't work, don't give a shit, just literally and figuratively eat their elders, devouring the status quo and infecting each other with shambling, unemotional anti-angst. It wasn't until the 2000s that my students embraced zombies as cool, and every year since then they've continued to worship the undead creatures. I can think of a number of reasons why they do this, and though George continues to reject his films' influence on culture, they have indeed done so in a complex way, by offering an outlet through which young people can act out their adolescent psyches in the face of the negative cultural values inherent in the Bush and Clinton years.

10 DUEL OF THE DEAD

"More brains!" —Zombie, *Return of the Living Dead*

"Choke on 'em!" —Captain Rhodes, *Day of the Dead*

Following *Dawn*'s success, Romero found no lack of projects, beginning with the long-gestating, highly personal fable *Knightriders* (1981). The film was originally conceived as a period piece depicting the dark—or at least grittier—side of medieval lore. In the wake of Romero's experience directing high-speed TV sports documentaries like *Driver: Mario Andretti*, however, the concept was retooled for modern-day motorcycle-riding knights. UFD committed some $4 million to the production, which chronicles uncompromising leader Billy Davis (a young, up-and-coming Ed Harris) and his colorful ragtag troupe on their peripatetic rounds playing small-time Renaissance Fairs while attempting to resist commercialism. They resolve numerous personal conflicts within the group—such as Billy's constant wrangles with macho would-be usurper Morgan (Tom Savini)—and slay the metaphorical dragons of societal suppression that stand in their way. While stirring in spots, the overlong (145 minutes in its *shortened* cut) odyssey suffers from tedious polemics, heavy-handed sentimentality, a paucity of adrenalizing action and a basically unsympathetic hero who comes off less as a shining idealist than a stubborn control freak.

The film has since won its fair share of followers via cable TV and home video exposure but at the time proved a major theatrical flop. At that point, Romero's imprimatur was synonymous with horror, and most audiences did not take kindly to his change of pace. Romero would concede financial failure but not utter artistic defeat. "I still don't believe its length was what caused its bad performance at the box office," he told author Paul R. Gagne. "Probably more to blame are its romantic idealism, to which some contemporaries said 'Feh!,' and its timid release pattern against a collection of summer 'blockbusters.' Because of prior successes, I was able to make *Knightriders*. Had *it* been a success, I would have been able to make some other nonhorror. You have to earn your stripes, I learned that. Happy thing that I love scare shows!"

Which is exactly where Romero went next, to the waiting arms of reigning fright icon Stephen King, for the E.C. Comics-inspired anthology *Creepshow*. Romero first bonded with King when the *Living Dead* legend had been considered to direct an adaptation of King's vampire novel *'Salem's Lot*, which, after a long stretch in development hell, ultimately saw the light of day as a TV project, sans Romero's participation. *Creepshow* promised to bring the director not only back into the fear-film fold but return him, at least partially, to his best-known area of eerie expertise: zombies. Dealing with his biggest budget to date, approximately $7.2 million, name actors ranging from E.G. Marshall to Adrienne Barbeau, and first major studio (Warner Brothers), Romero was relieved to learn he could still shoot the film in his beloved Pittsburgh.

Executed as simple *Grand Guignol*, darkly comic set pieces, *Creepshow*'s five tales offered audiences little of the cerebral sustenance found in *Night of the Living Dead*, *Dawn of the Dead*, or *Martin*, but they delivered the gory goods on a purely fun level. Best of the bunch is the lead-off tale *Father's Day*, wherein a murdered Dad (with a heavily made-up John Amplas cast as the zombie pop) rises from his grave to gain revenge against patricidal relatives and avaricious heirs. (When we first caught the pic at a Times Square venue back in 1982, the nabe's notoriously interactive audience quickly picked up on Pop's off-repeated on-screen mantra, and cries of "I want my cake!" threatened to drown out the rest of the film.)

The anthology takes a bit of a dip with *The Lonesome Death of Jordy Verrill*, a *Blob*-like vignette about space goo getting the better of a greedy hick played by author King himself in a manner broad enough to make Shemp Howard blush—in short, not a particularly pretty, nor especially funny, sight. It's back to Living Dead land—or, more accurately, sea—with the vengeance tale *Something to Tide You Over*. Wealthy TV exec Leslie Nielsen buries his cheating spouse (*Dawn*'s Gaylen Ross) and her paramour (Ted Danson) neck deep in the sand and waits for high tide to do the rest—a spectacle he watches via video remote. Natch, the drowned lovers resurface to do an understandably freaked-out Leslie in, zombie-style.

Sort of an EC Comics variation on *Who's Afraid of Virginia Woolf?*, *The Crate* casts Fritz Weaver as an academic who finds a monster in the titular box and employs it to off his vulgar, loud-mouthed wife (Adrienne Barbeau). *Creepshow* literally crawls to its conclusion with its second best story, the bug-happy *They're Creeping Up on You*, which pits a brilliantly evil E.G. Marshall against a seemingly endless supply of roaches (specially imported from Trinidad for the occasion). A wrap-around segment, featuring a young comic book reader (played by Joe [Son of Stephen] King) who inflicts an EC-style payback on his disapproving dad (the great character actor Tom Atkins), puts a satisfying coda on the anthology.

Creepshow opened to brisk box-office business in November 1982, eventually earning some $25 million. Critical reactions were mixed. Old pal Roger Ebert offered a big fat thumbs-up: "Romero and King have approached this movie with humor and affection, as well as with an appreciation of the macabre."

Former Romero collaborator John Russo also got behind the movie, telling contemporaneous interviewer Tim Ferrante, "I don't like all of George's films, but I was entertained by *Creepshow*. I used to read *Tales from the Crypt* when I was a kid, and to me, the movie was just like the comic books, and I think that some of the critics that didn't like the movie probably never read those comic books and didn't know what George was trying to do."

Newsweek's David Ansen was one of those critics who was

less enamored of the terror titans' collaboration, opining, "For anyone over twelve there's not much pleasure to be had watching two masters of horror deliberately working beneath themselves. *Creepshow* is a *faux naif* horror film: too arch to be truly scary, too elemental to succeed as satire."

In the end, money talked and *Creepshow*'s box-office success enabled Romero to walk into what he'd initially conceived as his greatest *Dead* epic of all, in his words "the *Gone with the Wind* of zombie films." As the director explains, "Suddenly, I got this conceit: Maybe I'll do one of these every ten years, reflect a little bit of what's going on. So *Day of the Dead* really grew out of that '80s feeling of giving up on everything—government, the military, faith in the financial systems."

Romero's first draft stretched to 204 pages and involved nothing less than a multitiered society where the lowest classes of humans are raised to feed zombies. In turn the undead are slated to be "tamed" to work as slaves to maintain the ruling elite, a variation on the original zombie concept as seen as early as 1932's *White Zombie*. UFD balked at ponying up the nearly $7 million required to film Romero's grandiose vision, so the director reluctantly agreed to halve his original scenario. (Some of the excised ideas, like the insulated hi-rise of the rich, would surface some two decades later in *Land of the Dead*.)

Day underwent many permutations, not only in the script and budget departments, but in some rather bizarre ways: There was even brief discussion about lensing it in 3D (a fate that would befall an ill-advised *Night of the Living Dead* remake in 2007) in a bid to mimic the modest success of *Jaws 3D*. Another possible option was rejected outright by Romero and producer Richard Rubinstein—making a milder, R-rated film for a major studio that could furnish the bucks needed to restore the original scale (at the expense of the more extreme zombie gore content).

Says Romero, "For me, the *Grand Guignol* is part of these films, part of their character. Regardless of how essential those sequences are to the art or drama of the film, for me, those sequences are part of the fun of doing this type of film. Like *Grand*

Guignol theater, it's doing it for the sake of the illusion, seeing how well an effect can be executed."

After much soul-wrestling, Romero put the finishing, in his mind diminishing, touches on his leaner—if not necessarily meaner—screenplay. "It's a completely different script; it was the only way I could make a movie given the dollars that were allotted. But I approached it seriously."

Romero retained lofty philosophical goals for the film, despite the budgetary setback: "It's about one of, not necessarily the last, but one of probably several nests of humanity that are left. As a military group they were there for research and, of course, now the need for what they are doing is all but gone: With society gone, who are they going to report to if they find anything out? All of a sudden, when that structure is gone, they don't quite know how to behave or they cling to old behaviors and no one talks to each other and no one communicates. So there's this sort of tragedy about how a lack of human communication causes chaos and collapse even in this small little pie slice of society."

In its final form, *Day* opens, like *Dawn* before it, with the female lead, scientist Sarah (Lori Cardille), dreaming. Here, we see part of her nightmare: She caresses a calendar image of a lush pumpkin patch, a vintage vestige of a vanished vista. Rows of zombie arms then punch through a white-brick wall, surrounding and barely missing her. Sarah awakes in a helicopter occupied, like the protagonists in *Dawn*, by four characters; the group also sports a gender and ethnic makeup similar to *Dawn*'s, including the obligatory (in a Romero zombie movie) black man, pilot John (Terry Alexander), flask-carrying Irish electronics expert McDermott (Jarlath Conroy), and Sarah's lover, jumpy military type, Miguel (Antone DiLeo).

The four are scouting Florida's West Coast for signs of life. After a desperate dash through a litter-strewn, zombie-infested Fort Myers (a scene filled with several imaginative bits, including zombies emerging from an abandoned movie theater), they find two soldiers guarding a pre-Gitmo, but post-Freedom Flotilla, zombie holding pen outside town. From there the four descend

DEATH CERTIFICATE

I the undersigned take full responsibility of viewing:
AN EVENING WITH THE UNDEAD

"NIGHT OF THE LIVING DEAD"
"BLOOD AND BLACK LACE"

And by signing my own death certificate I hereby release this theatre of any liability, should my death occur during and/or following the showing of the above mentioned motion pictures.

Cause of Death:_____

Time of Death:_____

_____
Ticket Holder's Signature

Hypes of the Living Dead: Walter Reade publicists raid William Castle's bag of flick tricks, with gimmicks ranging from faux insurance policies to bogus death certificates. (Courtesy Andrew Jones Collection)

He's coming to get you, Barbara: Judith O'Dea is ready for her close-up upon arriving at the ill-fated farmhouse. (Courtesy Andrew Jones Collection)

I'm ready for my close-up, Mr. Romero: Zombie volunteer catches up on her beauty rest between takes. (Courtesy Andrew Jones Collection)

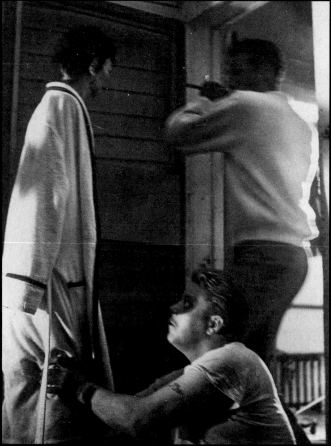

Don't get the wrong idea, Buddy: Crew member George Kosana, who also played Sheriff McClelland, steadies dummy about to be bludgeoned by Duane Jones. (Courtesy Andrew Jones Collection)

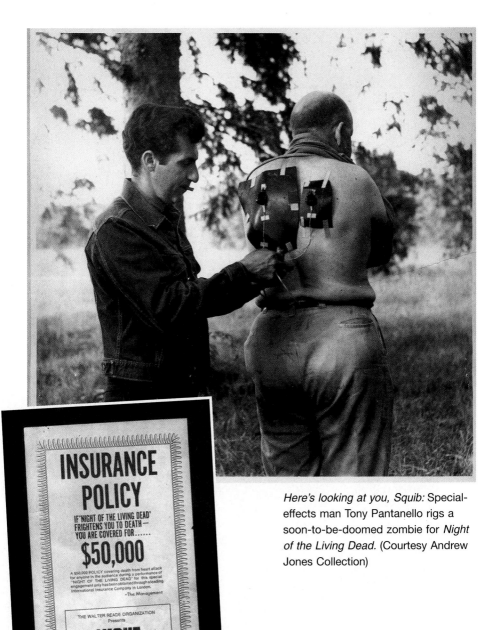

Here's looking at you, Squib: Special-effects man Tony Pantanello rigs a soon-to-be-doomed zombie for *Night of the Living Dead.* (Courtesy Andrew Jones Collection)

That's Exploitation II: The phony insurance policy was another exhibitor favorite in the golden age of movie promotion in the 1960s and '70s. If by chance you did die from fright, there's little chance your heirs could have collected that $50,000—there was no International Insurance Company in London. (Courtesy Andrew Jones Collection)

A Hardman is good to find: Karl Hardman (Harry Cooper) lends a helping makeup hand on the *Night of the Living Dead* set. (Courtesy Andrew Jones Collection)

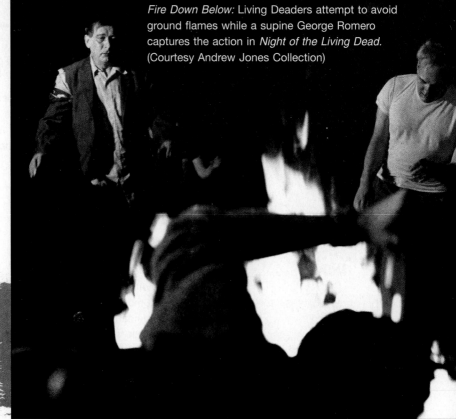

Fire Down Below: Living Deaders attempt to avoid ground flames while a supine George Romero captures the action in *Night of the Living Dead*. (Courtesy Andrew Jones Collection)

Launch of the Living Dead: George Romero (seated, *right*, guarding expensive camera) prepares to lead his troops into zombie battle. (Courtesy Andrew Jones Collection)

"All persons who die during this crisis from whatever cause will come back to life to seek human victims . . ." Charles Craig as the TV newscaster . . .

. . . and moonlighting as a zombie. (Photos courtesy Charles Craig)

Throwing in the trowel: Helen Cooper (Marilyn Eastman) loses argument with zombie daughter. (Courtesy Latent Image)

Like Chocolate for Blood: Bosco chocolate syrup was used—very effectively—to simulate blood. *From left to right:* Director George Romero (holding can of paint), Judith Ridley, holding can of Bosco, Karl Hardman, and Kyra Schon, who played Hardman and Eastman's zombie daughter. In forefront is Marilyn Eastman, imitating a hot fudge sundae. (Courtesy Latent Image)

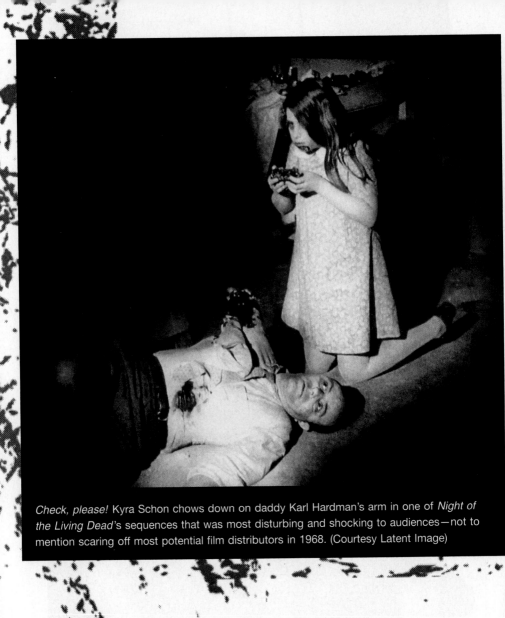

Check, please! Kyra Schon chows down on daddy Karl Hardman's arm in one of *Night of the Living Dead*'s sequences that was most disturbing and shocking to audiences—not to mention scaring off most potential film distributors in 1968. (Courtesy Latent Image)

Have a heart: Zombie extra enjoys a major human organ midnight snack.
(Courtesy Latent Image)

NIGHT OF THE LIVING DEAD
40th Anniversary 1968 – 2008
© 1968 Image Ten, Inc.

GEORGE KOSANA
(aka – Sheriff)

Yeah, they're dead. They're all messed up: Sheriff George Kosana utters the classic line, which he ad-libbed. (Courtesy Latent Image)

By George: Director George Romero, assisted by Gary Streiner, films a close-up of Judith O'Dea. (Courtesy Latent Image)

A Shot in the Dark:
Duane Jones blasts away
at zombie invaders.
(Courtesy Latent Image)

Heeeere's Johnny!
Russell Streiner comes
to get screen sister
Barbara (Courtesy
Latent Image)

Like a hole in the head: Scripter John Russo as a dead zombie. (Courtesy Latent Image)

What's Up, Chuck? Unsuspecting moviegoers were given barf bags. Some were actually utilized. (Courtesy Latent Image)

NIGHT OF THE LIVING DEAD

NO ONE WILL BE ADMITTED WITHOUT A STOMACH DISTRESS BAG!

GALLAGHER THEATER THURS 7:30

George Kosana, Russ Streiner, Judy O'Dea, George A. Romero, Kyra Schon, John Russo and Bill Hinzman

Night of the Living Dead
40th Anniversary 1968-2008

The Gang's All Here: At the *Night of the Living Dead* 40th anniversary.
(Courtesy Latent Image)

This Is Your Light: Screenwriter/zombie John Russo accepting a match from a local Pittsburgh TV newsman. (Courtesy John Russo)

Dead of Night: The solid citizens of Evans City, Pennsylvania, do the zombie stomp. (Courtesy Latent Image)

Bill Kills: Zombie Bill Hinzman attacks brother Johnny (Russell Streiner) as sister Barbara (Judith O'Dea) beats a hasty retreat. (Courtesy Latent Image)

Zombies R Us: The living dead descend on the farmhouse. (Courtesy Latent Image)

into an underground military installation—a vast, natural set where, like *Dawn*'s mall, most of the action unfolds—run by the crazed Captain Rhodes (Joseph Pilato) backed by a handful of surviving soldiers, most notably the aggressively foulmouthed Sergeant Steele (former pro footballer Gary Klar).

Sarah unites with fellow subterranean scientists, rational Dr. Ted Fisher (Romero regular John Amplas) and loony Dr. Logan (*The Crazies'* Richard Liberty), who seems more interested in teaching his living-dead charges tricks than in discovering a cure for the zombie plague, a cure that would probably be too late to implement in any case. Logan's prize pupil—and one of the film's true inspirations—is a semi-cognizant zombie the doc dubs "Bub." As interpreted by Howard Sherman, a versatile New York actor whose experience ranged from Shakespeare to mime, Bub supplies this otherwise dark and dour entry with its few moments of living-dead levity. Sherman not only channels Boris Karloff's Monster from *Frankenstein* and *Bride of Frankenstein* but adds highly inventive frills and flourishes of his own, most notably an extended bit with a tape recorder, rock music cassette, and headphones. He also attempts to "read" a paperback of *'Salem's Lot* (!). When another zombie subject, less cooperative than Bub, petulantly upsets a lab bench, Dr. Logan douses the lights and delivers the movie's classic line, "You can just sit there in the dark and think about what you've done."

As more of the soldiers become zombie chow, the situation further deteriorates when the deranged Rhodes demands John ready his chopper for an escape attempt, executing Fisher point-blank to emphasize his order. When the penned zombies break free of their bonds, wholesale carnage ensues, with the best revenge saved for Rhodes. After being wounded by a wildly handgun-firing Bub, the belligerent captain is torn in half and devoured by the zombies. Rhodes remains hardcore to the end, angrily instructing the zombies eating his intestines to "choke on 'em!" (a line improvised by Pilato on set and heartily endorsed by Romero). *Day* concludes much like *Dawn*, with survivors Sarah, John, and McDermott stranded on an island beach, facing an uncertain but none too rosy-looking future.

For the vast underground military complex, the Pittsburgh Film Commission suggested a former limestone mine in Wampum, Pennsylvania, since converted into a storage facility for everything from luxury yachts to feature-film negatives, including the Romero-referenced *Gone with the Wind*. As striking in its own way as the Monroeville Mall, the mine represents the latter locale's flip side—stygian and chilly, with the temperature set at an unwavering 55 degrees and with a high humidity that frequently caused equipment and zombie makeup malfunctions. The gray labyrinthine expanse proved a nightmare to light, while its windowless environment severely taxed cast and crew alike, mentally and physically. Recalls star Lori Cardille, "We all were sick a lot. One time I had a 104-degree temperature."

Transportation to and from the remote site posed further logistical problems. Many cast and crew chose to stay at a nearby Holiday Inn rather than endure the daily commute before and after long shooting days. Fortunately, Romero came to the set loaded for bear and ready to rumble, largely eschewing his usual free and easy improv approach for a more Hitchcockian rigor in order to meet his strict release deadline. Contractually, filming, which began in fall 1984, had to wrap by early winter 1985. *Day of the Dead* would also be the first film Romero wouldn't personally edit; he entrusted that task to longtime cohort Pasquale Buba.

Outdoor scenes were lensed in the vicinity of George and Chris Romero's second home on Sanibel Island, while nearby Fort Myers offered just the right amount of small-city urban decay to convey a zombie-plagued planet in serious decline, indeed on the likely brink of extinction.

As with *Dawn*, principal casting was conducted in New York City. In the case of Pittsburgh-based Lori (Daughter of Chilly Billy) Cardille, nepotism had nothing to do with it. The actress had rung up a number of legit credits since relocating to New York City, including ongoing roles in the soap operas *Edge of Night* and *Ryan's Hope*. After seeing her in a physically challenging lead role in the off-Broadway play *Reckless*, Romero decided he had his heroine.

Cardille freely admits to hating horror movies and rarely

watched her dad's show. "I really was terribly upset by those films," she says. "I used to think, 'What if I have to act in one of these?'" But when the opportunity arose, Cardille felt grateful for the chance—and the part as it was written. "He [Romero] could've made me this sexy little twit bouncing around with a gun—much more the sexual element. But he made her intelligent and strong. In fact, whenever I would try and make her a little more emotional, he would not allow me to do that." Cardille sums up Sarah as "an exaggerated woman of the '80s." Admits Romero, "I think I was still partly apologizing for the first film, where Barbara was just Jell-o."

While not as experienced as stage-trained actors like Cardille, Alexander, and Conroy, Pittsburgher Joe Pilato, who'd appeared in small parts in Romero's *Dawn of the Dead* and *Knightriders*, brought plenty of over-the-top intensity to his Rhodes role. "He [Romero] pretty much just gave it to me," Pilato says gratefully. "I don't know if he auditioned other people, but it was very quick. I came in and it was like, 'You got it'!" Pilato believed that a primary reason he won the role was due to *Day*'s drastic budgetary reduction, but his casting is consistent with Romero's past policy of going with his gut and trusting certain performers' naturalistic style regardless of professional pedigrees. "I'd rather shoot what the actor's doing than insist, for the sake of camera, any specific movement or line delivery or whatever," Romero says. "I'm relying on them to be there and understand what they're doing."

Easily the film's trickiest role was that of the soulful zombie Bub, brilliantly handled by improv ace Howard Sherman. "George said he wanted kind of an infant-like quality to him, that there was kind of an innocence about him, which totally freed my imagination. The way Bub moves is like a baby, a baby who hasn't mastered how to control the muscles." He also succeeded in locating the character's mental state: "A smart zombie is about as smart as a really dumb dog."

Once again, the filmmak-

> *"A smart zombie is about as smart as a really dumb dog."*
> —Howard "Bub" Sherman

ers had no shortage of zombie volunteers for the Pennsylvania mine scenes, with many extras returning from *Night* and especially *Dawn*, eager to trade their time for screen immortality, a dollar bill, and a hat reading "I Was a Zombie in *Day of the Dead*." Romero recalls, "I think the dean of Carnegie Mellon is in there with his wife. *I* wouldn't do it for a million bucks!"

Florida, though, proved an entirely different story. Not even a radio-station contest, created to round up zombies, made much of an impact. "We wanted to have this huge shot, with something like eight hundred zombies," Chris Romero says, "and we ended up getting thirty-six! I think they probably didn't have the Pittsburgh tradition of zombiehood." George Romero expressed identical disappointment, characterizing most of the Sunshine State volunteers as "a lot of people just goofing off." Cinematographer Mike Gornick adds, "They were just totally out of it and were kind of unruly and couldn't get into the flavor of being zombies. By the time we were shooting *Day*, we thought it was kind of universally understood how a zombie should respond!" But Tom Savini put it best: "When you're born in Pittsburgh, one of the things you want to be when you grow up is a zombie in a George Romero movie."

> "When you're born in Pittsburgh, one of the things you want to be when you grow up is a zombie in a George Romero movie."
>
> —Tom Savini

The seasoned specialty zombies—from a party clown (a concept later repeated in *Diary of the Dead* and homaged in *Zombieland*) to Bub—not only pulled their acting weight but benefited from what were far and away the best makeups of the original trilogy. Savini and assistants crafted some 200 zombie masks in all and engineered intestinal extractions that were, in their way, as radical as Rick Baker's morphing effects for 1981's *An American Werewolf in London*.

Says Savini, "In one of the scenes we tore a guy [Joe Pilato] in half. We filled the fake body with intestines and chicken parts and things like that. He was trapped underneath the floor so we could attach this body to him. Unfortunately, we had the entrails in a refrigerator and someone unplugged it two weeks before this scene, and they were rank, they were really awful! So the zombies had their noses stuffed with wax so they couldn't smell it, but this poor guy trapped in the floor, he was ready to throw up by the end of it, the smell was incredible."

Day of the Dead, which opened in limited release on the July 4th, 1985 weekend, garnered mixed reviews. *Night* crier and subsequent *Dawn* supporter Roger Ebert gave the film thumbs-down, a reaction shared, more predictably, by the *The New York Times'* Janet Maslin, who wrote, "Yes, there are enough spilled guts and severed limbs to satisfy the bloodthirstiest fan. But these moments tend to be clustered together, and a lot of the film is devoted to windy argument." The United States Conference of Catholic Bishops Office for Film and Broadcast remained consistent in its clerical views, categorizing the film as morally offensive, explaining: "Director-writer George Romero's third low-budget zombie chiller provides a loathsome and unimaginative mix of violence, blood, gore, and some sexual references demeaning to women." *Richmond News Leader* critic Dean Levi tossed the most (dis)gusto into his review, labeling *Day* "a cesspool of vile filth produced by sick minds for sick-minded people who delight in seeing viscera rawly ripped out of bodies, eaten and sucked on by deformed zombie extras." (Yum! We'll buy *that* for a dollar!)

Yours truly joined the side of the naysayers in our original *New York Daily News* Phantom of the Movies review. "In *Day*, Romero's zombies find themselves all messed up with no place to go, doomed to stagger on empty sans the shock value of *Night* or *Dawn*'s brilliantly retch-ed excesses. . . . *Day of the Dead* is not entirely bereft of redeeming moments, such as the scene that sees wacky scientist Dr. Logan attempt to civilize a captive zombie via standard behavioral techniques. *Day* also generates some genuine last-reel suspense (full of Tom Savini's usual expertly revolting makeup effects), but here it's a case of too much, too late."

Multiple viewings on VHS and DVD have caused us to upgrade our assessment, with a greater appreciation of the points Romero scores via his mega-volume onscreen science vs. military debates and his ability to create an overall mood of inescapable doom. In 1985, though, the film arrived as a disappointing experience. In the wake of *Night*'s radical, unrelieved nightmare and *Dawn*'s wild, ghoulish party atmosphere, *Day* indeed seemed like the day after, complete with deadening hangover.

Romero provides his own overview: "There are really split camps. There are some people you can't get'em away from the first film, that's their love. Then there are some people who just celebrate and party with *Dawn of the Dead*—it's sort of the wildest of the three; it was also the most popular. Then there are the real trolls who like *Day of the Dead*."

The director sides with the last-mentioned faction. "There's just something about *Day of the Dead* I really think works. It's become my favorite of the three films." On a more personal level, Romero notes, "The environment and the people that you're working with really play an important role in how you eventually reflect on the film and how you rank it. Everyone on the crew knew the script. I've been on sets where people don't even bother to read it. I've had set dressers that have no idea what should be this person's character: 'I put a pillow in there because I like the pillow.' Forget whether the character might like it or not."

Day's wider release in August 1985 was yielding slow but steady returns when the film was blindsided, bushwacked, and butchered by an uncomfortably ironic rival that came out of left field but originated a little too close to home.

While Romero had been enjoying celluloid success with *Martin* (critically, at least), *Dawn of the Dead* and *Creepshow*, his former partner John Russo split his time between writing generally well-received horror novels (e.g., *Indian Givers*) and participating in the creation of not-so-sterling films. The latter included *The Booby Hatch* (1976), a rather execrable softcore sex comedy in a vein previously mined by Alan Abel's *Is There Sex After Death?* and Robert Levy's *If You Don't Stop It, You'll Go Blind*, and the redneck-menace chiller *Midnight* (1982), a promising Russo-scripted terror tale done in by uneven acting and undernourished production values.

But Russo, along with fellow *Night* and Latent Image alums Russ Streiner and Rudy Ricci, had been nurturing a collective pet project since 1972, a *Night* sequel slated to be produced by their own company, New American Films. That proposed continuation, titled *Return of the Living Dead*, was scripted as a straightforward horror film: Following *Night's* conclusion, the mysterious zombie plague abates, but citizens live in fear of its revival. When the dead rise anew some ten years later, all hell breaks loose.

The project lay dormant until Russo wrote a novelization using that title in 1978. At that point, former partners Russo and Romero reached an agreement. Says Russo, "We exchanged releases where I gave George the right to produce and distribute *Dawn of the Dead* and he gave me the right to produce and distribute *Return of the Living Dead*," so long as *Return* was not promoted as a direct sequel to *Night*.

Three years later, in 1981, an independent producer named Tom Fox purchased the *Return* property outright. Romero wanted more aggressive steps taken so the public wouldn't confuse *Return* with *his* planned *Dawn* sequel, *Day of the Dead*. *Variety* further fogged the issue by erroneously connecting Romero with *Return*, reporting, "[Tom] Fox, who had an association with Romero, acquired the rights from Romero and his Pittsburgh partners."

The Laurel Group responded with a warning to Fox and projected producing companies (Orion Pictures and the British outfit Hemdale) to change the title and cease any further mention of Romero. *Variety* made amends by publishing some of those terms: "Your continual efforts over several years to unfairly trade upon our clients' reputation have confused the public, damaged our clients' property rights, and have made it evident that it is impossible for you to release any picture under the title *Return of the Living Dead* which would not continue to confuse the public and the industry." A precedent already existed: Chicago film distributor William Links had been successfully prevented from re-releasing the 1972 horror movie *Messiah of Evil* under the handle *Return of the Living Dead* in 1978. But when the new case went before the MPAA, that body, which had tangled with Romero and Rubinstein in the past, ruled against the pair.

Another two years passed before Fox finally got the project

rolling, hiring *Texas Chainsaw Massacre* auteur Tobe Hooper to direct and *Alien* co-scenarist Dan O'Bannon to rewrite the screenplay, which he did quite thoroughly. Even though all three originators receive story credit on screen, by the time O'Bannon got through rewriting it virtually all that remained of the Russo, Streiner, and Ricci script was that hotly contested title, *Return of the Living Dead*. Director Hooper ultimately left the project and the directorial chores were handled by scripter O'Bannon.

Because *Return* experienced problems of its own during its early production stages, its release was moved back to Halloween, 1985. But with some last-minute tinkering, chiefly the addition of more youth-oriented dark comedy and punk rock, the film was deemed ready for a summer launch—precisely the time when *Day* was going into wider release.

Return couldn't be more different than *Day* if it tried—and it did. According to Dan O'Bannon's version of the movie's genesis, "This independent producer Tom Fox bought *Return of the Living Dead*. I didn't want to make that script. I didn't think it was right to intrude so directly on Mr. Romero's turf. It was a serious sequel to *Night of the Living Dead*." The final cut is anything but serious, adopting a tone closer in spirit to *Creepshow* but armed with a freewheeling punk-rock 'tude.

The movie opens with the anti-disclaimer: "The events portrayed in this film are all true. The names are real names of real people and real organizations." O'Bannon's plot posits that *Night of the Living Dead* was based on a true incident involving army-owned corpses inadvertently re-animated by a toxic chemical called 2-4-5 Trioxin. Said dead were subsequently sealed in allegedly airtight drums and erroneously delivered to the Uneeda Medical Supply Company in Louisville, Kentucky. Needless to say, it's not long before they're on their unsteady feet again.

Return operates as a sharp spoof of *Night*, *Dawn* and imitators. Uneeda owners Burt (Clu Gulager) and Frank (James Karen, in a role originally intended for director O'Bannon—an occasional actor who'd impressed as "Pinback" in John Carpenter's cult debut *Dark Star*—but finally awarded to Karen following the latter's knockout audition), along with a pack of already seemingly brain-dead punks, are put through their paces by the cerebrum-starved zombies. Also joining the fray are local, possibly ex-Nazi mortician Ernie (Don Calfa) and Frank's nephew and assistant Freddy (Thom Matthews). Freddy, along with Frank, falls victim to the toxic gas and gradually joins the zombie ranks. Scream queen Linnea Quigley made her B-movie bones in *Return* by baring lots of living skin, though she cheated a mite by wearing a flesh-colored G-string.

The first all-out, balls-out *Living Dead* sendup, *Return* owes much of its success to its great ensemble comedy work, a result of two weeks of intensive rehearsals where the cast repeatedly ran through the script in sequence, like a live play. Says James Karen, "It helped everybody, and we all got to know each other. By the time we were shooting, we all had ideas about how to turn others on to interesting little things." The timing approaches the frenzied precision of a vintage Marx Brothers movie, powered by a scorching punk and metal soundtrack.

O'Bannon also contributed many key alterations to existing Romeran zombie rules. *Return*'s ghouls are not only stronger and faster than Romero's but can *talk*. Much of their screen time is spent demanding "Brains!" and "More brains!" Eating brains, it's explained by a captured old lady zombie (a brilliantly unsettling effect), eases the pain of being deceased. And Trioxin gas isn't limited to resuscitating only the recent dead; it seeps into the soil of the local cemetery where the punks are frolicking and revives long-deceased, near-skeletons, as well.

At the same time, O'Bannon's zombies can't be killed by destroying their brains; they can even be chopped into little pieces and those pieces will keep on coming to get you, Barbara. Only cremation can terminate these hardy horrors. In one inspired scene, a now-zombified Frank crawls into Ernie's crematorium in a ghoul suicide move (an idea O'Bannon credits to actor Karen). O'Bannon gets more cynical than Romero: At film's end, clueless authorities go *The Crazies* one better—they send in the nukes, leaving the zombies, and much of Louisville, in cinders. And, like *Day*'s Bub, *Return* introduces a memorable "personality" zombie in "Tarman," a drum-escaped corpse played in creatively elastic fashion by actor Allan Trautman.

At the box office, O'Bannon's newfangled rock'n'roll zombies ate Romero's living dead alive. Where UFD opted for a gradual rollout for *Day*, Orion went with a full-blast wide release backed by a gung-ho advertising campaign. Beyond that, *Return* obviously tapped into the tenor of the times and offered far more of what most contemporaneous zombie fans wanted: good sick fun. Following the horror hi-jinks of *Dawn*, *Day* was just too much of a downer.

Still, the timing of *Return*'s arrival, combined with the Russo, Streiner, and Ricci connection, struck Romero as a low blow of the highest order. "I was reviewed three times for that film. *Entertainment Tonight* announced it as 'George Romero's *Return of the Living Dead*!' Even people in Florida, who had been zombies in *Day* were going to see *Return of the Living Dead*, and they were calling us up and saying, 'Gee, I didn't see any Florida stuff!' I hated the way the whole thing went down. . . . It was all dirty pool, and I never want to get into anything like that again. Jack and I were trying to preserve our friendship during it all, and it got crazy. I think he was screwed as well as everyone else—the film is his in title only. It's a sendup, which is exactly what I worried it would be. That damages your ability to do it straight." (Romero would later soften his view regarding *Dead* spoofs, offering a far more positive take on the 2004 British farce *Shaun of the Dead*, even awarding co-creator Edgar Wright and star Simon Pegg zombie cameos in his 2005 *Land of the Dead*.)

That contention was borne out by the fact that, while Romero's zombies went into extended hibernation (due, in part, to the director's choice), O'Bannon's returned a scant three years later, though lightning (or Trioxin 2-4-5) failed to strike twice, at least not creatively. In the heavy hands of director and scripter Ken (*Meatballs Part II*) Wiederhorn, *Return of the Living Dead Part II* merely mimics the surface machinations of the first, minus that flick's satiric thrusts; indeed, it seems bizarrely geared to a preteen market, complete with young kid heroes, à la *Monster Squad* and *The Goonies*.

Brian Yuzna's 1993 *Return of the Living Dead 3*, at heart a nihilistic love story about a boy (J. Trevor Edmond) and his punkette zombie (Mindy Clarke), injects a bit more life into the

(text continues on p. 153)

Night of the Laughing Dead: Top 13 Zomcoms

Night of the Creeps (1986, Sony Pictures Home Entertainment)

Director Fred (*The Monster Squad*) Dekker successfully sends up the entire catalog of sci-fi/horror cliches in a witty romp replete with frat-house zombies, axe maniacs, exploding heads, and killer slugs from outer space. Inspirational line, courtesy of Detective Tom Atkins: "The good news is, your dates are here. The bad news is, they're dead."

Shaun of the Dead (2004, Universal Studios)

Brit slacker Shaun (Simon Pegg) finds his plans to put his life in order suddenly complicated by an influx of the living dead in Edgar Wright's highly imaginative romp, arguably the funniest zomcom since *Return of the Living Dead*.

Night of the Comet (1984, MGM Home Entertainment)

Valley gals Catherine Mary Stewart and Kelli Maroney inherit the Earth when a passing comet obliterates the population in Thom Eberhardt's clever black comedy. Zombies, mad scientists, and trucker Robert Beltran add to the fun.

Zombie Strippers (2008, Sony Pictures)

The titular characters prove both popular with and lethal to their brain-dead clientele in writer, director, and editor Jay Lee's zany spoof, one peppered with witty dialogue, copious (but never pretentious) literary references (Ionesco scores a major nod), zombie catfights, female flesh aplenty, Robert (Freddy) Englund and cartoon gore galore.

Planet Terror (2007, The Weinstein Company)

Science-warped mutant zombies have their way with imperiled humans in Robert Rodriguez's gung-ho homage to the over-the-top grindhouse flicks of the '70s, originally packaged with Quentin Tarantino's *Death Proof* as *Grindhouse* and crammed with dark laughs, action, gore, and gross outs.

Chopper Chicks in Zombietown (1991, Troma Entertainment)

Foxy motorcycle mamas save a small town from mad mortician Don (*Return of the Living Dead*) Calfa in a fun biker/horror hybrid. Says one resigned local resident: "Nobody ever gets out of here. You go to school here, get married, in-breed and die."

Zombieland (2009, Sony Pictures)

Despite some drifts into sentimentality, Ruben Fleischer's post-zombie apocalypse road trip boasts a number of genuinely funny bits (e.g., an abandoned supermarket filled with obese zombies), some legitimately grisly zombie kills (a mallet squashing zombie clown head), Woody Harrelson as a Twinkie-addicted zombie-basher and inspired dialogue.

Zombies! Zombies! Zombies! Strippers vs. Zombies (2007, In the Dark Entertainment)

Rival groups of snobby strippers and hostile hookers bury their cat-fighting hatchets to make a last stand for humanity against encroaching zombies at the Grind House strip club in a raw but funny farce filled with off-the-wall exchanges.

American Zombie (2008, Cinema Libre)

A virus causes a few thousand disparate people in the L.A. area to technically stop living and become mixed-up zombies in Grace Lee's clever living deadpan send up of whiny "outsider" groups and pretentious documentarians alike.

Fido (2006, Lionsgate)

Comic Billy Connolly plays a retro-futuristic family's loyal (but still hungry) zombie pet and slave in a clever flick, directed by Andrew (*Night of the Living*) Currie that merges a '50s-style setting with Romeroesque *Living Dead* licks.

I Was a Zombie for the F.B.I. (1984, Rykodisc)

Intrepid F.B.I. agents played by real-life cousins James Rasberry and Larry Raspberry [sic] battle evil aliens out to zombify the American citizenry with their zombie-making "zomball" in this fun, low-key, black-and-white '50s-style indie spoof structured as a vintage six-chapter serial.

Tokyo Zombie (2005, Anchor Bay Entertainment)

Slacker buds and would-be warriors Micchan (Show Aikawa) and Fujio (Tadanobu Asano) confront the undead in Sakichi Sato's darkly goofy, consistently amusing Japanese zomcom, complete with zombie gladiator action.

Death Becomes Her (1992, Universal Studios)

A Z-video concept gets the Hollywood megabuck treatment, with surprisingly felicitous results, as clever dialogue, dark wit, swift pacing, and splatstick effects bring this dueling dead-bimbos (Goldie Hawn vs. Meryl Streep) comedy to often riotous life. Even Bruce Willis, with a Forry Ackerman makeover, is funny here.

franchise, which went dormant until a sudden revival in the 2000s, produced the abysmal, nearly amateur-level sequels *Return of the Living Dead: Necropolis* (2005) and *Return of the Living Dead: Rave to the Grave* (2007), both appropriately lensed in the Ukraine near the Chernobyl nuclear disaster site and broadcast on the Channel Formerly Known as Sci Fi.

Romero would later reflect in a *VideoScope* interview:

I just don't like the *Return of the Living Dead* films mainly because I think they ripped Jack Russo off. He wrote *Return of the Living Dead*, and they bought it from him on the promise that they would use his script and involve him in it. The moment the deal was closed, they walked away and wrote their own thing. So Jack really had nothing to do with that script and that pisses me off. I just thought it was unethical.

Russo, though, apparently took the whole process in stride. "I thought Dan [O'Bannon] did a marvelous job, and I liked the movie. Dan and I got along superbly well, and he very much liked my novelization of the script."

American Werewolf in London director John Landis perhaps puts *Return* in its most accurate perspective: "What I liked was the shamelessness of it."

Zombie Movie Milestones:
Stuart Gordon's *Re-Animator*

1985 was nothing if not a banner year for zombie films. In addition to the dueling undead of George Romero's *Day of the Dead* and the John Russo–inspired *Return of the Living Dead*, Chicago-based director Stuart Gordon, of the Organic Theater fame, became the first to mesh old-school H.P. Lovecraft with new wave zombies in his 1985 breakthrough screen debut *Re-Animator*. Loosely adapted from Lovecraft's short story *Herbert West: Re-Animator*, the film focuses on some grisly fun and games at the Miskatonic, Massachusetts, Med School morgue, where precocious mad scientist Herbert West (Jeffrey Combs) is perfecting a secret serum to re-animate the dead. To this end, he recruits fellow med student Daniel Kane (Bruce Abbott) and a number of soon-to-be-lively cadavers.

Gordon keeps the demented action moving at a brisk pace. To learn why a murdered, revivified, and then lobotomized (!) med-school dean (Robert Sampson) delivers his naked blond daughter (Barbara Crampton) to the severed-but-still-living head of a lascivious brain surgeon (David Gale)—well, you'll just have to see for yourself. Suffice it to say that no previous film had mixed copious gore (a reported then-record-setting twenty-four gallons of blood!) and dark guffaws to such scintillating effect.

Re-Animator began life as a planned stage production until Gordon, co-scripter Dennis Paoli and fellow writer William Norris retooled the concept as a thirteen-episode half-hour TV series. When Gordon met producer Brian Yuzna, the latter persuaded him to go the low-budget Hollywood film route instead, eventually inking a distribution deal with Charles Band's modest but open-minded B-movie factory, Empire Pictures. First-time filmmaker Gordon hired sure-handed cinematographer Mac Ahlberg (himself an occasional director) to help show him the visual ropes and a top-notch makeup effects crew to bring his particularly grisly-looking zombies to vivid, horrifying life.

Budgeted at $900,000, *Re-Animator*, released October 18, 1985, proved a steady box-office earner and a major critical hit. Roger Ebert wrote: "I walked out somewhat surprised and reinvigorated (if not re-animated) by a movie that had the audience emitting taxi whistles and wild goat cries." Even *The New York Times'* Janet Maslin was moved to note: "*Re-Animator* has a fast pace and a good deal of grisly vitality. It even has a sense of humor, albeit one that would be lost on 99.9 percent of any ordinary moviegoing crowd."

The film would lead to two less laudatory, though still largely satisfying, Yuzna-directed sequels, *Bride of Re-Animator* (1990) and *Beyond Re-Animator* (2003), both returning the entertaining Mr. Combs to the title role. That intense thespian makes no bones about his affection for his career-launching character. "The meatier parts in anything, either a movie or a play," he notes, "are usually the ones who are out of the norm, who are not your everyday run-of-the-mill persons. You have a coat rack with a lot of hooks on it."

From the get-go, Combs and Gordon agreed on the actor's approach to the part. As Combs states:

> I don't go at it saying, "Okay, I'm going to play a mad scientist."
> That's not even part of the equation. I don't think of Herbert West
> as being crazy or insane; he's merely brilliant and gifted and ego-
> centric and arrogant and ambitious and lets nothing get in the
> way of his goal, and it's everyone else's labeling that says he is
> mad. . . . It's everyone else who *just doesn't understand*. So even if
> I do come across as maybe scaring you, that's good, but I didn't go
> at it saying, "I'm going to scare you." He's obsessed. He's gonna be
> the sperm that's gonna fertilize the egg and nothing is going to
> get in his way.

As for the film itself, Combs recalls:

> A lot of happy accidents made that piece come together. The cast-
> ing was great. I think I was right for my role but everybody else is
> right for theirs, too. It's directed with such energy and honesty,
> the editing is great, [composer Richard Band's] music's spot-on.
> A lot of things have to come together in order to make a movie
> something special. It's a mysterious alchemy to put together
> a wonderful movie like that.

Director Gordon, who has followed that film with a string of quality, if modestly budgeted, creations that include *From Beyond* (1986), *Edmond* (2005), and *Stuck* (2007), credits *Re-Animator* with kick-starting his career but, like Romero, expresses wariness about continuing down that one-way street. "First, I should say it's a wonderful thing because it got me started, and I've been working ever since thanks to the success of that first movie. But it also becomes negative because every executive thinks that everything else you do is going to be exactly like *Re-Animator*. That was one of the reasons I didn't want to do the sequels; I don't want to get that pigeonholed. I like doing horror, but I like doing other things as well, so it is a mixed blessing, I guess."

DESECRATION
OF *THE DEAD*

I don't like sharks; I'm not a good enough swimmer.
—George Romero

Shortly following the *Return* vs. *Day* debacle, the original holy grail of zombie films, *Night of the Living Dead*, suffered its first direct indignity: In 1986, Hal Roach Studios issued a colorized version of the film on VHS, at a reported cost of some $250,000, more than twice *Night*'s original budget. *Night* had long been pirated theatrically, with inferior prints making the grindhouse and drive-in rounds, and, in the early '80s, the movie's public domain status caused it to become one of the first films to flood the nascent Beta and VHS markets, with myriad bottom-feeding outfits distributing the title to burgeoning video outlets. But Roach's edition represented the first instance of tampering with the actual content and compromising the movie's essential documentary feel. That charge was refuted at the time by Rob Word, then Roach's senior vice president of production and marketing. "When the original was shot," he rationalized, "news crews were still filming in 16 mm black-and-white, but now we're used to seeing that stuff in color."

The colorization process proved an artistic disaster and outraged dedicated *Dead*heads who couldn't abide the mood-ruining hues. Romero agreed, "I just think it's silly. I don't like to watch it in color. It looks awful, and it kills the gag in the beginning. The whole gag is, there's this guy walking across the cemetery for like two minutes, and we think it's just a human. But now that he's *green*, we don't think he's human."

Oddly, one of the few defenders of the process was the cemetery zombie himself. As a photographer, Bill Hinzman had snapped the shoot's only color photos and later said of the new version, "I watched it in color and the choice is there for people to watch it that way or to continue seeing it in black-and-white. Personally, and I may be speaking for some of the original stockholders as well, it just brought around more notoriety for the picture. I think it's neat."

Night would undergo three additional colorizations, one by Anchor Bay Entertainment in 1997, which at least opted for flesh-toned zombies, and two by colorization specialists Legend Films, in 2004 and 2009, the last adding a 3D process as well.

Although Romero temporarily abandoned his Living Dead, he kept busy in the fright field. He co-produced Laurel's *Creepshow*-inspired cathode horror anthology series *Tales from the Darkside* (1984–1988) and wrote the spooky pilot episode *Trick or Treat*, directed by actor Bob Balaban. Despite the positive reception the episode earned, Romero had mixed feelings about surrendering creative control. "It was the first time I ever sent anything off to military school, to be directed by someone else. I didn't like being in that position." Romero's disaffection increased when his suggestion to shoot the pilot in Pittsburgh was overruled and filming was relocated to New York City.

Romero hung on with the show for a time, penning the excellent second-season episode *The Devil's Advocate*, featuring Jerry Stiller as a shock jock from hell (literally!), and adapting the short stories *Baker's Dozen* and *The Gingerbread Witch*. But Romero decided that television was not his ideal media métier, at least not *Darkside*, whose episodes often suffered from undernourished budgets (roughly $100 grand per). Consequently, he declined opting into Laurel's subsequent series *Monsters*, though he did adapt a Stephen King short story, *Cat from Hell*, for the 1990 big-screen *Tales from the Darkside: The Movie*.

Romero remained in an anthology groove, however, scripting the less successful—but still mostly fun—Michael Gornick-directed sequel *Creepshow 2* (1987), a project shorn of shining stars (though it did boast George Kennedy, Lois Chiles, and a rare appearance by Dorothy Lamour) and trimmed from five stories to three, involving a killer statue, a killer oil slick, and (what else?) a killer corpse. The last appears in the film's best tale, *The Hitchhiker*, complete with a cameo by Stephen King as a dimwitted trucker. (When we saw the movie in Times Square, audience members again chanted, "I want my cake!" but this time their prayers went unanswered.)

It was around this time that Romero and longtime Laurel Group partner Richard Rubinstein parted ways. While there was no reported rancor involved, increasing creative differences divided the pair. As Romero noted, "He was the kind of guy who would say, 'Oh, I give George all the freedom in the world'—but it was only 'cause he wasn't interested. I could never sit down with Richard for two days straight, with no sleep, and talk story."

Linking up with current producer Peter Grunwald, Romero followed *Creepshow 2* with a writing and directing for-hire job for Orion Pictures, *Monkey Shines* (1988). Romero adapted Michael Stewart's novel about a psycho simian (played by a primate named Boo) and a quadriplegic (Jason Beghe) she's been trained to aid but winds up tormenting—sort of a *Misery* with monkeys. Not the most promising premise ever to scamper down the scare-pic pike, and not even as proven a frightmeister as George Romero could yield real chills from the uninspired situation. *Monkey Shines* does proffer sights previously unseen onscreen, though. It's the first flick, for starters, that tries to wring gut-wrenching suspense from a climactic showdown whose vital and unlikely components are: a motionless quadriplegic; an equally immobile voice-controlled computer; a half-dead scientist (John Pankow) shot through with enough barbiturates to "bring down King Kong"; and a cute little hyperactive, capuchin monkey running amok with a straight razor (!).

John Russo, meantime, busied himself adapting his own slasher novel, *The Majorettes* (1986), for the home video screen, with direction by Bill Hinzman and largely indifferent results.

"When you start tampering with a classic, there's always the potential of a backlash."
—Russ Streiner, on the 1990 remake of Night of the Living Dead

Hinzman, in turn, would further clutter the celluloid graveyard with the 1988 misfire *Flesh-eater* (video title: *Night of the Living Zombies*), in which he not only directs but scripts and resurrects his Cemetery Zombie. The latter character serves as the mute star of a mindless romp that rips off *Night of the Living Dead* with inept abandon, from redneck posses shooting zombies to ghouls going after a pack of brain-dead teens holed up in a remote house.

At this point, it seemed unlikely that Romero, Russo, Russ Streiner, and Bill Hinzman would ever wind up back on the same team. But that's precisely what happened when plans arose in 1990 to remake the original *Night of the Living Dead*, under the auspices of prolific schlock manufacturer Menahem Golan. Romero and Russo buried the legal hatchet (there never had been a personal one, according to both men) with a scheme to cash in on the property with a proper copyright and, at last, recoup some long-lost revenue. Russ Streiner explains, "Part of the reason to do that remake was rooted in that copyright problem. We felt that if we got many of that same group of people back together and remade the picture that in some way it would help shore up the copyright on the original picture." Streiner allowed that, in exhuming the hallowed *Dead*, the group might be treading on dangerous ground. "When you start tampering with a classic, there's always the potential of a backlash."

Armed with a relatively lavish $4.2 million budget, Russo and Russ Streiner signed on to produce, while Romero executive-produced and revised the original script. Tom Savini logically came onboard to handle the special makeup effects, then was persuaded to direct as well. "When George handed me the script, he said use the script as a guide, change whatever you like. If you have any questions, I'll answer them honestly, but I'm not going to tell you what to do. This is your movie."

Prior to the film's release, Russ Streiner made the prophetic statement: "George based his script on the 1968 version, but there are a couple of things in it that are new that should surprise people. You won't be totally confident about what's going to happen next."

Confidence seems to be one of many key ingredients lacking in the new, decidedly unimproved *Night of the Living Dead*. Indeed, if ever a movie begged to have a bullet put through its head, it's this one. Its inability to recreate even a soupçon of an iota of the original's black magic makes one appreciate all the more the sheer alchemy that informed the 1968 film.

Right from the opening scene (which Savini wanted to lens in black and white with a gradual bleed into color), the mood is all wrong. The iconic car rolls up a similar cemetery road, located in Washington, Pennsylvania, but this time in bright, sunny spring rather than bleak, ominous autumn. Scripter Romero awkwardly rewrites siblings Johnny's (Bill Moseley) and Barbara's (Patricia Tallman) dialogue, lending it a needlessly sour rather than ominously teasing tone. And now, in another hollow *faux au courant* detail, it's their formerly abused mom, not anonymous pop, lying in the grave awaiting their annual wreath.

The acting also contributes to the early warning signs of the disaster that lies ahead. Unlike Streiner in the original, Moseley, normally a fine actor, can't manage a decent Boris imitation when he utters *Night*'s signature line, "They're coming to get you, Barbara!"—delivered first in voice-over, with the camera still a long distance from the car, then repeated, just as poorly, in the cemetery. Romero and Savini attempt a fake-out when the expected initial cemetery zombie is revealed as another confused, fleeing citizen, who's rapidly followed by the *real* cemetery zombie, a dude in makeup so exaggerated, he instantly gives the game away.

Johnny's murder represents another blown opportunity. Says Savini in the accompanying DVD featurette *The Dead Walk*: "I wanted his death to be more graphic than in the original film. In fact, we even built this lovely dummy of Bill Moseley, and I had the zombie crush his head. Again, it's more emotional when they see it happen." Not, unfortunately, when viewers see an *obvious* dummy; in the 1968 version, the thudding sound effect, sickening in its finality, brilliantly sold the horror of Johnny's demise.

Barbara's subsequent sprint to the farmhouse is filmed without sufficient suspense-generating cuts, Ben (Tony Todd) no longer literally pops up out of nowhere but simply pulls into the driveway in his pickup after running over another zombie dummy—etc., etc., ad nauseam, ad infinitum, whichever arrives first.

Savini's dinner theater-level rehash trashes the original film's genius at virtually every turn. The door-boarding scenes seem to drag on for an eternity sans energy or suspense. The characters are coarser and more broadly drawn. Ben and Harry Cooper (Tom Towles) go at it full blast with barely a second's provocation, while Tom (William Butler) and Judy Rose (Katie Finneran), formerly just Judy, are recast as rednecks. Helen Cooper (McKee Anderson) is reduced to cipher status and daughter Sarah (Heather Mazur), in Kyra Schon's Karen role, supplies scant menace. Worse, her classic matricide occurs in a perfunctory offscreen moment, while her shocking cannibalization of her dear, old dead dad is dropped entirely. True, the creators were contractually bound to bring in an R-rated product but that didn't demand stripping the film of its total terror potential.

Likewise excised are most of the TV studio sequences and the trip to D.C. to interrogate clueless officials. Indeed, nearly all the script revisions are ill advised: Ben's transformation into a zombie packs no punch, nor does Barbara's point-blank execution of a surviving Harry (who, after being wounded by Ben, hides out in the attic). As the film grinds through its pointlessly retooled paces, it exhibits little in the way of charm, atmosphere, or tension, with loudly trumpeted "jump" scares replacing the original's hard-earned chills. Gone are the nightmare quality and documentary feel.

The actors, though more experienced, largely lack the authenticity the earlier, less polished cast exhibited. Todd, a reliable pro who'd soon go on to greater fame as the eponymous specter in Clive Barker's *Candyman* franchise, turns in the best work, offering a thoroughly professional, if a bit more macho impersonation of the late Duane Jones's performance as reluctant hero, Ben. (Ving Rhames, who'd later turn up in both the *Dawn of the Dead* and *Day of the Dead* remakes, was originally considered for the role, as were Laurence Fishburne and Eriq LaSalle.)

Tallman's shotgun-toting, Sigourney Weaver-ized Barbara comes across not so much strong as aggressively unpleasant. (On the plus side, her overly intense delivery of the Ed Wood-worthy line "Whatever I lost, I lost a long time ago, and I do not plan on losing anything else" at least elicited some laughs from an otherwise increasingly hostile audience at the *Fangoria* screening we attended.) Accomplished character actor Towles, excellent as the title psycho's accomplice Otis in John McNaughton's cult classic *Henry: Portrait of a Serial Killer* (1986), appears especially constrained as the monotonously written, perpetually P.O.'d Harry (in this version, a part tailor-made for Joe Besser). His on-screen lament, "Damn it, we've heard all this before!" rings all too sadly true.

Only in the area of the zombie makeups does the remake partially succeed; under special effects experts Everett Burrell and John Vulich's supervision, the living dead match the sophistication of *Day of the Dead*'s zombies. And this time the filmmakers had the luxury of auditioning the zombies. Russ Streiner recalls, "Extras drove from Kentucky to be in the remake. They had to expand their extras casting because the turnout for these zombies was so great."

Savini even felt the need to hire a zombie movement instructor, though that didn't work out as well as hoped. "It backfired on us," he admits. "People were just doing incredibly wild things. It wound up: 'Just move slow.' It was the same thing I think that George said to his zombies in the original film." But minus the original's ambient sense of inescapable dread, the zombies seem more like ambulatory set decorations than legit threats.

In short, even if collecting overdue *Living Dead* debts was the remake's sole raison d'être, fans had a right to expect better, especially considering the talents involved, leading with Romero (who even cut back on his usual cameo, appearing only as a radio voice near film's end).

Not surprisingly, initial critical reaction was largely negative, with Roger Ebert granting the remake only one out of four stars and rejecting the film's chief point: "The ending of the movie, with its bonfire and tortured freeze-frame scenes, is apparently intended to suggest that we really are no better than the zombies, a conclusion which, even based on the evidence of the characters in this movie, I have trouble accepting." Though disparaged in its day, the remake has more recently garnered kinder attention in some circles, particularly from those mostly younger viewers averse to watching black-and-white movies.

As for the filmmakers, Savini posed the leading rhetorical query: "Why on Earth would you dare to remake a classic?" Today, John Russo expresses a similar sentiment. "The remake would probably have been a great box-office success if the original had never been made. But it suffers from being compared to the original. The original has the magic that persists to this day, and that level of magic was not achieved by the remake, even though we tried hard. Overall, the picture did not turn out as well as we hoped. This was not all Tom's fault."

> "I still have nightmares that I'm on that movie set, directing that movie, and waiting for the sun to come up, so I could just stop shooting and go home."
>
> —Tom Savini, on directing the remake of Night of the Living Dead

At the end of the *Night*, Savini adopted a far harsher view of the entire ordeal. "That was the worst experience of my life. Everybody had a different idea, or wanted a favor. I've learned that even if they're your best friends, if it's your vision, then you should stick with it, because nobody stabs you in the back worse than your best friends. . . . I still have nightmares that I'm on that movie set, directing that movie, and waiting for the sun to come up, so I could just stop shooting and go home."

Watching the film makes it abundantly clear that Savini, whose previous directorial experience had been limited to a trio of *Tales from the Darkside* episodes, sorely lacked Romero's camera command. Actor Tom Towles, however, at least partially exonerated the debuting director in a *VideoScope* interview:

It was not a comfortable time for Tom for a number of dark and personal reasons. Things in his personal life collapsed in on him almost from the first day of shooting onwards. Nevertheless, I thought that his intellectual, creative and emotional fortitude throughout it was impressive. He hung in there and tried to keep it all together. First-time directors are challenged in ways that they cannot possibly anticipate, which is why I have so much respect for them when they succeed.

While the *Night* remake disillusioned many *Dead*heads, the franchise would receive an even harder slap in its living dead face later that decade.

Zombie Movie Milestones:
Peter Jackson, on *Dead Alive*

Long before Peter Jackson made his international blockbuster mark with the *Lord of the Rings* trilogy, his 1992 *Dead Alive* (originally *Braindead*) aspired to be—and arguably became—the goriest zomcom ever committed to celluloid. Jackson's frantic tale, set in 1957, gets off to a relatively sedate start. After fending off offended natives played by the real-life Fijian Rugby Team, a New Zealand zoo official captures a vicious "Sumatran Rat Monkey" in the wilds of King Kong's mythical stomping ground, Skull Island (the auteur would return to the locale for his far bigger-budgeted 2005 *King Kong* redo). Once the caged critter sinks its teeth into nerd Lionel's (Timothy Balme) overbearing mom (Elizabeth Moody), the pic's pace and body count pick up considerably. Lionel soon has his hands (and basement) full of cannibalistic zombies—former neighbors all—who threaten his burgeoning romance with lovely Spanish lass Paquita (Diana Penalvar). She complains early on: "Your mother ate my dog!" To which Lionel responds, "Not all of it." When Lionel's crude, avaricious, inheritance-seeking Uncle Les (Ian Watkin) hosts a populous party at Lionel's zombie-infested home, the scene and screen are set for a non-stop zombie gore orgy that pulls out all the splatter stops, highlighted by our hero's lawnmower shredding of a slew of unlucky stiffs.

> Joe Kane: Dead Alive *may be the gore movie to end all gore movies. Was that your intent from the outset?*
>
> Peter Jackson: *Dead Alive* was made because I was a fan of those sorts of movies. I love *Re-Animator,* I love the *Evil Dead* films. If it hadn't been for those films being made, *Dead Alive* probably wouldn't have existed. You don't want to do a rip-off of *Evil Dead* or *Re-Animator*. You want it to have its own identity. It's a responsibility of anybody who tackles an over-the-top gory zombie movie: you've got to look at what the gore quotient is and try and top it.
>
> JK: *How did you stage the lawnmower scene?*
>
> PJ: We had two or three cameras going through some of that stuff. I think the one group of people that need the biggest

congratulations are the zombie extras. They were twenty or twenty-five very brave people. We had the lawnmower—it wasn't, obviously, a real lawnmower, it was this fake fiberglass thing we had made that had these hoses that were connected to a huge pump that was in turn connected to this massive 44-gallon drum of fake blood that was maple syrup with food coloring. We'd sort of tested this thing with water and we'd seen the water spurting out, yet we didn't know what it was going to do to the syrup—we hadn't done it with human beings before. My only instruction really to the extras was to be as brave as they possibly could and to throw themselves against the mower till we yelled, "Cut."

JK: *You also have the initially reluctant heroine, Diana Penalver, eventually taking charge.*

PJ: I didn't want to make a film where the female characters just sit around and scream and get terrified. I wanted Lionel's girlfriend to be doing as much as he is. The funny thing is neither Tim nor Diana were horror fans. Tim said he'd never seen a horror film. So I gave him *Evil Dead 2* and *Dawn of the Dead* on videotape before we started the film. He came in the next day, gave them back to me and said, "Uh yeah, I get the idea." Diana absolutely *hated* horror films. The first special-effects scene we did with Diana is where she's cutting through a zombie hand with a pair of nail scissors. She's cutting through the wrist of a zombie that's clamped around Lionel's throat. It was just a rubber hand with some blood tubes in it. She was chopping away and the blood was spurting in a very realistic way and I'm thinking, "Great, this is looking good." And then when I yelled "Cut!", I looked up at her and she was crying. But she got used to it after a while.

JK: *How would you like audiences to regard* Dead Alive?

PJ: *Dawn of the Dead* I think of as the zombies in a shopping mall. And *Re-Animator* is the zombies in the medical laboratory. And *Evil Dead* is obviously the zombies in the cabin. I hope people think of *Dead Alive* as the one with the guy with the zombie mother in the 1950s.

12 DESECRATION OF THE DEAD, PART 2: THE SEQUEL

> If I fail, they write me off as a statistic. If I succeed, they
> pay me a million bucks to fly out to Hollywood and fart.
> —George Romero

Before participating in the misguided *Night of the Living Dead* **remake,** Romero had reteamed with *Dawn* investor and fellow fright-meister Dario Argento on *Two Evil Eyes*. That collaboration didn't see limited U.S. theatrical release until 1991, a year after the *Night* redo, but proved a fruitful fright-film reunion, at least for the duo's fans. Here, the famous fear auteurs' double visions of Edgar Allan Poe add up to two hours of solid shocks.

Romero returns to living dead territory with an updated account of Poe's *Facts in the Case of M. Valdemar*, a sardonic narrative in an E.C. Comics/*Creepshow* vein that reunites that movie's alums E.G. Marshall, as a lawyer, and Adrienne Barbeau, as Jessica (she's the soon-to-be-merry widow of an aged, dying millionaire). Jessica's doctor beau (Ramy Zada) uses hypnotism to control the ailing codger's mind while keeping him alive long enough for his will to go into effect. Trouble ensues when those selfsame hypnotic techniques prevent the tycoon's brain from expiring even after his body bids adieu. Romero draws upon his sharply honed scare skills to milk the straightforward story for a fair amount of chills.

Argento exhibits even more ambition in his ultra-eclectic update of Poe's *The Black Cat,* weaving in threads from such other Poe stories as *The Pit and the Pendulum* and *The Cask of Amontillado,* while Harvey Keitel contributes a strong turn as feline-phobic crime photographer Rod Usher. Argento probably had enough material and energy to go feature length with his segment, which, at roughly sixty-five minutes, ultimately suffers from a truncated feel. *Two Evil Eyes* may not break new genre ground, but the film covers its oft-trod terror turf with sure footing by a pair of pros.

The film's overall creative success notwithstanding, Romero recalls the experience with mixed emotions. "Dario shot his half of the film in Pittsburgh as well, then they took the movie back to Europe to finish it. They did all the post-production on it over there. Then they opened it in Europe, but they never got a good distributor for it over here. I liked it a lot. Had it been made for a studio and gone out with a good campaign, I thought it could have done a little business."

Romero yet regrets surrendering post-production control:

I wish I could have had a chance to be involved in the finishing of it. The tracks aren't as good. Pino Donaggio did a nice score, but I think they missed a couple of opportunities. But what are you gonna do? Contractually, I was supposed to be able to do it but I think they had money problems too. They did invite me over for the last few days of post, but at that point there was nothing that could be done, so I bailed out.

In the States, the VHS market was the ultimate target. "They were looking forward to video; I think they released only a couple of hundred prints. They put it out there so maybe it has a little visibility so when it goes to video, people have heard about it."

Following an onscreen cameo as one of Hannibal Lecter's (Anthony Hopkins) jailers in Jonathan Demme's Pittsburgh-shot *The Silence of the Lambs* (1991), Romero next joined forces with former collaborator and fellow terror titan Stephen King for the major studio (Orion Pictures) production *The Dark Half.* Timothy Hutton does a solid job in dual roles as Thad Beaumont, an author who literally becomes his own worst enemy when his pseudonymous alter ego George Stark (Hutton again) transforms into a flesh-and-blood doppelganger with demands of his own. When Thad refuses to cooperate with his titular bad self, Stark executes a series of vicious slayings that implicate his creator as the perp. A promising premise grows increasingly strained as the reels roll on, but on a creepy, sadistic level *The Dark Half* works fairly well, as Romero manages to yield maximum gore and shock value from Stark's vile, escalating rampage.

Romero has long felt drawn to the theme of duality: "I've often worked with the 'monster within' theme. The *Living Dead* films even have a little touch of that." But the filmmaking experience again turned out to be less than ideal. As before, the director, who also adapted King's novel for the screen, felt uncomfortable working within the studio system. "On the one hand, you have a lot more talent because you have the money to pay for that talent." On the downside, "The more money people spend, the more uptight they get, the more reluctant they are to leave it up to the filmmaker. An extra $100,000 doesn't get you an extra $100,000; it gets you an extra $90,000. An extra million gets you maybe $400,000."

Beyond the monetary squabbling inherent in the system, Romero has had a perennial problem: He doesn't like dealing with those suits who confuse power with creativity, people whose goals, besides making money, are winning the petty pissing wars that unfold behind the scenes, often to the detriment of creating a good film or even making that desired dough. As Romero has stated, "I'd love to make a big movie. I'd love to make a *Batman* movie or something like that. I probably don't want to make it under the kind of conditions that you're forced [into] to make those kinds of films."

Like *Two Evil Eyes*, *The Dark Half*, which wrapped in March 1991, lingered for over a year in celluloid limbo. Says Romero, "Orion ran into trouble and I guess all their pictures wound up on the shelf. You have these visions—after you put the time and energy into something—that it just goes to in-flight or video." At least *The Dark Half* did see the cinematic light of day, even if it earned mostly mixed reviews and disappointed at the box office, taking in some $10 million domestically.

Over the next several years, Romero would virtually vanish from the public radar screen when, despite his insights into and abhorrence of the mainstream movie establishment, he became totally trapped in a well-paying but invisible Hollywood development hell, attached to projects that were either scrapped (e.g., an adaptation of Whitley Streiber's *Unholy Fire* and a remake of *The Innocents,* based on Henry James's *The Turn of the Screw*) or assigned to other directors (notably, 1999's *The Mummy*). Still he kept chasing the dangling Hollywood carrot.

"It was very frustrating," Romero remarks. "We had a housekeeping deal at New Line for a couple of years, and they never made a movie with us (my partner Peter Grunwald and I). When we left New Line, we wound up with the rights to one project that was then picked up by MGM, and they developed it for a year and a half. Never made it. The same project went to Fox under Chris Columbus's company. They developed it for another year. The studio never made the movie. In the meantime, I was just completely frustrated and I lost *The Mummy* because of that project. It was ready to go, and they wouldn't let us off the contract on this other film they never made, so I wound up losing *The Mummy*. Mine was very different, though. Mine was really sort of a homage. It was very noir and really a throwback to the old one. Nothing at all like what they eventually did to it. But it was ready to roll, and we couldn't get out of the contract. Then we worked on *Goosebumps* for a while and then Fox got into some kind of a feud with Scholastic, and they decided not to make that one. So that was six or seven years!"

In 1998, Romero returned to both his zombie and commercial roots, directing a 30-second live-action ad promoting the video game *Resident Evil 2* for the Japanese market. That second-generation game, like the original *Resident Evil* game, borrowed heavily from the director's own *Living Dead* films. Romero then signed on to write a script for the first *Resident Evil* movie, a fairly faithful adaptation of the game. Producing company Capcom executive Yoshiki Okamoto told *Electronic Gaming Monthly* that "Romero's script wasn't good, so Romero was fired." In a *DGA* magazine interview, Romero explained, "I don't think they were into the spirit of the video game and wanted to make it more of a war movie, something heavier than I thought it should be. So I think they just never liked my script." Scripting and directorial assignments eventually went to Paul W. S. (*Event Horizon*) Anderson.

While Romero endured this fiscally rewarding but creatively stonewalled period, former partner Russo dramatically upped his Pittsburgh production slate, directing the horror film *Heartstopper* (1991), a relatively lavish (roughly $1 million) effort bolstered by B-list names like Michael J. Pollard and Moon Unit Zappa. That film remains among Russo's fondest projects. "My favorite of the horror films I directed is *Heartstopper*, a.k.a. *Dark Craving*, although some scenes were cut by the distributor from the DVD release that should never have been cut because they make some of the following scenes appear illogical. This movie was based on the best novel of the fifteen I have had published." Russo soldiered on with several lower-profile efforts, including the mini-budgeted, shot-on-video sequel *Midnight 2* (1993), the holiday horror quickie *Santa Claws* (1996), and the immortal party flicks *Scream Queens Swimsuit Sensations* (1992) and *Scream Queens Naked Christmas* (1996).

> "Marilyn Eastman and I had the idea around the same time. We were inspired by the success of the Star Wars *rerelease.*"
>
> —John Russo, on Night of the Living Dead, *30th anniversary edition*

In 1998, Russo and three key fellow original *Night* alums—Russ Streiner, Bill Hinzman, and Karl Hardman—committed what many *Dead*heads rate as an unthinkable cultural crime: In a deal with Anchor Bay Entertainment, designed to promote the dawn of the DVD age via a digitally remastered *Night of the Living Dead*, 30th anniversary edition, they exhumed *Night's* corpse for a blasphemous posthumous makeover, adding newly filmed scenes and inserts along with an inappropriate synth score.

Russo retraces the origins of that dubious brainstorm. "Marilyn Eastman and I had the idea around the same time. We were inspired by the success of the *Star Wars* rerelease. George Romero and I were going to write the new scenes, and George was going to direct. But by the time we got a deal with Anchor Bay, George was tied up with *Resident Evil* and other projects, and he couldn't be involved. So I wrote the new scenes and directed them." In a contemporaneous *Entertainment Weekly* interview, however, Romero denied any intended involvement with the project, stating "I didn't want to touch *Night of the Living Dead,*" adding that "no bad blood" existed between Russo and himself.

The new, decidedly unimproved version opens with two drivers transporting the electrocuted corpse of the soon-to-be Cemetery Zombie (Hinzman) in a pickup truck (the same model as seen in the original film) to the burial ground, with another nearby boneyard subbing for the original Evans City site. Kinfolk of one of the late killer's victims await graveside to make sure the murderer's really dead, while an unhinged-looking Reverend Hicks (shamelessly overacted by Scott Vladimir Licina, who also composed the new score) prepares to preside over the proceedings.

After these characters depart, a not only obviously older but significantly heavier Hinzman (30 years of graveyard grub apparently agreed with him) rises awkwardly from his coffin, the drivers flee, and we cut to the opening of the original film—Johnny and Barbara's car rolling up that road to hell. The intrusive footage gratuitously serves to add artistic injury to insult by negating the original's nearly instant plunge into pure nightmare turf by delaying and deflating the siblings' abrupt encounter with the undead menace.

Other mutilations mar the narrative: A car crash results in a family of zombies (played by the filmmakers' relatives) who join a group of fellow new ghouls pointlessly intercut, at basically arbitrary intervals, with scenes of the original Living Deaders. When Ben turns on the radio, we hear a new narration offering more explanation, with voice-over supplied by original *Night* TV announcer Charles Craig. Said narration now grows so ludicrously narrow-focused that it even details what happened at Beekman's Diner, giving us more of Ben's personal backstory.

The *30th Anniversary* version works in an absolutely awful "epilogue" where Reverend Hicks, the first human to have survived a zombie bite, is interviewed by a TV reporter (Debbie Rochon) at the Ormsby Medical Center and pronounces the zombies' presence on the planet a punishment from God. Licina not only plays the admittedly thankless role way over the top, but his metal-Satanic style, complete with shaved skull and eccentrically manicured facial topiary, is totally out of keeping with the era and setting. Russo and crew then unceremoniously cut back to Ben's execution and the rest of the original ending.

Accompanying the film is a frequently downright delusional DVD commentary wherein the participants, particularly Russo and Russ Streiner, can't seem to see the incongruities obvious to the even semi-attentive viewer. Streiner purrs over how "the footage blends in so well" (it doesn't) and "how delicately the original music has been blended with the original" (ditto).

In another interview, Russo boasts how they used "the same film stock as before, the same lenses, and, in some cases, the exact same lights. We tried to be real faithful to the original. The new material involves concepts we discussed doing thirty years ago but didn't have the time or money to accomplish."

The film, Russo claims, is "not tampered with, just broadened. You have more things explained that weren't before. We've just augmented the original storyline. The story is tighter, and it makes more sense. It gives the movie a more modern pace." He goes on to comment, "I'm extremely proud of everyone who worked on this. In a lot of ways, it's easier to make a movie from scratch than to do something new and refreshing with a thirty-year-old movie. . . . our objective in doing the new scenes with the new characters was to add to the movie, not destroy its impact. I think it plays just as well as it ever did."

As noted, *Dead*heads disagreed, often vehemently. Wrote *Zombie Movies: The Ultimate Guide* author Glenn Kay, "The additional scenes feature modern-looking actors and noticeably longer takes than the 1968 film, so they stick out like a comical

Debbie Rochon, on Digging Up *The Dead*

In the summer of 1998, John Russo put together a deal with Anchor Bay to fund a new version of *Night of the Living Dead* called *The 30th Anniversary Edition*. He was charged with adding eighteen minutes of new footage to create what the copyright offices would consider a "new film."

Over the years the film was dubbed and redubbed over and over, seeing releases by countless companies. I had once asked John about the legal aspects of this pirating, and he said they had no way of getting the money to sue every company that released it in North America and overseas. With such companies, you would have to hire a lawyer in that state or that country to represent you—a dauntingly expensive task. So in order to get any sort of copyright ownership back to all the original filmmakers, a new version was planned.

Initially, George Romero was rumored to direct, but he was hired to helm *Resident Evil.* With George out of the picture, John Russo, Russ Streiner, Karl Hardman, Marilyn Eastman, and Bill Hinzman soldiered on to shoot the eighteen minutes needed to create a copyrightable version of the film. This would allow them to have ownership of the new version, plus include a newly remastered, pristine version of the original on the disc. For what many consider the biggest cult film in the world, and one of the most influential horror films ever made, it seemed like a novel idea to have all of the filmmakers finally able to make a few bucks from the original classic.

John had asked me to be a reporter in some of the new scenes that were shot. Being such a huge fan of the movie, it was impossible to say no. I mean, who wouldn't want to be cut into their favorite film? The additional scenes added a little bit of backstory to the first zombie, played by Bill Hinzman, and also introduced a priest character, who was bitten by Hinzman's zombie but somehow survived.

The first time I saw the new version, in 1999, I thought the footage matched perfectly. I was not thrown off by the new scenes and was very anxious for the release! I knew there would be a shitstorm to deal with, but I also felt that there would be a section of the horror audience who would enjoy it and would be able to distance themselves from the original enough to watch this movie with an open mind. And certainly if they knew *why* it was done, then they would be pulling for all the filmmakers, rejoicing in the fact that they would finally be able to make a few bucks from their opus.

Not the case.

The viewing public really detested this version and everyone involved was vilified. Maybe it was a lesson to be learned. Maybe it should not have been done. Maybe it even damaged some careers. Actually, it *did*.

From my standpoint, it was an extremely exciting shoot working with all the original *Night* people, and I was thrilled to be in it. If I were to do it all over again—the answer is, yes, I would. I have never been one to wring my hands in worry over what others might think. It would have been great if George had been involved, for sure, but I have a deep friendship with most of the other original Image Ten folks and I hold that to this day. We had a blast. However, recently seeing the movie on DVD on an HD digital TV, the footage no longer matches because of the über-hyper clarity. This is a case of technology not aiding in the viewing experience. Now the "new" scenes jump out much more and the film seems even more disjointed than ever. *If only it was degraded a few generations and it would have all blended together more . . . ?* I can't say I think the movie is great, and I know from first-hand experience that it suffered a massive hate wave from fans and industry people, but as far as experiences go, I wouldn't trade it for the world.

sore thumb." The Web site DVD Verdict's critic raged, "The acting in the new opening is horrible and clearly in a different style than that of the actors in the original film. . . . The poor editing also creates a ton of confusion if you have not seen the original film before, cutting out key points to the plot and lessening the impact of certain scenes. . . ."

Splatter.com's reviewer vented, "Unlike the *Star Wars* special edition, which restored lost footage and added new special effects, Russo's tragic mistake of a movie adds brand new footage, introduces new characters who have nothing to do with the events in the original film, and, perhaps worst of all, adds a totally new film score, performed on a synthesizer! What amazes me is that Romero didn't insist on having his name completely removed from this version of his film." (The original 1968 closing credits unspool intact at the new version's conclusion.)

"Russo managed to singlehandedly ruin what he created. Fans of the original will literally feel sick watching it. Then the rage will set in. The video box claims the film has been 'expanded and enhanced' to celebrate its 30th anniversary, but it's only been raped and pillaged."

Ain't It Cool News cyber suzerain Harry Knowles went so far as to threaten supporters of Russo and crew's remix with excommunication from his sacred geek domain. Even tainted actor and composer Scott Vladimir Licina felt moved to post a lengthy mea culpa on allthingszombie.com, though, judging by the ensuing comments, most *Dead*heads were not appeased.

As for Romero, he told a *VideoScope* interviewer, "I don't agree with all the stuff he [Russo] does. I've told him. We talk about it, but we're still good buddies. That was one of the things that I told him I thought was dumb! He showed it to [then-wife] Chris and I one day when it was just finished, hoping that we would have nice things to say and neither of us did. I just thought it was ridiculous. That one wasn't about the protection of copyright or reestablishing copyright or anything. The remake was. The principal reason we did the colorized version and the remake was to try to help reestablish some kind of copyright."

Obviously, the only feasible aim of this exercise in celluloid grave-robbing had to be to squeeze a few more bucks out of a cadaver some of whose creators refused to let rest in peace. The exercise might not quite equate with painting a moustache on the Mona Lisa but, for *Dead*heads at least, it certainly smacked of egregious sacrilege. John Russo may have opined on the commentary track that, "We have our cake and eat it too," but *Dead*heads would more likely echo Joe Pilato's Captain Rhodes in *Day of the Dead*: "Choke on 'em!"

Zombie Movie Milestones:
Danny Boyle on *28 Days Later*

A psychological rage virus, unwittingly unleashed by animal-rights activists who break into a chimp-research facility, transforms the vast majority of the British citizenry into hyperactive zombies in Danny (*Trainspotting, Slumdog Millionaire*) Boyle's suspenseful 2002 chiller *28 Days Later*. While openly "quoting" from George Romero's original zombie trilogy, especially *Day of the Dead*, with a dash of the same director's *The Crazies* (echoes of *The Last Man on Earth* and *The World, the Flesh and the Devil* are also in evidence), Boyle and screenwriter Alex (*The Beach*) Garland bring enough fresh energy and ideas to the ghoul table to make *28 Days Later* a major addition to the living-dead ranks.

Our story centers on young hospital patient Jim (Cillian Murphy), who awakes, naked and alone, to a London stripped of human life. As he wanders the streets, Jim is rescued from rampaging "infecteds" by armed fellow survivors Selena (Naomi Harris) and Mark (Noah Huntley). After Selena is forced to gore-kill an infected Mark, she and Jim hook up with Frank (Brendan Gleeson) and daughter Hannah (Megan Burns). The disparate, desperate quartet embarks on a road trip (the film's most exciting extended sequence, including a rabid attack by a young zombie boy that packs a literal wallop) to follow what may or may not be an illusive signal emanating from a nearby military encampment (where the action gets a tad *too* close to *Day of the Dead* territory for comfort).

28 Days Later enjoyed some notoriety when it was rereleased in the summer of 2003, after its initial, generally successful 2002 theatrical run, complete with an alternate ending. The DVD edition boasts *three* separate climaxes. If you can get past the copious Romero lifts, you'll likely deem *28 Days Later* one of the most intense, least winking chillers of the new millennium's debut decade.

Joe Kane: *What was it that attracted you to the horror/ zombie genre?*

Danny Boyle: It wasn't so much the horror or the zombies, really. It was two elements, and this is the god's honest truth, this isn't a publicity answer: When Alex Garland wrote this script, it was like 40-50 pages long. And it was a total zombie genre kind of adventure-type film. Now these two ideas in the beginning of it, as soon as I read them I knew I wanted to make the film, and it's weird because the rest of the film, at that point, I didn't think was very good. But he had these two ideas—that there was a psychological virus that was released from a laboratory, which I thought was a brilliant shift on the normal cliché biological viruses. So you cut into that world of slight sci-fi, which I thought was a great premise for a film. And on the next page he had this image of this man walking 'round a deserted London on his own in pajamas. I thought, "That's it for me—I want to make that film." And the rest of it I didn't much like because it *was* a zombie film, really, with lots of attacks and all this kind of stuff. So we worked on it for like eight months, a year, and we tried to make it a more emotional journey than a zombie film normally is. I mean, I love doing the zombies, or the "infecteds" as we called them, but, thematically, I wanted to work up something that was more vulnerable and valuable than zombies and their victims normally are in genre films. That was the idea.

JK: *And there is more character development than you usually see.*

DB: I hope so. It was very much my wish and my desire that you should get attached to the young guy and the girl as well. And when Brendan Gleeson, the taxi driver, dies, you should feel heartbroken, really, and bereft. So I wanted it to be a real emotional journey. And that catches people by surprise in a way, because the way our film is advertised, or the way the kind of general atmosphere of the film enters the public consciousness, you know, they think horror or stuff like that. But when we showed the film early on, women really liked the film, and I was very pleased about that—because women on the whole don't go to zombie films. They're not lining up outside for zombie movies. And it's done very well—we're very fortunate. We've been very lucky—and lucky is a terrible word to use, of course—it coincided with a kind of ratcheting up of world tension and world paranoia, really, about our safety and our vulnerability. I think that's one of the reasons the film has done as well as it's done. It's met that mood; it's coincided with that shift, I think.

JK: *I think that the Gleeson character, and even Mark in the beginning, they bared their souls, and they don't live long enough to attack once they're infected, so it's shocking when they have to be killed.*

DB: Absolutely. It's also why you've gotta do the film without stars, right? Because as soon as you put a star in a film, there's kind of an agenda where you know they're gonna survive basically and they're gonna be the story. Whereas the idea of this is that you have no idea about who could be the lead, who you're really gonna follow, or what's gonna happen to them—anybody could get killed at any moment.

JK: *In the DVD commentary, you mention you visually referenced real-life events, like Bosnia.*

DB: I have the biggest collection of photography books you've ever seen—it's obscene! And I kind of work from images and pictures and a lot of this stuff in the film was drawn on, either directly or as an inspiration, for certain images of ways that you create in the audience the idea of an apocalypse, without the resources to decimate everything. You know, we didn't have the money to do it on a huge kind of Hollywood-type scale, but there are ways that you can psychologically do it. One of the big ones was an empty London, which is unrealistic, of course, because the city would not look like that; there'd be wrecked cars everywhere, there'd be bodies everywhere. But you have to try and find kind of a poetic image for it that people buy, and they don't care that it's not absolutely literally real.

JK: *And the collected bodies, that's almost a subliminal refer-*

ence to those photos that people might see in newspapers but not really remember.

DB: That's right. There's a lot of stuff happened in Europe and before that in Africa over the last ten to fifteen years that was visual inspiration for the film in a way. And you're right—I think those images lodge in people's brains and though they don't recollect them, specifically, they do resonate in some way.

JK: *Did you use any CGI?*

DB: A lot less than we thought we were gonna have to. We thought we'd have to do a lot of removals because we'll never get the motorways empty and we'll never get the city empty. But actually, just sort of the way we approached it, we actually succeeded, ironically, in doing those things very, very cheaply and very quickly. So we didn't do a huge amount of CGI. You have to paint out the occasional plane. And also traffic lights, 'cause you can't turn them off. But basically what you're seeing is what was there, for those few moments.

JK: *How about the explosions? They were real?*

DB: We did the explosions for real. I had a running battle with my producer over that, who was determined to do it as a model to save some money. And I was absolutely adamant I was gonna blow that gas station up. We'd have these running rows where I'd say, "Look, nobody's gonna *care* that it's a low-budget British film! They're not gonna say, 'Oh that was okay, the explosion—never mind, they didn't have much money.' They're just gonna go, 'That's shit—why isn't it as good as *The Matrix*?'" That's what's cruel about cinema. People pay the same price to get into *The Matrix* as they do to see a low-budget British film. They have a right to make those demands of a film. So I was determined to blow it up. And we blew it up. And my goodness me, that was a fantastic explosion!

JK: *And you shot the whole film on digital?*

DB: Except for the sequence right at the end when they're in the lake district to actually close the film. The beauty of celluloid—and it is a more lyrically beautiful medium—was meant to kind of breathe life back into the film, but, of course, it wasn't a particularly nice day in the lake district, so you don't sense it as much as we'd planned, because the good old British weather let us down. But the rest of it was shot on digital, yeah.

JK: *You couldn't really tell.*

DB: Again, the same thing I said about the explosion, we didn't want people to be making allowances for the film at all. We shot it on digital video for all sorts of different reasons, some to do with being able to keep control of the film because we keep the costs down and some to do with the fact it's curiously appropriate for a film about survivors that these cameras are used, because these cameras are survivors as well—you would still be able to use these cameras if you could find batteries. Because they're people cameras, everybody knows how to use them. They're not like movie cameras which, you know, need training to use. So there was something wonderful about using them like that.

JK: *They're spontaneous, too.*

DB: It allowed us to do the film sequentially. I've never shot a film sequentially before. Because there's a lot less fuss, you're a lot more flexible, so we sort of broke some of the rules which we'd previously worked by with this approach.

JK: *You mention something on the DVD commentary about how you could speed it up?*

DB: Yeah, the other thing that happened was when you get interested in these cameras, and you get into the menus that are inside them, they've got all these tricks, some of which are really disgusting—you know, you can set everything sepia like old Edwardian photographs—all this tacky, typical kind of Japanese consumerism! You can make everybody kind of sparkle and things like that. But there are certain things you can do that are extraordinary—you have this motion-capture thing where it kind of imitates frame captures, so you can photograph at like 16,000 frames a second, rather than 24 frames, which would be the regular speed. It doesn't *actually* do that, it's a fallacy, but you do get that *effect.* When quick motion and high-contrast motion are captured, it's slightly unreliable and sort of snatches at the image, and I find it a wonderful way of portraying the infecteds, or the zombies if you like, because I was able to move very, very quickly. And when you photograph them moving very, very quickly in certain light conditions, it felt like they'd been speeded up and yet they didn't look like an old movie, Keystone Kops or anything. So that was a great discovery for me.

JK: *The effect ups the anxiety level.*

DB: Unnerving, yeah. I can't quite explain it, but the effect definitely makes people anxious.

JK: *You also mention borrowing from Romero.*

DB: Yes. Alex Garland is a huge Romero nut, really. He knows everything about it. There was too much Romero in the script, I thought, and we tried to scale it back, but there are still a *lot* of references, if you like, or homages to Romero. But they're really more from the writing than from me. I sort of tried to keep clear of the films as much as possible. Alex was very keen on them—well, I knew he was—and I thought it would be a better balance if I kept clear of them.

JK: *The only one that seemed extreme was the Bub character, though it didn't play out quite the same way.*

DB: It didn't play out the same way, but yeah, you're right, that was very close. Alex did acknowledge where we were borrowing; he wasn't trying to keep it secret, if you like.

JK: *The film was re-released with one of the alternate endings following the credits?*

DB: We didn't have enough money to shoot the original ending, so we finished the film with a little ending that we did in London, which is very bleak and very cheap. They leave, and he ends up in a hospital bed, the same place he is at the beginning.

JK: *I thought that was the best ending. It almost could have been a nightmare he had.*

DB: Yeah, it was very interesting. But then Fox saw the film and, of course, understandably, from a studio point of view, it's a very, very bleak ending and they said, "Hey guys, here's some more money, please go and shoot your original ending in the lake district." So we said, "Okay, okay." So anyway we changed that ending. We went and shot it and then we had two endings. And of course the studio loved the optimistic ending—well, "optimistic," fifty million people are dead, it's not really optimistic, but there's some hope. So we argued and we argued and argued. Then we tested it—Fox paid for us to test it twice—and when I saw it at a run that ending you're talking about is really *bleak*. I mean, it's really tough. And I went with the ending that originally came out. And ironically, of course, which is how I began this story, irony of ironies, Fox said we'd like to put out both endings in America!

13 REBIRTH OF *THE LIVING DEAD*: THE PROMISED *LAND*

I feel secure around zombies.
—Asia Argento

In 2000, George Romero ended an involuntary seven-year screen absence with the direct-to-video domestic release of the French-financed (a reported $5 million) *Bruiser*, a violent fable starring Jason Flemyng as suicidal corporate drone Henry. When Henry slaps on a mask crafted by his obnoxious boss's alienated spouse (Leslie Hope), he discovers that it provides him with the courage to vent his pent-up lethal rage at his many enemies' expense. Dubbed "The Faceless Killer" by the media, our loser "hero" looks to settle the score with his vile magazine owner employer (a wildly overacting Peter Stormare, of *Fargo* fame) and other office offenders.

Bruiser boasts several well-executed set pieces plus a fine performance by *Creepshow* alum Tom Atkins as a skeptical detective. Otherwise, it largely lacks the Romeran thrills and shock value fans had come to expect. In many ways, *Bruiser* harks back to *Jack's Wife*, a film rich in ironies and ideas but sometimes uncertain in execution. Following in the brilliant footsteps of the somewhat similarly themed *American Psycho* (2000) and *Fight Club* (1999) didn't help either, though *Bruiser* has garnered its share of boosters over the years, including the writer/director himself.

As Romero told a *VideoScope* interviewer, the film ranks high among his favorite efforts and experiences: "I love it . . . I think it's a pretty interesting idea. But even more than that is how successfully you think you executed it and what kind of an experience it was making it. We were really working with wonderful people. It was just a wonderful time. . . . I always felt that *Martin* was the best executed or the closest of my films to what I had originally written on the page, and *Bruiser* probably comes in second."

While Romero, by this point a chronic development hell recidivist, returned to projects that would ultimately not reach the screen with him at the helm, in 2004 Universal Studios shocked old-school *Dead*heads by funding a big-budget remake of *Dawn of the Dead*. It was a move inspired by the success of Danny Boyle's *28 Days Later* (2002) and the sustained visibility of Romero's high-profile *Dawn* title. The property was licensed from Romero's former partner, New Amsterdam Entertainment head Richard Rubinstein, and assigned to debuting feature-film director Zach Snyder. Script credit went to Troma grad James (*Tromeo and Juliet*) Gunn, with reported major uncredited assists from writers Michael (*The Player*) Tolkin and Scott (*Minority Report*) Frank.

Universal assembled a highly capable A-minus cast that included *Pulp Fiction* player Ving Rhames (earlier, a candidate to portray Ben in the 1990 *Night of the Living Dead* remake), Sarah Polley (*Go*), Jake Weber (*The Cell*), and Matt Frewer (*Max Headroom*). While Romero had nothing to do with the project, three original *Dawn* actors—Ken Foree, Scott Reiniger, and Tom Savini—turn up in cameos, as a televangelist, general, and sheriff, respectively. In another nod to the original, an upscale mall department store bears the name Gaylen Ross, while an obese survivor is moved through the mall via wheelbarrow, like Reiniger's injured Roger. The new *Dawn* even appropriated the original's tagline, "When there's no more room in hell, the dead will walk the earth," again uttered onscreen by Foree.

Several passing references to *Night of the Living Dead* also surface, when a car crashes into a gas station and explodes like *Night*'s pickup truck and when Polley—after hearing indistinct radio reports and escaping her hubby's attempts to break the windows with a rock like the Cemetery Zombie—rams her vehicle into a tree à la Barbara. The film even includes an oblique reference to *Carnival of Souls*, in the character of an atheistic church organist.

The *Dawn* redo gets off to an energetic start with a scene reminiscent of *The Crazies'* opening—a man, secretly infected by a zombie bite, goes nutzoid in a normally somnolent suburb, leading to his nurse wife's (Polley) frenzied flight through streets choked with zombie violence and chaos. Ultimately, she joins a group of fellow refugees (a much larger cast than in the original) at a Milwaukee 'burb mall to make a desperate stand against the rabid zombie hordes.

Ontario, Canada's abandoned Thornhill Square Shopping Center replaced Pittsburgh's Monroeville Mall, with all-new storefronts constructed specifically for the shoot. Oddly, most corporate brand names refused to give permission for onscreen product placements, apparently viewing the zombie genre as a disreputable association; only Panasonic and Roots lent their assent to appear in the film.

Dawn stalls out a bit during its second act, where many of the characters' charisma shortages, at least compared to the original, show through. The zombie attacks supply some much-needed adrenaline, though, as does the swiftly paced, action-packed last-reel escape sequence. *Dawn* also presents one of screen zombiedom's strongest closing sequences, continuing the horrific story via *Blair Witch*-style video camera grab shots (even as the end credits scroll). Other neat touches include the birth of a zombie baby and a gruesomely inventive chainsaw mishap. The influence of the then-recent horror hit *28 Days Later* is most apparent in the zombies themselves—a fast-moving mob of relentless cannibal killers bald on recognizable individual traits (few zombie close-ups last more than a second or two). The film met with generally positive reviews and a healthy box-office haul, even ousting Mel Gibson's controversial *The Passion of the Christ* from the top spot after a reign of several weeks.

Romero felt ambivalent about the end results, offering an accurate appraisal. "It was better than I expected it was going to be, but I thought it was an action film. It lost its soul. In a way, it lost its reason for being. And I don't like fast-moving zombies, so that wasn't my cup of tea at all! But it was a fun ride. It had a couple of good action set pieces and a couple of neat script ideas. I was thinking it would be just nothing, and I thought it was pretty entertaining."

Ironically enough, it was *Dawn*'s monetary success (over $100 million worldwide) that helped enable Romero to find funding to revivify his long-dormant zombies with *Land of the Dead* (2005), likewise via Universal Studios. The director enjoyed by far his largest *Dead* budget to boot, a bit over $15 million. While not technically a sequel, *Land*'s events occur shortly after *Day of the Dead* left off. To mark his return to the Living Dead fold after two decades, Romero honors his original *Night of the Living Dead*, opening his new film—following the vintage Universal globe-encircling airplane logo—with black-and-white images depicting the aftermath of a zombie apocalypse while a radio broadcast furnishes the historical exposition. Romero had hoped to incorporate clips from *Night*, *Dawn*, and *Day* but rights issues dashed that plan.

We next cut to the present, where Romero, seemingly possessed by the spirit of John Carpenter, eschews his usual siege situation, takes his zombie act on the road, and juices the horror with amped-up action. Sort of an escape from (a zombie-infested) Pittsburgh (though the actual city is never named), *Land* even features Carpenteresque characters. Leading the way is maverick hero Riley (Simon Baker), head of a raiding party sent ever farther afield to scavenge goods for transport to the city, one ruled with a platinum fist by mega-rich Kaufman (Dennis Hopper) and enforced by his henchmen and paramilitary minions. Kaufman and crew are safely (for the moment) ensconced in Fiddler's Green, a luxury hi-rise for the elite that towers above semi-wasteland streets inhabited by the poor, while the lumpen prole zombies wander outside the manned, electrified gates.

Meantime, in the outer regions, Riley, his disfigured, sharp-shooting partner Charlie (Robert Joy)—who, in another *Night* nod, first appears onscreen looking like a zombie—and rival Cholo (John Leguizamo) loot abandoned stores for supplies while mowing down scores of shambling zombies from their monster tank/armored RV combo, affectionately dubbed Dead Reckoning. The scenes immediately evoke parallels with occupied Iraq, just as *Night's* search-and-destroy posse footage mirrored events in 1960s Vietnam, as Dead Reckoning rolls through a devastated deathscape. This peripatetic premise allows for some first-rate, up-close-and-personal zombie carnage, with Cholo's lethal raid on a liquor store furnishing a gore highlight. While *Land's* specialty zombies, like angry, gargantuan Big Daddy (Eugene Clark)—the Living Dead's Bub-like insurgency leader—look more spectacular than ever (courtesy of special-effects ace Greg Nicotero), they're too often interspersed with all-too-obvious animatronic zombies spraying CG blood.

Back in the city, Riley and Charlie save renegade Slack (Asia [Daughter of Dario] Argento) from eating zombie death in a grotesque gladiatorial battle (a riff earlier seen in 2002's *Tokyo Zombie*, though it's doubtful Romero would have caught that particular flick). Cholo, meanwhile, who suffers from thwarted class aspirations, attempts to buy his way into Fiddler's Green but is rejected by arrogant boss Kaufman. Out for revenge, Cholo and cohorts commandeer Dead Reckoning and threaten to destroy Fiddler's Green via the vehicle's long-range guns if their extortion demands aren't met.

While Cholo had longed to fit in, Riley's sole goal is getting out, and he's promised that chance if he and his crew can stop the dangerous renegade. Following some high-voltage action sequences, Riley and Cholo find common ground and join sides.

Under Big Daddy's increasingly cognizant supervision, the zombie army descends on the city and Fiddler's Green, leading to grand scenes of mass human and zombie destruction. The story is told the untamed Romero way, at least in the unrated cut released on DVD. (The trimmed theatrical version represented the first official *Dead* film to carry an "R" rating.) Cholo, though since bitten and zombified, realizes his revenge by catching up with Kaufman, who's trying to flee in a Lincoln Continental (a reference to Karl Hardman's *Night* car).

As the zombies overrun the city, Riley and crew head for Canada. Before they leave, femme cohort Pretty Boy (Joanne Boland) locks Big Daddy in her cross-hairs, but Riley commands her to stand down since the dead, like themselves, are "just looking for a place to go." The gap separating humans from zombies continues to narrow in Romero's ongoing saga.

As in his previous zombie films, Romero works ample political commentary into the mix. In the early going, the living dead are easily distracted by fireworks ("sky flowers")—as Roger Ebert points out in his positive critique, a seeming reference to the U.S.'s then-recent "Shock and Awe" policy deployed against Iraq, backfiring tactics that served mostly to help incite an incipient insurgency. Kaufman and his makeshift cabinet also openly ape the George W. Bush administration. According to Romero, "Hopper modeled his performance after Rumsfeld. Thematically what this film is about is a bunch of people trying to live as though nothing has changed or, at least, that's what the administration believes. The protagonists understand that the world has completely changed."

Romero adds that he spent more time with Hopper talking about the largely dashed hopes of the '60s than discussing the script. Like many pre-boomer idealists, both men wholeheartedly latched on to the decade, siding with a generation a few years younger than themselves. While Hopper later turned Republican, Romero has yet to let go of those ideals. "The underbelly in all my movies is a longing for a better world, for a higher plane of existence, for people to get together," he told *American Film* journalist Dan Yakir back in 1981. "I'm still singing those songs."

As in his earlier films, Romero works in a number of neat, nearly subliminal touches. Zombie heads emerge from the water à la the ever-pursuant phantoms in a signature moment in Herk Harvey's *Carnival of Souls*. On a tour of the city, the camera pans past a postapocalyptic Punch and Judy-style puppet show, where Romero puts in his requisite cameo as the voice of the unseen puppeteer: "Take that, you scary zombie!" Much later, after the zombie Armageddon, the puppets lie lifeless on their little stage. On an even grislier note, Romero, with more than a little help from effects ace Greg Nicotero, includes a "Night of the Living *Head*" moment when Big Daddy angrily stomps on the dome of a decapitated comrade.

With zombies proliferating in pop culture at an exponential rate, Romero expressed his wish to reestablish his *own* zombie tenets in *Land of the Dead*: "There seems to be some confusion about how you become a zombie, that you have to be bitten, which isn't the case. One of the things we wanted to establish here was that anyone who dies becomes a zombie. If you get bitten, you get infected and become a zombie that much sooner because you die that much sooner." On a more esoteric note, he points out, "There's an issue we've not dealt with in zombie films: Can there be zombie animals? We actually had a scene written for dead rats. It was a very, very elaborate scene in the early days of the script, and it just would've been impossible to pull off. But," Romero adds, in his best Hitchcock impersonation, "it's a topic that I might have to visit." (In the interim, zombie-animal buffs can scope out the Living Dead dog and cat in pal Stephen King's *Pet Sematary* and the titular fowls in Lloyd Kaufman's *Poultrygeist: Night of the Chicken Dead*.)

Romero not only enjoyed his most lavish budget to date with *Land*—which still, according to the director's calculations, totaled less than half the *Dawn of the Dead* remake's outlay—but the highest-profile cast of any of his *Dead* films. Ardent Romero fans Hopper and Leguizamo were eager to sign on, while for Asia Argento the film represented a homecoming of sorts: "To me it reminds me of my childhood," she says. "I feel secure around zombies." Filming in Toronto (where he now lives) and Hamilton, Ontario, Romero employed mostly Canadians in the rest of the roles, including such well-known homegrown thespians as Robert (*Atlantic City*) Joy, Peter (*Saw VI*) Outerbridge, Earl (*The Sweet Hereafter*) Pastko, and Alan (*Narc*) Van Sprang.

While not a blockbuster, *Land of the Dead*, released in June 2005, fared fairly well at the domestic box office, earning some

$40 million. Critical reception was generally positive. Roger Ebert applauded *Land*'s political and social subtexts, awarding the film three out of four stars, while *VideoScope* reviewer Robert Freese wrote, "Romero delights us with extended scenes of nail-biting suspense, as well as his patented sledgehammer, goose-you-out-of-your-seat shock scenes," and *The New York Sun* hailed it as "the American movie of the year." Even the oft-dismissive *New York Times* lent its voice to the overall chorus of approval, labeling *Land* "an excellent freakout of a movie."

Kudos came as well from fellow filmmakers, who rightly hold Romero in high esteem. *Hellboy* helmer Guillermo del Toro raved, "Finally someone was smart enough to realize that it was about time, and gave George the tools. It should be a cause of celebration amongst all of us that Michelangelo has started another ceiling. It's really a momentous occasion."

Those same tools should *not* have been extended to director Jeff Broadstreet, who perpetrated the unauthorized 2007 *Night* remake, *Night of the Living Dead 3D*. The resurrected three-dimensional format does nothing to help this desecration of Romero's oft-violated *Dead*; the flick rips off the original when convenient and deviates (poorly) when not. Not surprisingly, in place of Romero's cross section of credible characters, we get the expected lot of contemporary idiots—lamely sarcastic obnoxoids with flea-sized attention spans and all the charm of rotting meat. The dialogue suffers mightily under the anti-inspiration of scripter Robert Valding, while the EC Comics-style zombie designs lack the stark terror of Romero's more realistic shambling-corpse conceptions.

Worse, the filmmakers see fit to pay hypocritical homage by incorporating TV clips of the original that only serve to accentuate this "re-imagining's" flagrant flaws. At the risk of indulging in gratuitous *haigiography*, we must say that Sid Haig's wonderfully eccentric perf as a mad mortician reps *Night 3D*'s sole plus, and fans of that talented actor, whose own career had been re-animated by Rob Zombie via choice roles in *House of 1000 Corpses* (2003) and *The Devil's Rejects* (2005), can be forgiven for tuning in. Otherwise, this rates as yet another travesty, like *Day of the Dead: Contagium*, that deserves to be soundly spanked by the Living Dead Anti-Defamation League.

In more positive *Dead* developments, *Land*'s success soon landed Romero back in the zombie driver's seat, albeit in a much more modest model. After a collaboration with the manufacturer Hip Interactive on a video game entitled *City of the Dead* reached a dead end in 2006, Romero worked on a Webcast project called *Zombisodes*, short films depicting the behind-the-scenes run-up to his new film, *Diary of the Dead*. *Diary* began lensing in Toronto in June of that year and, with its $2 million budget, marked a return to the grassroots guerrilla filmmaking of *Night of the Living Dead*.

"This film is not linked to the others," Romero explains. "It's going back to the beginning and starting over. It's more like *Night of the Living Dead*. . . . It's not like we're suddenly in a world which is inhabited by zombies. It's the kind of film that I sort of cut my teeth on and love doing."

It was difficult for many *Dead*heads to conceive of the ultimate horror-film innovator chasing the *Blair Witch*'s tail, but Romero felt that was the best approach to take to explore today's emerging egalitarian media and ADD-addled culture. As Romero told an interviewer, "It's a lot of information and oftentimes that information is opinion or perspective. It's completely unmanaged. I find it frightening."

Diary's simple premise sees University of Pittsburgh film student Jason Creed (Josh Close) video-record a road trip undertaken with several fellow students that quickly detours into a perilous trek through a zombie-infested wasteland (Creed continues to capture it on tape). Radio reports warn of an outbreak of living dead cannibals. The group undergoes further grisly encounters at a hospital. After a stay at a heavily armed urban camp, where a voluminous response to Jason's Internet-uploaded videos attest that many other people continue to survive, they arrive at his squeeze Debra's (Michelle Morgan) house. They battle her undead family, and, finally, hole up at the mansion of fellow student Ridley (Philip Riccio) for a *Night of the Living Dead*–like showdown.

Romero may be making cogent points about today's shallow,

callow, hi-tech, low-wattage youth, but his characters here don't arouse much in the way of audience interest or empathy. That extends to his own generational more or less stand-in, boozy, arrogant faculty advisor Andrew Maxwell (Scott Wentworth). While *Diary* is always competent and, at times, compelling, the film had the misfortune to debut theatrically on the outsized heels of *Cloverfield*, a similarly home-video-lensed affair that yields greater suspense and scares, and enjoyed far wider release and buzz.

Diary does incorporate some undeniably clever flourishes—flesh-eating living-dead party clowns have always been a fave in these parts, and Romero trots out a great one in Bupkes (Kyle Glencross), while deaf-mute Amish farmer/zombie-fighter Samuel (R.D. Reid) represents another memorable figure. Romero also works in a neat critique aimed at horrordom's current obsession with fast-moving monsters, along with a classic brain-melting-by-battery-acid zombie kill and other memorable bits. But, overall, *Diary* plays more tired than Dead, more self-imitation than fresh exploration. On the upside, as with the original *Night* and *Dawn*, Romero concludes this chapter on a truly disturbing note that questions the worth of the human species.

Starting his four-week shoot in mid-October 2006, Romero jettisoned his preferred method of shooting reams of multi-angled coverage for paring and shaping in the cutting room in favor of the mostly single-camera long takes dictated by the story. To facilitate that process, he relied more on sketches for preplanned shots. Romero was prepared to shoot the film as a $250,000 direct-to-DVD project if need be, so he didn't feel unduly hampered by his limited budget.

Beginning with *Land*, Romero succeeded in basically recreating Pittsburgh in Toronto, which he still finds much preferable to working within the major studio system: "You really need a relationship with the key people—A.D., script supervisor, director of photography, most importantly, and editor, probably even more importantly," he maintains. "So I wound up meeting a whole bunch of new people. [Otherwise] you get to meet the DP three days before you go to camera. You don't have time to sit down and get drunk and talk about what you want to do." To further speed the filming along, Romero made extensive, if inexpensive, use of CGI, adding effects in post-production rather than creating them on the spot.

In many ways, the resultant lean, mean production stands in stark contrast to his relatively lush, name-studded *Land* experience. Still, a number of high-profile fans managed to get in on the act, with Quentin Tarantino, Stephen King, Simon Pegg, Wes Craven, Guillermo del Toro, and M. Night Shyamalan all contributing cameos as various radio newscasters. In homage to the film that started it all, sound bites from the original *Night of the Living Dead* are also integrated into the final cut.

Romero had nothing but praise for his nimble Canadian cast. "They had a lot of theater experience. I think they could have gone from scene one all the way to the end of the movie, all in a single shot." Romero also put in one of his more prominent cameos, as an on-air police official. And while the story called for fewer zombies, the filmmaker maintains, "There aren't as many zombies, but a couple of zombies can go a long way, if they're the right zombies."

Critical response was mixed. Roger Ebert gave an enthusiastic thumbs-up: "While horror provides the marketing hook, Romero's movies are even more entertaining for their zesty sociopolitical satire, and like its ancestors, *Diary* explodes like an undead noggin with that stuff. . . . You may not believe in zombies, but the un-named dread in the air of *Diary of the Dead* is recognizably believable because we live with it now." *The New York Times* offered a more measured take: "There's some striking filmmaking in *Diary of the Dead*, but there's also a lot of less-than-elegant speechifying. . . . The problem with *Diary of the Dead* is that it doesn't get into your body; it doesn't shake you up, jolt you, make you shiver and squeak. It's clever . . . it just isn't scary."

Though *Diary* barely cleared the $5 million domestic box-office mark, Romero scored the necessary financing for his next descent into zombiedom, *Survival of the Dead*, which went into platform release in May 2010. He offered his take on his latest excursion into *Living Dead* Land:

Because *Diary of the Dead* was produced on a low budget, it wound up making a great deal of money worldwide. So the producers wanted another one . . . quickly. All five of the *Dead* films I'd made had been to some extent inspired by current events—by what the world looked like (to me)—when each was made. Now I was faced with making a sixth film without any immediate stimulation. So I decided to use a more universal theme. War. The idea that humankind seems incapable of "burying the hatchet"—age-old angers and enmities prevail even when the world is on the brink of total disaster. I also decided to have some fun stylistically. The theme was a timeless one, so I wanted to give the film a timeless feel. I'd always wanted to make a western, so I took a minor character from *Diary of the Dead*, a sergeant in the National Guard who appears for a minute or so, and took him and his three buddies off on their own adventure. In an attempt to escape the chaos on the mainland, the Guardsmen take a ferry to a small island off the coast of Delaware, assuming there will be fewer of the dead to deal with. The problem is there are two feuding families on the island. The Guardsmen end up with a much larger problem on their hands. The dead are controllable. The living can't be controlled.

I had all of my department heads watch an old western called *The Big Country*, in which Burl Ives and Charles Bickford fight a feud to the death. We set out to model *Survival of the Dead* after *The Big Country*. I think it works quite well. And I was able to indulge myself by throwing in some real *Loony Tunes* moments that come close to slapstick. Then, as we were working on the film, headlines started to appear about how rage was becoming regrettably acceptable. Entertainers, sports figures, politicians were suddenly unable to disagree without being disagreeable. The United States has high-ranking members of the Senate sniping at each other in the foulest of ways, and the public, taking license from the bad behavior of their leaders, has begun to behave badly in very dangerous ways. So, purely by accident, *Survival of the Dead* is quite current, I think, in its socio-political criticism.

Romero's reputation was further cemented in 1999, when *Night of the Living Dead* was named to the National Film Registry as a film judged "culturally, historically or aesthetically significant." The movie also earned inclusion in the 2010 Academy Awards horror-movie tribute.

14 *DEAD AHEAD*

Unlike fellow frightmeister Wes Craven, whose mega-success with the *Scream* series enabled him to lens his box-office-challenged dream project, the inspirational Meryl Streep vehicle *Music of the Heart* (wherein violins replaced violence as the filmmaker's focus), Romero has yet to find financing for *his*. "I'd love to do *Stranger in a Strange Land*," he once told yours truly, "but I think that'd be pretty tough. And I have a version of *Tales of Hoffman* I've been working on over the years, something I keep going back to—a futuristic version that takes place in space."

While the jury's still out whether or not those visions will reach the screen, George Romero, like many of the greats, has no intention of hanging up his megaphone. Over the past couple of years, he's been linked with a variety of potential projects, including writing and directing a sequel to *Diary of the Dead*. One thing is for certain: He won't stay idle.

Nor are the zombies his films have inspired likely to shamble off any time soon; on the contrary, their influence on international pop culture continues to expand exponentially. Over 100 artists worldwide, using techniques ranging from traditional animation to claymation, collaborated on director Mike Schneider's visually arresting feature-length *Night of the Living Dead: Re-Animated* (2009), which keeps the original movie soundtrack intact to back the fresh kaleidoscopic imagery. Writer and director Zebediah DeSoto plans a 2011 launch for his animated 3D take *Night of the Living Dead: Origins*, with a voice cast that includes 1990 *Night* remake alums Tony Todd and Bill Moseley, along with *Day of the Dead*'s Joseph Pilato as Harry Cooper.

On television, *Dead*heads witnessed a bizarre sight when Patricia Arquette's Allison Dubois dreamed she was a character in *Night of the Living Dead* and, via the magic of CGI, entered that nightmare world in *Bite Me*, the 2009 Halloween season episode of the psychic series *Medium*. That riff echoed an earlier one employed by director Anthony Hickox in his trippy 1988 big-screen horror homage *Waxwork*. TV series, ranging from *South Park* to *The Simpsons*, have likewise referenced *Night*, while in 2010, AMC greenlit a proposed series pilot, directed by frequent Stephen King helmer Frank (*The Mist*) Darabont, based on the comic book *The Walking Dead*. CBS had earlier, in 2007, commissioned a zombie TV pilot called *Babylon Fields* but never broadcast the show. In England, *Dead Set*, a mock reality TV zombie apocalypse miniseries set in the *Big Brother* house, aired on E4 in October, 2008.

Night of the Living Dead has also been reinterpreted in at least two stage musical incarnations. In 2002, writer Thomas Hoagland and composer Chad Kushuba presented *Night of the Living Dead: The Musical* in Detroit, while a different tuner with the same title surfaced in Aurora, Illinois in 2007 (book by Jack Schultz and songs by Schultz and Kathleen Dooley). A *Night of the Living Dead* movie musical has also been making the film-festival rounds, while *Eat Me: A Zombie Musical*, featuring The Falsies, enjoyed its digital debut in 2009 via Amoeba Films.

Zombies have found a particularly prolific niche on the pop-music scene. Some of the higher-profiled living dead ditties include the Cranberries' protest song "Zombie," The Misfits' "Night of the Living Dead," Rob Zombie's "Living Dead Girl," Ozzy Osbourne's "Zombie Stomp," The Zombie Girls' "Zombie Girl," Jonathan Coulton's "Re: Your Brains," The Cramps' "Zombie Dance," and our high-concept fave, The Zombeatles' "A Hard Day's Night of the Living Dead." Oddly enough, the original British Invasion band The Zombies have yet to sing about their namesakes, though rapper Aesop Rock raided *Night of the Living Dead* for clips to insert into his "Coffee" music video.

And speaking of video, video games have long enjoyed a symbiotic relationship with Romero-styled zombies, with the films spawning games and vice versa. Venerable game franchises

Zombies of Antiquity

Earliest known zombie joke, translated from the original hieroglyphics:

RAMSES: My zombie has no nose.
FUAD: How does he smell?
RAMSES: Awful.

House of the Dead and *Resident Evil* still reign near the top of the list, despite competition from scores of rivals, while live games like "Humans vs. Zombies" (sort of a "Died and Seek") continue to gain popularity on college campuses and other locales where the living and dead mingle.

Zombies likewise flourish in contemporary literature. Beyond the expected comic books, graphic novels, and pulp fictions, the living dead have crashed the bestseller lists via Max Brooks's *Zombie Survival Guide* and *World War Z* (eventually to be a major motion picture), along with Seth Grahame-Smith's Jane Austen meets George Romero mashup *Pride and Prejudice and Zombies*. We're still waiting for *Of Mice and Men-Eating Zombies*, wherein George is forced to shoot Lenny in the head after the latter is bitten by rabid rabbits and comes back as a . . . zombie! To say nothing of *The Old Man and the Z*.

Even as improbable a venue as reality has been turned into a mass zombie stage, with "zombie walks" becoming a way of life in virtually every state in the Union and many sites abroad, routinely attracting thousands of participants in zombie garb and guise. The earliest known pageant, dubbed "The Zombie Parade," unfolded in Sacramento, California, back in 2001, while such variations as Pittsburgh's Monroeville Mall "Walk of the Dead" and Minneapolis' "Zombie Pub Crawl" (we'll drink to that!) are held yearly. Grand Rapids, Michigan's first Zombie Walk claims the (unverified) Guinness World Record for top turnout with over 8,000 Living Deaders reporting for duty, while the Zombie Independent Film Festival, hosted by the Holiday Star Theater in Park Forest, Illinois, hopes to best the record in 2010. Withal, it's easy to see why many folks feel that dead is the new eighty.

The beauty part about zombies is that they are infinitely elastic symbols that can mean all things to all people, different croaks for different folks, if you will. Equal parts aggressors and victims, they can represent the usurpers, as in *Night of the Living Dead*, the oppressed, as in *Land of the Dead*, or the manipulated, mesmerized masses, as in *Dawn of the Dead*. Even more than casual Fridays, zombies may be our contemporary corporate-driven consumerist culture's biggest safety valve: You can pretend to *be* one and stand up for your zombie rights, or you can hunt them down and kill them sans a shred of conscience. To paraphrase Pogo *and* George Romero, "We have met the zombies and they are us."

YOUR OFFICIAL "Z"WARDS

Best Zombie Movie: *Night of the Living Dead* (1968)

Best Zombie: Cemetery Zombie (Bill Hinzman), *Night of the Living Dead*; runner-up: Bub (Howard Sherman), *Day of the Dead* (1985)

Best Zombie Musical: *Michael Jackson's Thriller* (1983); runner-up: *The Incredibly Strange Creatures Who Stopped Living and Became Mixed-Up Zombies* (1964)

Best Zombie Song: "The Zombie Stomp," The Del Aires, *Horror of Party Beach* (1964)

Best Zomcom: *Re-Animator* (1985)

Best Zombie Walk: Vampira, *Plan 9 from Outer Space* (1959); runner-up: David Emge, *Dawn of the Dead* (1978)

Best Zombie Movie Titles: *A Virgin Among the Living Dead* (1973)—a good way to retain that status; *Erotic Nights of the Living Dead* (1979)—when good zombies go bad; *Nudist Colony of the Dead* (1991)—'nuff said

Best Zombie Documentary: *Document of the Dead* (1985/2010)

Best Zombie Mockumentary: *American Zombie* (2007)

Best *Dead* Remake: *Dawn of the Dead* (2004)

Worst *Dead* Remake: *Night of the Living Dead 3D* (2007)

Best *Dead* Sequel: *Dawn of the Dead* (1978)

Worst *Dead* Sequel: *Children of the Dead* (2001)

Most Surreal Zombie Movie: *Let's Scare Jessica to Death* (1971)

Most Cerebral Zombie Movie: *They Came Back* (aka *The Revenants*, 2004)

Best Zombie Quote: "They're dead. They're . . . all messed up." Sheriff McClelland (George Kosana), *Night of the Living Dead*

Best Zombie Tag Line: "When there's no more room in hell, the dead will walk the earth." *Dawn of the Dead*

First Zombie-Movie Oscar: *Death Becomes Her* (1994), makeup effects

Best Zombie Incantation: "Oh, sacred masters of the sky, instill our fighting cadavers with kicking, slashing strength to execute righteous slaughter! Show us bloodshed like it used to be!" *Raw Force* (1981)

Best Military Zombies: Richard Backus, *Deathdream* (1974); runner-up: David (Shark) Fralick, *Uncle Sam* (1997)

Best Zombie Fighters: Valley gals Catherine Mary Stewart and Kelli Maroney, *Night of the Comet* (1984)

Best Zombie Tykes: *The Children* (1980) (Don't forget to "Cut off their hands!")

Best Living Dead Pet: Zombie cat, *Pet Sematary* (1990)

Best Joe Franklin Cameo in a Zombie Movie: *Ghoul School* (1991)

EPILOGUE OF THE LIVING DEAD:
WHERE ARE THEY NOW?

Marilyn Eastman (1927–). In addition to acting in films like
Houseguest (1995) and *Santa Claws* (1996), Marilyn Eastman
continued operating Hardman Associates with business and life
partner Karl Hardman until their retirement in 1999. Today,
Marilyn occasionally appears at horror-film conventions.

Karl Hardman (1927–2007). A frequent guest, with longtime partner
Marilyn Eastman, on the horror-film convention circuit, Karl
Hardman passed away in 2007 after a battle with pancreatic
cancer. On her Web site, daughter Kyra Schon notes he "was
nothing like old Harry in real life, thank God, yet he agreed that
the cellar was the safest place."

Bill Hinzman (1936–). While largely inactive behind the camera, the
Cemetery Zombie continues to act in movies, like *The Drunken
Dead Guy* (2005), *Shadow: Dead Riot* (2006), and *River of
Darkness* (2010). He is a frequent guest at horror-film conventions.

Duane Jones (1936–1988). While he acted in the occasional film,
most notably Bill Gunn's 1973 cult fave *Ganja and Hess*, Duane
Jones devoted most of his shortened life to acting and directing
on New York City stages, as well as teaching those crafts in
college. He died of cardiac failure at age 51.

George Kosana (1936–). Former Image Ten production manager
and zombie killer Sheriff McClelland is a frequent horror-film
convention guest and recently returned to the screen with a role
in *Incest Death Squad* (2009).

Judith O'Dea (1945–). The erstwhile Barbara divides her time
between acting assignments in films like *Women's Studies*
(2010) and *Timo Rose's Beast* (2009) and overseeing O'Dea
Communications. The latter company "specializes in oral
presentation training—how to organize, visualize, and effectively
deliver powerful, persuasive presentations."

Judith Ridley (1948–). After playing Judy in *Night of the Living
Dead* and Lynn in *There's Always Vanilla*, Judith Ridley dropped
out of the acting game, married Russell Streiner, and worked as

a food stylist, arranging cuisine for TV commercials. She's currently employed as a librarian.

George A. Romero (1940–). Veteran auteur and *Night* director and co-writer George Romero continues to maintain a busy, high-profile filmmaking pace, most recently helming *Survival of the Dead* (2010). Projected future films include *Diamond Dead* and *Solitary Isle.*

John A. Russo (1939–). With Russ Streiner, John Russo is a co-mentor of the John Russo Movie Making Program at DuBois Business College in DuBois, Pennsylvania. He continues to keep busy in the trenches as well, with film projects (*Escape of the Living Dead*), novels and comic books, and he is a frequent horror-film convention guest.

Kyra Schon (1957–). After hanging up her trowel, Kyra Schon worked in several professions, including schoolteacher. She is a frequent, welcome, and witty guest at horror-film conventions. "Although I didn't pursue a career in films," she says, "I do feel that my role as Karen Cooper has enhanced my life. I've been afforded the opportunity to get to know people that I otherwise would never have met."

Gary Streiner (1946–). *Night* soundman Gary Streiner spent most of his working life in the advertising world, where he was a key member of the team that created the Jerry Seinfeld American Express campaign. He later filmed and co-produced the Seinfeld theatrical documentary feature *Comedian* (2002) and currently organizes the annual Living Dead Festival in Evans City, Pennsyvania.

Russell Streiner (1940–). In addition to partnering with John Russo in the John Russo Movie Making Program, former "Johnny" Russ Streiner currently serves as chairman on the Board of Directors of the Pittsburgh Film Office.

Keith Wayne (1945–1995). Keith (Tom) Wayne represents the *Night* crew's most tragic story—he ended his life with a self-inflicted gunshot. As John Russo told us: "Keith Wayne had become a successful chiropractor in Charlotte, North Carolina, and also was a champion weightlifter with lots of trophies in major competitions in the 'odd lifts,' as opposed to the Olympic lifts. My understanding is that he suffered for years from clinical depression. He had two teenage daughters and was going through a divorce, which probably contributed to his suicide. Very sad, because he was extremely talented, especially as a singer."

NIGHT OF THE DIGITAL DEAD: YOUR OFFICIAL LIVING DEAD FILM AND DVD LIST

Titles are followed by release date, home video label and date, and director (D), screenwriter (S), cast, and running time.

n.i.d. = not in distribution

George Romero's *Dead* Films

Night of the Living Dead: The Original Classic (1968) (Elite
  Entertainment, 2002)
Night of the Living Dead: 25th Anniversary Edition (Tempe Video
  VHS, 1993, n.i.d.)
Night of the Living Dead: 30th Anniversary Edition (Anchor Bay
  Entertainment, 1998)
Night of the Living Dead: 40th Anniversary Edition (Dimension
  Extreme, 2008)
  D: George Romero. S: George Romero, John A. Russo. Duane
  Jones, Judith O'Dea, Karl Hardman, Marilyn Eastman, Judith
  Ridley, Keith Wayne, Kyra Schon. 96 mins.

Dawn of the Dead: Ultimate Edition (1979) (Anchor Bay
  Entertainment, 2004)
Dawn of the Dead Blu-ray Disc (Anchor Bay, 2007)
  D/S: George Romero. David Emge, Gaylen Ross, Ken Foree,
  Scott Reiniger, Tom Savini. 126 mins.

Day of the Dead (1985) (Anchor Bay Entertainment, 2003)
Day of the Dead Blu-ray Disc (Anchor Bay, 2008)
  D/S: George Romero. Lori Cardille, Terry Alexander, Joseph
  Pilato, Jarlath Conroy, Richard Liberty, John Amplas. 102 mins.

Night of the Living Dead (1990) (Sony Pictures Home
  Entertainment, 1999)
  D: Tom Savini. S: George Romero. Tony Todd, Patricia Tallman,

Tom Towles, McKee Anderson, William Butler, Kate Finneran,
Bill Moseley. 92 mins.

Land of the Dead: Unrated Director's Cut (2005) (Universal Studios
Home Entertainment, 2005)
D/S: George Romero. Simon Baker, Dennis Hopper, John
Leguizamo, Asia Argento, Robert Joy, Eugene Clark. 97 mins.

Diary of the Dead (2007) (Dimension Extreme, 2008)
D/S: George Romero. Josh Close, Michelle Morgan, Shawn
Roberts, Amy Ciupak Lalonde, Joe Dinicol, Scott Wentworth. 95
mins.

Survival of the Dead (2010) (Magnet Entertainment, 2010)
D/S: George Romero. Devon Bostick, Kathleen Munroe, Kenneth
Welsh, Athena Karkanis, Alan Van Sprang, Julian Richings. 90
mins.

George Romero's Non-*Dead* Films

Season of the Witch (a.k.a. *Jack's Wife*) (1972)/*There's Always
Vanilla* (1972) (Anchor Bay Entertainment, 2005)
D/S: George Romero. Jan White, Ray Laine, Ann Muffly, Bill
Thunhurst, Joedda McClain, Neil Fisher. 130 mins./89 mins.
D: George Romero. S: Rudy Ricci. Ray Laine, Judith Ridley,
Johanna Lawrence, Richard Ricci, Roger McGovern. 93 mins.

The Crazies (Blue Underground, 2003); Blu-ray (Blue Underground,
2010)
D/S: George Romero. Lane Carroll, W.G. McMillan, Harold Wayne
Jones, Lloyd Hollar, Lynn Lowry, Richard Liberty. 103 mins.

O.J. Simpson: Juice on the Loose (1975) (Vidmark Entertainment
VHS, 1998, n.i.d.)
D: George Romero. S: Neil Fisher. O.J. Simpson, Howard Cosell.
47 mins.

Martin (1977) (Lionsgate Home Entertainment, 2004)
D/S: George Romero. John Amplas, Lincoln Maazel, Christine
Forrest, Elayne Nadeau, Tom Savini, Sarah Venable. 95 mins.

Knightriders (1981) (Anchor Bay, 2007)
D/S: George Romero. Ed Harris, Gary Lahti, Tom Savini, Amy
Ingersoll, Patricia Tallman, Christine Forrest. 145 mins.

Creepshow (1982) (Warner Home Video, 1999)
D: George Romero. S: Stephen King. Hal Holbrook, Adrienne
Barbeau, Fritz Weaver, Leslie Nielsen, E.G. Marshall, Carrie Nye.
120 mins.

Creepshow 2 (1987) (Anchor Bay VHS, 1997, n.i.d.)
D: Michael Gornick. S: George Romero. Lois Chiles, George
Kennedy, Dorothy Lamour, Tom Savini, Domenick John,
Stephen King. 89 mins.

Monkey Shines: An Experiment in Fear (1988) (MGM Home
Entertainment, 1999)
D/S: George Romero. Jason Beghe, John Pankow, Kate McNeil,
Joyce Van Patten, Christine Forrest, Stephen Root. 115 mins.

Tales from the Darkside: The Movie (1990) (Paramount Home
Entertainment, 2001)
D: John Harrison. S: Michael McDowell, George Romero.
Deborah Harry, Christian Slater, David Johansen, Julianne
Moore, James Remar, Rae Dawn Chong. 93 mins.

Tales from the Darkside: Seasons 1–3 (1984–1988) (CBS
DVD/Paramount)
D: Various. S: George Romero, others.

Two Evil Eyes (1991) (Blue Underground, 2003); Blu-ray (Blue
Underground, 2009)
D: George Romero, Dario Argento. S: George Romero, Dario
Argento, Franco Ferrini. Adrienne Barbeau, E.G. Marshall, Harvey
Keitel, Madeleine Potter, John Amos, Kim Hunter. 115 mins.

The Dark Half (1993) (MGM Home Entertainment VHS 1993,
n.i.d.)
D/S: George Romero. Timothy Hutton, Amy Madigan, Michael
Rooker, Julie Harris, Robert Joy, Beth Grant. 122 mins.

Bruiser (2000) (Lionsgate, 2001)
D/S: George Romero. Jason Flemyng, Peter Stormare, Leslie
Hope, Nina Garbiras, Tom Atkins, Andrew Tarbet. 99 mins.

John Russo's *Living Dead* Films

Night of the Living Dead. 30th anniversary edition (1998) (Anchor
Bay Entertainment, 1998)

D: George Romero, John A. Russo. Duane Jones, Judith O'Dea, Karl Hardman, Marilyn Eastman, Scott Vladimir Lucina, Debbie Rochon. 93 mins.

Children of the Living Dead (2001) (First Look Pictures, 2001)
D: Tor Ramsey. S: Karen L. Wolf. Producer: John A. Russo. Tom Savini, Marty Schiff, Damien Luvara, Jamie McCoy, Sam Nicotero, Heidi Hinzman. 90 mins.

Escape of the Living Dead (2011) (TBA)

John Russo's Non–*Living Dead* Films

The Booby Hatch (a.k.a. *The Liberation of Cherry Janowski*) (1976) (Synapse Films, 2009)
D: Rudy Ricci, John A. Russo. S: Rudy Ricci, John A. Russo. Sharon Joy Miller, Rudy Ricci, Doug Sortino, David Emge. 86 mins.

Midnight (1981) (Lionsgate, 2005)
D/S: John Russo. Lawrence Tierney, Melanie Verlin, John Amplas, John Hall, Charles Jackson, Doris Hackney. 94 mins.

The Majorettes (1987) (Shriek Show, 2004)
D: S. William Hinzman. S: John A. Russo. Kevin Kindlin, Terrie Godfrey, Mark V. Jevicky, Sueanne Seamens. 92 mins.

Voodoo Dawn (1991) (Vidmark VHS, 1992)
D: Steven Fierberg. S: Jeffrey Delman, Evan Dunsky, Thomas Rendon, John A. Russo. Raymond St. Jacques, Gina Gershon, Theresa Merritt, Tony Todd. 84 mins.

Heartstopper (1991, n.i.d.)
D/S: John A. Russo. Kevin Kindlin, Moon Unit Zappa, Tom Savini, Michael J. Pollard, John Hall. 90 mins.

Midnight 2: Sex, Death and Videotape (1993) (Sub Rosa Studios, 2008)
D/S: John A. Russo. Matthew Jason Walsh, Jo Norcia, Chuck Pierce, Lori Scarlett. 72 mins.

Santa Claws (1996) (E.I. Independent Cinema, 2006)
D/S: John A. Russo. Debbie Rochon, Grant Kramer, John Mowod, Dawn Michelucci, Marilyn Eastman. 83 mins.

Saloonatics (2002) (n.i.d.)
D/S: John A. Russo. Chuck Corby, Debbie Rochon, Bruno
Sammartino, Tom DeJohn, Heidi Hinzman. 90 mins.

Bill Hinzman's *Living Dead* Film

Revenge of the Living Zombies (a.k.a. *Flesheater*) (1988) (Shriek
Show, 2003)
D/S: S. William Hinzman. Bill Hinzman, John Mowod, Leslie
Ann Wick, Kevin Kindlin. 88 mins.

Return of the Living Dead Series

The Return of the Living Dead: Collectors Edition (1985) (MGM
Home Entertainment, 2007)
D/S: Dan O'Bannon. Clu Gulager, James Karen, Don Calfa,
Thom Mathews, Linnea Quigley, Beverly Randolph. 90 mins.

Return of the Living Dead Part II (1988) (Warner Home Video, 2004)
D/S: Ken Wiederhorn. James Karen, Thom Mathews, Michael
Kenworthy, Marsha Deitlein, Suzanne Snyder. 89 mins.

Return of the Living Dead 3: Unrated (1993) (Trimark
Entertainment, 2001, n.i.d.)
D: Brian Yuzna. S: John Penney. Mindy Clarke, J. Trevor
Edmond, Kent McCord, Sarah Douglas, James T. Callahan, Mike
Moroff. 97 mins.

Return of the Living Dead: Necropolis (2005) (Lionsgate, 2005)
D: Ellory Elkayem. S: William Butler, Aaron Strongoni. Aimee-
Lynn Chadwick, Cory Hardrict, John Keefe, Peter Coyote. 88
mins.

Return of the Living Dead: Rave to the Grave (2007) (Lionsgate,
2007)
D: Ellory Elkayem. S: William Butler, Aaron Strongoni. Aimee-
Lynn Chadwick, Cory Hardrict, Jenny Mollen, Peter Coyote. 86
mins.

Remakes of *The Living Dead*

Night of the Living Dead 3D (2007) (Lionsgate, 2007)
D: Jeff Broadstreet. S: Robert Valding. Brianna Brown, Joshua
DesRoches, Sid Haig, Greg Travis, Johanna Black. 80 mins.

Night of the Living Dead: Reanimated (2009) (Wild Eye Releasing, 2010)
D: Mike Schneider. 96 mins.

Night of the Living Dead: Origins (2011) (TBA)

Sequels of *The Living Dead*

Dawn of the Dead (2004) (Universal Studios, 2004); Blu-ray (Universal Studios, 2008)
D: Zack Snyder. S: James Gunn. Sarah Polley, Ving Rhames, Jake Weber, Mekhi Phifer, Ty Burrell, Matt Frewer. 99 mins.

Day of the Dead (2008) (First Look Pictures, 2008); Blu-ray (First Look Pictures, 2008)
D: Steve Miner. S: Jeffrey Reddick. Mena Suvari, Nick Cannon, Ving Rhames, Michael Welch, Christa Campbell, Matt Rippy. 86 mins.

Day of the Dead 2: Contagium (2005) (Anchor Bay, 2005)
D: Ana Clavell, James Glen Dudelson. S: Ana Clavell, Ryan Carassi. Laurie Baranyay, Stan Klimecko, John Freedom Henry. 103 mins.

Documentaries of *The Living Dead*

Autopsy of the Dead (Zero Day Releasing, 2009)
D: Jeff Carney. S: Jeff Carney, James Cirronella. S. William Hinzman, Kyra Schon, Gary Streiner, Regis Survinski, Charles Craig, Joseph Unitas. 144 mins.

Dead On: The Life and Cinema of George A. Romero (2008) (TBA)
D/S: Rusty Nails. George A. Romero, Dario Argento, Danny Boyle, Quentin Tarantino, John Waters, Rob Zombie. 120 mins.

The Definitive Document of the Dead: The Special Edition (1985/2010) (Synapse Films, 1998, 2010)
D: Roy Frumkes. S: Roy Frumkes. George Romero, Tom Savini, Michael Gornick, Scott Reiniger, Roy Frumkes, Sukey Raphael. Narrated by Susan Tyrrell. 91 mins.

Fan of the Dead (2003/2009) (Cheezy Flicks, 2010)
D/S: Nicolas Garreau. 52 mins.

Midnight Movies: From the Margin to the Mainstream (2005) (Starz Home Entertainment, 2007)
D: Stuart Samuels. S: Stuart Samuels, Victor Kushmaniuk. Perry Henzell, Alejandro Jodorowsky, David Lynch, Richard O'Brien, George Romero, John Waters. 88 mins.

Night of the Living Dead: 25th Anniversary Documentary (1993) (Tempe Video, 1993)
D/S: Thomas Brown. George Romero, John A. Russo, Wes Craven, Sam Raimi, Russell Streiner, Karl Hardman. 83 mins.

One for the Fire: The Legacy of "Night of the Living Dead" (2008) (*Night of the Living Dead 40th Anniversary Edition*. Dimension Extreme, 2008)
D: Robert Lucas, Chris Roe. S: "Half Breed" Billy Gram. 80 mins.

Feature-Film Goofs on *The Living Dead*

Flight of the Living Dead: Outbreak on a Plane (2007) (New Line, 2007)
D: Scott Thomas. S: Sidney Iwanter, Mark Onspaugh, Scott Thomas. David Chisum, Kristen Ken, Kevin J. O'Connor, Richard Tyson. 89 mins.

Knight of the Living Dead (2005) (n.i.d.)
D: Bjarni Gautur. S: Bjarni Gautur, Hoddi Bjornsen. Hoddi Bjornsen, Andri Kjartan, Steiner Geirdal, Bjarni Gautur. 83 mins.

Last of the Living (2008) (Echo Bridge Entertainment, 2009)
D/S: Logan McMillan. Morgan Williams, Robert Faith, Ashleigh Southam, Emily Paddon-Brown, Mark Hadlow. 88 mins.

Night of the Creeps: Director's Cut (1986) (Sony Pictures, 2009)
D/S: Fred Dekker. Jason Lively, Steve Marshall, Jill Whitlow, Tom Atkins, Allan Kaysel, David Paymer. 90 mins.

Night of the Living Dorks (Die Nacht der lebenden Loser) (2004) (Anchor Bay, 2007)
D: Matthias Dinter. Tino Mewes, Manuel Cortez, Thomas Schmieder, Collien Fernandes, Tim Wilde. 89 mins.

Poultrygeist: Night of the Chicken Dead (2006) (Troma
Entertainment, 2009)
D: Lloyd Kaufman. S: Daniel Bova, Gabriel Friedman, Lloyd
Kaufman. Jason Yachanin, Kate Graham, Allyson Sereboff, Robin
L. Watkins, Joshua Olatunde, Caleb Emerson, Rose Ghavami,
Lloyd Kaufman. 103 mins.

Shaun of the Dead (2004) (Universal Studios, 2004) Blu-ray
(Universal Studios, 2009)
D: Edgar Wright. S: Simon Pegg, Edgar Wright. Simon Pegg, Kate
Ashfield, Lucy Davis, Nick Frost, Dylan Moran, Bill Nighy. 97
mins.

Short Spoofs of *The Living Dead*

Night of the Living Bread (1990)
D: Kevin S. O'Brien. 8 mins.

Night of the Living Dead Mexicans (2008)
D: Nicholas Humphries. 6 mins.

Night Off of the Living Dead (2004)
D: Richard Matthews. 28 mins.

Night of the Living Jews (2008)
D: Oliver Noble. 20 mins.

Opening Night of the Living Dead (2008)
D: Shalena Oxley. 3 mins.

Opening Night of the Living Dead (2009)
D: Jonathan McDevitt. 19 mins.

Paris by Night of the Living Dead (2009)
D: Gregory Morin. 12 mins.

Animated Shorts of *The Living Dead*

Bump in the Night: Night of the Living Bread (1995) (Ncircle
Entertainment, 2007)
D: Various. 25 mins.

Night of the Living Doo (2001) (*Scooby-Doo: The Mystery Begins*,
Warner Home Video, 2009)

D/S: Chris "Casper" Kelly, Jeffrey G. Olsen. Voice cast: Scott Innes, Grey DeLisle, B.J. Ward, Frank Welker, Gary Coleman, Mark Hamill. 20 mins.

Night of the Living Duck (1988) (*Space Jam: Two-Disc Special Edition*, 1996)
D/S: Greg Ford, Terry Lennon. Voice cast: Mel Blanc, Mel Torme. 7 mins.

Redubs of *The Living Dead*

Night of the Day of the Dawn of the Son of the Bride of the Return of the Revenge of the Terror of the Attack of the Evil, Mutant, Alien, Flesh Eating, Hellhound, Zombified Living Dead Part 2: In Shocking 2-D (1991) (n.i.d.)
D/S: James Riffel. 96 mins.

Night of the Living Dead: Rifftrax (2008) (Legend Films, 2008)
Voice cast: Mike Nelson, Kevin Murphy, Bill Corbett.

SOURCES

Author interviews: Danny Boyle, Jeffrey Combs, Tim Ferrante, Roy Frumkes, Stuart Gordon, Peter Jackson, Judith O'Dea, George Romero, John Russo, and others.

Bibliography

Andrews, Mark. "Hartman remembered as powerlifter, singer," *The Cary News* (9/13/95).

Biodrowski, Steve. *Cinefantastique.*

Canby, Vincent. "Getting Beyond Myra and The Valley of the Junk," *The New York Times*, July 5, 1970.

Collum, Jason Paul. *Assault of the Killer B's*. Jefferson, N.C.: McFarland & Co., 2004.

Danville, Eric. "I Was a Kiddie Cannibal!" *VideoScope* #20, Fall 1996.

DuFoe, Terry & Tiffany. "Dean of the Dead: George Romero Redux!" *VideoScope* #52, Fall 2004.

Ebert, Roger. *Night of the Living Dead* review, *The Reader's Digest*. *Re-Animator* review, *Chicago Sun-Times* (10/18/85). *Dawn of the Dead* review, *Chicago Sun-Times* (5/4/79). *Night of the Living Dead* (1990) review, *Chicago Sun-Times* 1990. *Land of the Dead* review, *Chicago Sun-Times* 2005. *Diary of the Dead* review, *Chicago Sun-Times* 2007.

Electronic Gaming Monthly (1/27/01).

Ferrante, Tim. "The Other Living Dead Guy," *Fangoria* #32 (1984), "A Farewell to Duane Jones," *Fangoria* #80 (1989), "*Night of the Living Dead*: 20th Anniversary, Part 1 & 2," *Fangoria* #71, 72 (1988), "The Dawn Patrol," *Fangoria* #119 (1992), "Uncle George Remembers," *The Bloody Best of Fangoria* #7 (1988).

Freese, Rob. "Lynn Lowry: Drive-in Diva," *VideoScope* #63, Summer 2007.

Gagne, Paul R. *The Zombies That Ate Pittsburgh: The Films of George A. Romero*. New York: Dodd, Mead, 1987.

Ben Hervey. *BFI Film Classics: Night of the Living Dead*. London: Palgrave Macmillan, 2007.

Higashi, Sumiko. *Night of the Living Dead: A Horror Film About the Horrors of the Vietnam Era.*

Kael, Pauline. *5001 Nights at the Movies.* New York: Henry Holt and Company, 1991.

Kane, Joe. *The Phantom of the Movies' VideoScope: The Ultimate Guide to the Latest, Greatest, and Weirdest Genre Videos.* New York: Three Rivers Press, 2000.

Kay, Glenn. *Zombie Movies: The Ultimate Guide.* Chicago, IL: Chicago Review Press, 2008.

Maslin, Janet. *Re-Animator* review, *New York Times* (10/18/85). *Dawn of the Dead* review, *New York Times* (4/20/79).

McDonagh, Maitland. *Broken Mirrors, Broken Minds.* New York: Citadel Press, 1994.

McDonagh, Maitland. *Filmmaking on the Fringe: The Good, Bad, and the Deviant Directors.* New York: Carol Publishing, 1995.

Nash, Jay Robert & Ross, Stanley Ralph. *The Motion Picture Guide 1927–1983.* Chicago, IL: Cinebooks, 1985.

Orr, J. Peter. "Coloring the Living Dead." *Fangoria* #72 (1988).

Paffenroth, Kim. *Gospel of the Living Dead: George Romero's Visions of Hell on Earth.* Baylor University Press, 2005.

The Phantom of the Movies. *The Phantom's Ultimate Video Guide.* New York: Dell Publishing, 1989.

Russo, John. *The Complete Night of the Living Dead Filmbook.* Pittsburgh: Imagine, 1985.

Stein, Elliot. "The Dead Zones: George A. Romero at the American Museum of the Moving Image," *The Village Voice*, 2003.

Variety. Review of *Night of the Living Dead* (10/15/68).

Voisin, Scott. *Character Kings: Hollywood's Familiar Faces Discuss the Art & Business of Acting.* Albany, GA: BearManor Media, 2009.

Waddell, Calum. "Tough Enough: Screen Heavy Tom Towles," *VideoScope* #74, Spring 2010.

Weaver, Tom. *Return of the B Science Fiction and Horror Movie Makers: The Mutant Melding of Two Volumes of Classic Interviews.* Jefferson, N.C.: McFarland & Co., 1999.

DVDography

The American Nightmare: A Celebration of Films from Horror's Golden Age of Fright (Docurama Films, 2004).

Autopsy of the Dead (Zero Day Releasing, 2009).

The Crazies (Blue Underground, 2003): Audio commentary.

Dawn of the Dead: Ultimate Edition (Anchor Bay Entertainment, 2004): Audio commentaries, *The Dead Will Walk* featurette.

Day of the Dead (Anchor Bay Entertainment, 2003): Audio commentaries, *The Many Days of Day of the Dead, Day of the Dead: Behind the Scenes* featurettes.

Diary of the Dead (Dimension Extreme, 2008): Audio commentary, *The Roots: The Inspiration for the Film* featurette, *For the Record: Feature-Length Documentary on Film's Cast, Crew & Creation.*

Document of the Dead: The Special Edition (Synapse Films, 1998): Audio commentary, interview segments.

Land of the Dead: Unrated Director's Cut (Universal Studios Home Entertainment, 2005): *Bringing the Dead to Life, Zombie Effects: From Green Screen to Finished Scene* featurettes.

Martin (Lionsgate Home Entertainment, 2004): Audio commentary, *Making Martin: A Recounting* featurette.

Midnight Movies: From the Margin to the Mainstream (Starz Home Entertainment, 2007).

Night of the Living Dead: The Original Classic (Elite Entertainment, 2002): Audio commentaries, *The History of Romero's Company—The Latent Image* featurette, *Video Interview with* Night of the Living Dead's *Judith Ridley, Original Shooting Script.*

Night of the Living Dead: 30th Anniversary Edition (Anchor Bay Entertainment, 1998): Audio commentary, *30th Anniversary Behind-the-Scenes* featurette.

Night of the Living Dead: 40th Anniversary Edition (Dimension Extreme, 2008): Audio commentaries, *One for the Fire* documentary, *Speak to the Dead: A Q&A with Co-Writer/Director George Romero, Ben Speaks: The Last Interview with Actor Duane Jones.*

Night of the Living Dead (1990) (Sony Pictures Home Entertainment, 1991): *The Dead Walk* featurette.

The Return of the Living Dead (MGM Home Entertainment, 2007): Audio commentaries, *The Decade of Darkness, Return of the Living Dead: The Dead Have Risen* featurettes.

Season of the Witch/There's Always Vanilla (Anchor Bay Entertainment, 2005): Audio commentaries, *The Directors: George Romero* featurette.

Radio/TV

Land of the Dead: George A. Romero Tribute Reel (Spike TV).
NPR National Public Radio.
Zombie Mania (Starz Entertainment).

Web sites

About.com
Big Bad Wolf
Cinefantastique Online
Classic Horror Film Board
Dread Central
DVD Verdict
Fangoria.com
Homepage of the Dead
Icons of Fright
Internet Movie Database
Kyra Schon: The Ghoul Next Door
LifeWhile
Pop Matters
Splatter.com
UGO.com
VH1.com
Videoscopemag.com
Wikipedia

NIGHT OF THE LIVING DEAD

THE ANUBIS

screenplay by Jack Russo

Jack Russo
527 Farnsworth Ave.
Clairton, Pa.

Night of the Living Dead

It is an ordinary dusk, of normal quiet and shadow. The grey sky contains a soft glow from the recent sun, so that trees and long blades of grass seem to shimmer in the gathering night. There is the rasp of crickets, and the rustle of leaves in an occasional whispering breeze.

Transitions are easy and gradual, with relaxed studies of earth, grass and leafy branches on a high mounded hill. Revelation of cemetery markers does nothing to disrupt the peacefulness of our established mood; when awareness comes, it is almost as though we have known where we were all along. We are in a typical rural cemetery, conceivably adjacent to a small church ... although the presence of a church is felt rather than confirmed. The stones range from small identifying slates to monuments of careful design ... an occasional Franciscan Crucifix, or a carved image of a defending angel. Over a hundred years of death indicated in stones syllabic with their year and the status of the families they represent.

Over the other night sounds is added the gravel-rumble of a slow-moving car. A wider shot reveals the car and the mounded cemetery, as the car pulls into the gate and moves down one of the cemetery roads. The car passes in extreme foreground and moves away from the camera. In the breeze of its passing, the dead leaves that clutter the little road swirl and move. Beyond the distant trees, the last receding grey of dusk is surrendering to the black. The car continues.

When the car stops, we feel the absence of its sounds ... replaced by the crickets and the subtle wind. Even as the car is still rocking slightly from its stopping action, we cut to a shot through the driver window at the occupants of the car.

The driver is a young man in his mid-twenties, and his passenger is a young woman, his sister. The man is in shirt sleeves with a loosened tie. His suit-coat is on the clothing hook over the back seat. The girl is wearing a simple but attractive summer suit, with the jacket removed and folded on her lap. She is fussing with her purse, while the man shuts off engine, lights, and leans back to

yawn and stretch his legs. The girl closes a potato chip bag,
brushes crumbs, fluffs her hair ... typical feminine gestures after
a long ride. The man stretches again.

BARBARA: THEY OUGHT TO MAKE THE DAY THE TIME CHANGES THE
FIRST DAY OF SUMMER. THEN TWO GOOD THINGS WOULD
HAPPEN ALL AT ONCE.

A little laugh from the man as he straightens his tie.

BARBARA: I LOVE THE LONG DAYS AND THE EXTRA SUN.

JOHN: A LOT OF GOOD THE EXTRA DAYLIGHT DOES ME. I LOST AN
HOUR'S SLEEP. AND IT'S DARK ALREADY, AND WE STILL
HAVE A THREE-HOUR DRIVE, AND WE WON'T GET BACK TILL
AFTER MIDNIGHT.

Barbara reaches down to put her shoes on:

BARBARA: IF IT REALLY DRAGGED YOU THAT MUCH, YOU WOULDN'T
DO IT.

JOHN: ARE YOU KIDDING? I CERTAINLY DON'T WANT TO BLOW
SUNDAY ON THIS SCENE. WE'RE GONNA EITHER HAVE TO
MOVE MOTHER TO PARKVILLE OR MOVE THE GRAVE TO
PITTSBURGH.

BARBARA: OH, YOU'RE JUST BEING SILLY. MOTHER CAN'T MAKE A
DRIVE LIKE THIS.

John reaches to the back seat and produces a flowered, cross-shaped grave ornament. In the center of
the cross, in gold script on a red field, is written
"We Still Remember."

JOHN: LOOK, TWENTY-FIVE DOLLARS ... "WE STILL REMEM-
BER" ... I DON'T, YOU KNOW IT ... I DON'T
REMEMBER WHAT THE GUY LOOKS LIKE.

BARBARA: JOHNNY ... IT TAKES YOU FIVE MINUTES.

JOHN: THREE <u>HOURS</u>--NO, <u>SIX</u> HOURS ... SIX HOURS AND FIVE
MINUTES.

Barbara continues to primp and straighten her outfit. John hands her the grave ornament and leans
forward to struggle into his suit jacket.

JOHN: MOTHER WANTS TO REMEMBER. SO WE HAVE TO DRIVE

FOUR-HUNDRED MILES TO PLANT A CROSS ON A GRAVE. AS
IF HE'S STARING UP THROUGH THE GROUND TO CHECK OUT
THE DECORATIONS ... (He points at the cross inscrip-
tion) ... <u>WE</u> HAVE TO REMEMBER ... AND SHE STAYS AT
HOME.

BARBARA: JOHNNY, WE'RE HERE ... ALL RIGHT?

She opens her door and turns to step out. John takes
the keys from the ignition and drops them into his
pocket. He reaches for his door handle ... "... WE
ON ... ARE WE ON? ..." a metallic radio voice. John
starts and looks down at the car radio. The voice
hesitates. Ticker-tapes and typewriters are dim in
the background. The voice sounds just slightly
excited.

VOICE: ... ER ... LADIES AND GENTLEMEN ... WHAT? ...

John, still staring at the radio, laughs slightly:

JOHN: HEY ... HEY, BARB, YOU KNOW THE RADIO'S BEEN ON ALL
THIS TIME ...

(Tighter Shot of Radio)

VOICE: LADIES AND GENTLEMEN ... PLEASE FORGIVE ... WHAT ...
HEY, YOU GOT A SIGNAL, CHARLIE? ...

JOHN: IT MUST HAVE BEEN THE STATION

VOICE: ... DO NOT BE AL... .

John clicks the radio off. He gets out of the car and
walks around the front of it, trotting to catch up
with his sister. It is obvious that she didn't hear
him. He catches up to her and starts to repeat his
discovery about the radio.

JOHN: HEY, THE RADIO IS OKAY, IT'S JUST ...

Barbara is more interested in finding the row con-
taining their father's grave.

BARBARA: YOU REMEMBER WHICH ROW IT'S IN?

JOHN: (Momentarily forgetting the radio) HUH? OH, IT'S OVER
HERE, I THINK ...

They start in his suggested direction.

JOHN: DID YOU HEAR THE RADIO?

BARBARA: (Looking ahead, trying to spot the grave) HMMM?

JOHN: THE RADIO'S FIXED. MUST'VE BEEN THE STATION, NOT
THE RADIO.

BARBARA: (Still searching intently, she tosses this line away)
GOOD ... YOU WON'T BE AS BITCHY DRIVING HOME.

Their jibes at each other are not really in anger, but
are typical of brother-sister annoyance. They walk
through the row of grave stones in the growing darkness.

JOHN: (Making conversation, with no more significance than
a comment about the weather) NOBODY AROUND.

BARBARA: WELL, IT IS LATE. IF YOU'D GET UP A LITTLE
EARLIER ...

JOHN: I ALREADY LOST AN HOUR'S SLEEP ON THE TIME CHANGE.

BARBARA: OH, SOMETIMES I THINK YOU COMPLAIN JUST TO HEAR
YOURSELF TALK.

JOHN: AN HOUR EARLIER AND IT'D STILL BE LIGHT. (He squints
into the dusk) IT'S HARD ENOUGH TO FIND IN THE LIGHT.

BARBARA: THERE IT IS. (She points)

They move toward a grave with a standard rectangu-
lar stone. It is an unkept grave, its outline cropped
and overgrown with grass and wilted flowers.

John takes the flowered cross and, stepping close to
the headstone, embeds its wire-prong base into the
earth, as he rambles on:

JOHN: WONDER WHAT HAPPENED TO THE ONE FROM LAST YEAR.
EVERY YEAR, TWENTY-FIVE BUCKS FOR ONE OF THESE
THINGS, AND THE ONE FROM LAST YEAR IS GONE ...

We hear Barbara's voice. The camera stays on John as
he builds up some dirt around the base of the ornament.

BARBARA: THE FLOWERS DIE ... AND THE CARETAKER OR SOMEBODY
TAKES THEM AWAY ...

JOHN: (Standing, brushing himself off) YEAH, A LITTLE SPIT
AND POLISH AND THEY CAN SELL THEM AGAIN. I WONDER
HOW MANY TIMES WE'VE BOUGHT THE SAME ...

He doesn't finish; in standing he sees his sister with a pair of rosary beads and he stops talking.

She is praying silently, looking down at the ground. John straightens his tie and buttons his jacket. He steps behind his sister, puts his hands in his pockets, and rocks nervously on one foot. She continues to pray. John looks around the cemetery.

The stones are soft and white ... they seem very pale. There are a few moving shadows. The sounds of the night seem louder, but this is only because they have stopped talking. The situation does not seem ominous. John is merely bored. In the distance, a huddled figure is walking among the graves.

JOHN: (Glancing at his watch) C'MON, BARB, CHURCH WAS THIS MORNING ...

The girl continues her prayers. John lights a cigarette, idly exhales the first puff of smoke and looks around again. The huddled figure still moves slowly among the graves. John turns to his sister and is about to say something but sees her making the sign of the cross and dropping her beads in her purse.

She turns from the grave and they both start to walk slowly away.

JOHN: (Slightly uncomfortable about urging her to leave) WELL ... I MEAN ... PRAYIN'S FOR CHURCH.

BARBARA: I HAVEN'T SEEN YOU IN CHURCH LATELY.

JOHN: WELL, GRANDPA TOLD ME I WAS DAMNED TO HELL ... (He says this lightly, looking ahead to a large tree. He smiles.) YOU REMEMBER? RIGHT HERE ... I JUMPED OUT AT YOU FROM BEHIND THAT TREE ... GRANDPA GOT ALL EXCITED ... 'YOU VAN BE DEMD TOAYELL' ... Barbara smiles.

JOHN: RIGHT HERE, I JUMPED OUT FROM BEHIND THAT TREE AT YOU.

Barbara expresses annoyance.

JOHN: YOU USED TO BE SO SCARED HERE.

BARBARA: JOHNEEE! (With forced irritation)

JOHN: (Laughing, playfully) YOU'RE STILL AFRAID ...

BARBARA: STOP IT ... I MEAN IT ...

JOHN: (Mockingly) ... THEY'RE GONNA GET YOU, BARBARA ...

BARBARA: STOP IT ... YOU'RE IGNORANT ...

JOHN: THEY'RE COMING FOR YOU, BARBARA ... THEY'RE GONNA GET YOU ...

(He leers at her, as though he is about to pounce).

BARBARA: (Becoming a little nervous) JOHNNY, STOP ...

JOHN: (Mockingly ominous) THEY'RE COMING OUT OF THEIR GRAVES ... AFTER YOU ... THEY'RE COMING ... TO GET YOU ...

With this, John throws up his arms and his voice rises. The figure moving among the graves stops, and stands for a moment. Barbara glances toward the figure and momentarily her anxiety turns to embarrassment.

BARBARA: JOHN, STOP BEING A CHILD!

The shadowy figure starts to move a little faster, through a row of graves which intersects perpendicularly with the path along which Barbara and John are walking.

BARBARA: (As we cut back to her) YOU'RE ACTING LIKE AN IDIOT.

John speaks in a low tone now, glancing at the figure as they draw closer in their penpendicular paths. John's remarks now are directed to Barbara, as though he didn't want the old man to hear ...

JOHN: HERE COMES ONE OF THEM NOW ...

BARBARA: (Walking faster) HE'LL HEAR YOU ...

JOHN: COMING TO GET YOU ...

Barbara purses her lips in anger ... the couple is now only a few yards from intersecting their path with the old figure ...

JOHN: (In a mocked-panic whisper) I'M GETTIN' OUTA HERE ...

He bolts and runs up the path.

BARBARA: JOHN ...

Embarrassed, she cuts herself short and continues to walk, more rapidly now. Up the path, beyond the intersection of the man's row, John stops, laughing, and turns to look back at his sister. She is near the place where the paths meet, and so is the old man. We cut close to her. She is looking down in embarrassed silence, aware of her proximity with the old man. She feigns poise, and as she makes the intersection looks up nervously to deliver a socially necessary smile to the old mourner ...

The old man lunges at the girl, his hand grabs at her hair. A frightened gasp chokes her. She is coughing. The man grips her arm and slashes at her clothing. She flails about choking, trying to yell ...

JOHN: (Horrified) HEY ... GOD ...

The man is all over Barbara, unable to hold her in her violent flailing. His grabbings tear her jacket and scratch her face. He seems to be trying to bite her arm. John leaps at the man. The three fall to the ground, Barbara kicking, and beating with her purse. John gets a firm hold on the man and Barbara is able to wrench free. The man is thrashing wildly at all parts of John's body. They struggle to their feet, the figure thrashes, beats, tears like an animal ... John clutches at him and they fall in a heap. In the darkness, their form is as one thrashing thing.

Barbara screams wildly. The two men make animal sounds. One figure gains the advantage and slams his fists down against the other's head.

Barbara is panic-stricken. Her screams turn to frenzied gasps as she finds a tree limb and snatches it up. But when she looks up, she sees that one has vanquished the other. She stops in her tracks. Night sounds. A close shot makes it clear that John is lying limply on the ground with the other man hunched over his form. The man is doing something

with the limp body, still ripping at it ... perhaps
groping for money ... Barbara cannot tell ...

BARBARA: JOHNNEEE ...

The old man freezes and looks up. The girl raises her
club and rushes toward him. He jumps into a half-
standing position, like an animal hunched to
spring ...

Barbara stops in her tracks. The man is breathing
heavily. She starts to back away. The man holds very
still. She backs further ... faster ... total fear.
The man starts to move slowly ... cat-like ... he steps
over the body. Barbara drops the club and breaks
into a dead run down the path. She screams. The man
moves after her, but he is considerably slower than
she, with seeming difficulty in moving. He appears
almost crippled.

In a flailing run, Barbara reaches the car, sobbing.
She yanks open the door. She can hear the man drawing nearer. She scrambles into the front seat and
slams the door shut ...

No Key.

The man draws nearer, seeming to move faster, more
desperate to reach the girl. Barbara sobs ... she
clenches the steering wheel. The driver's window is
open; she struggles to roll it up ... then pushes the
lock button. The man is upon the car. Barbara dives
across the seat to slam down the passenger-side lock
button. The man rips at the door handles and pounds
violently at the car. The girl starts screaming
again. The man ... pounding ... clawing ... he grabs
a stone from the road ... the passenger window shatters into thousands of little cracks. Another pound
sends the stone through the window, and hands grab
through the opening to peel away the flaked glass in
sections. Barbara's screams become more violent.
She summons enough presence of mind to reach for the

emergency brake. The man pounds and flails at the
window. The car, at the top of a long grade, slowly
starts to drift. The man struggles to hold it ... to
rip out the glass ... his arm breaks through, his
sleeve is ripped and tattered ... the hand grabs at
the inside of the door ... the car moving faster ...
the man struggles to cling ... he is forced to trot
after the car ... faster ... he loses his footing ...
grabs at the fender, the bumper ... he falls into the
road ... the car gains momentum. The man regains his
footing and starts after the car. It is moving
faster. Barbara is frozen in the driver's seat,
clenching the wheel. The road ahead is black ... the
speed is frightening ... she pulls the light switch ...
the headlights dance beams of light among the trees.
The beams reveal the grade in the road, which is nar-
rowing to one car width; and, about two hundred feet
ahead, the downhill grade ends and an uphill grade
begins. In desperation, the girl looks out the rear
window. Against the sky, in the light from the cemetery gate, the man is still coming after her. In
panic, she looks about. She is still in the cemetery
proper. Rows of graves on both sides of the road. No
lights from houses, no signs of life. The car slows ...
its momentum carries it some distance up the upgrade. Barbara glances backward ... the man is moving faster toward her ... she is terrified ... the car
reaches a full stop. There is increased panic in her
face ... as she forgets herself and the car begins to
drift backward ... toward the man, as he draws
nearer. The car picks up momentum, carrying her toward her pursuer.
She grabs at the emergency brake and yanks it tight,
the lurch of the car throwing her against the seat.
She struggles with the door handle; the button pops
up ... the man draws nearer ... she breaks from the

car. The man keeps coming, desperately trying to
move faster ... Barbara runs, off the roadway and
onto the turf of the cemetery. She falls ... kicks her
shoes off ... gets up and keeps running. The man is
still after her.

She reaches a low stone wall which marks the end of
the cemetery. She struggles over it and looks ahead
for a moment to get her bearings. Across a main
highway is a darkened gasoline station, and beyond it
an old house. She pants heavily, glancing up and
down the highway ... but there is no sign of traffic.
The man is nearing the low cemetery wall. She breaks
into a run across the highway.

The gasoline station shows no signs of life. It is old
and decrepit. One light is out over the pumps. The
pumphouse and surroundings are nearly lost in
shadow. Some fifty yards away, there is the old
house. She runs toward it.

She presses against the side of the house, in a darkened corner, trying to look up into the window.
Across the highway, she sees her pursuer struggle
over the little wall, and in his clumsiness fall grov-
elling on the ground.

In panic, she runs to the rear of the house and into
the shadows of a small back porch. Her first impulse
is to cry out for help, but she silences herself in
favor of trying to stay hidden. She gasps, trying to
hold her breath. Silence ... night sounds ... and the
sounds of the man's running footsteps slowing to a
trot ... then a walk ... the footsteps stop.

Barbara quickly glances about. There is a rear window. She peers through it, but inside everything is
dark. The pursuing footsteps take up again. She
presses back against the door of the house, and her
hand falls on the doorknob. She looks down at it,
grabs it with a turn, and the door opens.

She enters quickly, as quietly as possible, and closes
the door softly behind her, bolting it and feeling in
the darkness for a key. Her hand finds a skeleton
key, and she turns it, making a small rasp and click.
She leans against the door, listening, and can still
hear the distant footfalls.

Barbara finds that she is in the kitchen of the old
house. She gropes through a door and into a large
living-room ... no sign of life. Her impulse is to cry
for help, but again she stops herself for fear of
being heard by the man outside. She darts back to
the kitchen, rummages through drawers in a kitchen
cabinet, and finds the silverware. She chooses a
large steak knife and, grasping it tightly, goes to
listen at the door again. All is quiet. She goes back
into the living-room. Beyond it is an alcove that
contains the front entrance to the house. She rushes
to the front door and makes sure it is locked. Cautiously, she pushes back a corner of the curtain to
see outside. The view overlooks an expansive lawn,
large shadowy pine trees, and the service station
across the road. There is no sign of the attacker.
Suddenly, there is noise from outside: the pounding
and rattling of a door. Barbara drops the curtain
edge and stiffens. More sounds. She hurries to a
side window. Across the lawn, the man is pounding at
the door to the garage. She watches, her eyes wide
with fear ... The man struggles with the door, then
looks about and picks up something and smashes at it.
In panic, Barbara pulls away from the window.

Across the room is a telephone. She rushes to it and
picks up the receiver ... dial tone ... she frantically
dials the operator ... some buzzes and clicks ...
then ... "I'M SORRY ... OUR LINES ARE BUSY ... WOULD
YOU HOLD THE LINE PLEASE ... I'M SORRY ... OUR LINES
ARE ..." She quickly depresses the receiver but-

tons ... lets them up and dials again ... long
pause ... she can hear sounds from the gas station ...
"I'M SORRY ... OUR LINES ..."
She depresses the buttons again ... dials 411 for information ... another long pause ... then the rasp of
a busy signal. The noises from the service station
have stopped. She listens for a moment ... she shudders with fear ... notices a telephone directory in a
stand near the phone. Frantically, her fingers
search the pages for the emergency numbers ... the
police. She dials shakily, but before she has dialed
the last numbers the raspiness of the busy signal
comes over the receiver. She depresses the buttons
again ... footsteps ...
She puts the phone down and rushes to another window. A figure is crossing the lawn, coming toward
the house. It is a different figure, a different man.
She runs to the door and peers out through the curtains again. The man still walks toward the house. A
shadow darkens a strip of window at the left of the
door. Its abruptness startles her.
She peels back a corner of the curtain and sees the
back of the first attacker not ten feet away, facing
the man who is approaching. The attacker moves toward the new man. Barbara freezes against the door,
and glances down at her knife ... she looks back out
at the two men.
They join each other under the dark, hanging trees,
and stand, looking back toward the cemetery. From
inside the house, Barbara squints, trying to see. Finally, the attacker moves back across the road, in the
direction of the cemetery. The other man approaches
the house, seeks the shadows of a tree, and stops ...
in an attitude of stolid watching ...
Barbara stares, but can see little. She lunges toward
the phone again ... dials the operator ... the same

recorded message. She barely stops herself from
slamming down the receiver.

Then suddenly a distant sound ... an approaching
car. She scampers to the window and looks out. The
road seems empty. But after a moment a faint light
appears, bouncing and rapidly approaching ... a car
coming up the road. Barbara reaches for the doorknob, edges the door open very slightly ... the light
spills dimly over the area. There, under the great
tree in the lawn, is the silhouette of the second man.
Barbara shudders ... she is afraid to make her break
for the approaching car. The figure appears to be
sitting, quite still, its head and shoulders slumped
over ... it seems to be looking right at the house.
The car speeds by ... Barbara just stares at the figure. She cannot run. She closes the door and backs
into the shadows of the house.

She turns to see all around her. The large dreary
rooms are very quiet, cast in shadow ... she spies a
stairway ... runs toward it still carrying the knife
and starts up the stairs. The camera is level with
her eye, and picks up her view of the stairs as she
runs up ... panting and frantic she climbs, her hand
grazing the bannister ... still at her eye level, the
camera starts to pick up the top of the stairway ...
the floor of the second landing ... a brief glimpse of
something on the floor there ... she continues to
climb ... the floor of the landing ... zoom in ...
toward camera, the hand of ... a corpse.

Barbara stops ... the corpse is almost skeletal with
its flesh ripped from it, and it lies at the end of a
trail of blood. Screaming in absolute horror, Barbara almost falls down the stairs ... she is gag-
ging ... she breaks for the door, unlocks it, and
flings herself out into the night, completely unmind-
ful of consequences ...

She is bathed in light ... two headlights are screech-
ing toward camera ... the sounds of a vehicle stopping. Barbara covers her face with her arms.
Someone rushes toward her ...

VOICE: "ARE YOU ONE OF 'EM?"

She stares, frozen.

A man stands in front of her. He is large and crude,
in coveralls and tattered work shirt. He looks very
strong, and perhaps a little stupid. Behind him is an
old, battered pick-up truck, which he has driven
right up onto the lawn of the house. He holds a large
jack-handle in his hand, and stands there panting.
Behind him, the man at the tree still stands.
Barbara is still frozen ...

VOICE: The man shouts again: "ARE YOU ONE OF 'EM? I SEEN 'EM
TO LOOK LIKE YOU ..."

The man at the tree moves forward ... Barbara
screams and steps back ... the truckdriver spins to
face the other man. The other man stops in his
tracks. The truckdriver backs protectively toward
the girl, while the other stands, just watching. Finally, the truckdriver siezes Barbara's wrist and
pulls her into the house, slamming the door behind
them.

Barbara falls back against a wall. The truckdriver
locks the door and throws the bolt. He is breathing
hard. He turns to look at the girl. She brings the
knife up in a defensive gesture ...

TRUCKDRIVER: (soothingly, in a drawl, almost as he would address a
scared rabbit): "AAW RIGHT ...'TS AWRIGHT NOW ..."

She stares widely at him.

He immediately concerns himself with his surroundings. He moves into the next room to check the windows. He tries a lamp, it lights, he turns it off.
Barbara weakly lowers the knife and falls to a sitting position in a chair. She watches the man in-

tently ... he calls to her from the other room ...

TRUCKDRIVER: "DON'T YOU MIND THE CREEP OUTSIDE ... I CAN HANDLE
HIM ... THERE'S PROBLY GONNA BE LOTS MORE OF 'EM ...
SOON'S THEY FIN' OUT ABOUT US ... AHM OUTA GAS ...
THEM PUMPS OVER THERE IS LOCKED ... IS THERE FOOD
HERE? ... AH GET US SOME GRUB ... THEN WE BEAT 'EM
OFF AN' SKEDADDLE ..."
She just stares at him.

TRUCKDRIVER: "AH GUESS YOU PUTTZED WITH THE PHONE ..." (He grabs
it ... dials ... listens ... slams it back down. He
looks at Barbara. She is shivering.)

TRUCKDRIVER: "IT AIN'T NO GOOD NOWAY. MIGHT'S WELL HAVE TWO TIN-
CANS AND A STRING ... YOU LIVE HERE?"
She remains silent, looking toward the top of the
stairs. The man follows her stare and starts toward
the stairs ... halfway up he sees the corpse and
stops ...

TRUCKDRIVER: "OH ... BEJESUS ..." (He stares for a moment, then
slowly backs down the stairs.)
At the bottom of the stairs, he just looks at the girl
shivering with shock in her chair. Then he forces
himself back into action.

TRUCKDRIVER: "WE GOTTA BUST OUTTA HERE ... GIT TO WHERE THERE'S
SOME FOLKS ... SOMEBODY WITH GUNS OR SOMETHIN ..."
(He quickly moves toward the kitchen.)

TRUCKDRIVER: "AH'LL TRY TO SCARE UP SOME GRUB."
He enters the kitchen and starts to rummage. He
flings open the refrigerator and the cupboards.
Finding a stack of large paper grocery bags, he opens
one and starts to fill it with things from the refrigerator. He hurls the stuff into the bag. He is interrupted by Barbara's voice ...

BARBARA: (weakly) "WHAT'S HAPPENING?"
The man looks up at her ...

BARBARA: (repeating): "WHAT'S HAPPENING?" (She shakes her head
in fright and bewilderment.)

The truckdriver looks at her. She stands like a
frightened child in the kitchen doorway. He is
amazed at her question. A shattering crash startles
them. The man drops the groceries and siezes his
jack-handle. He runs to the front door and looks out
through the curtained window. Another shattering
sound. The first attacker has joined the second man
at the old pick-up truck, and with great sticks the
two are smashing out the headlights.

TRUCKDRIVER: "TWO OF 'EM."

Once the lights are battered out, the two men outside
start to beat at the body of the truck. The truckdriver spins and lunges toward the girl.

TRUCKDRIVER: "HOW MANY OF 'EM ... HOW MANY ..."

She backs further away ... the truckdriver lunges
again, this time in desperation to make her understand ...

TRUCKDRIVER: "HOW MANY ... COME ON, NOW ... AH KNOW YOU'RE
SCARED ... BUT AH CAN HANDLE THEM TWO BOHOPPERS ...
NOW HOW MANY MORE IS OUT THERE ... THAT TRUCK'S OUR
ONLY CHANCE TO GIT OUTTA HERE ... HOW MANY ... HOW
MANY ..."

He grabs her shoulders and she struggles against him,
thrashing hysterical ...

BARBARA: I DON'T KNOW ... I DON'T KNOW ... WHAT'S HAPPEN-
ING? ... I DON'T KNOW WHAT'S HAPPENING ..."

She breaks into hysterical sobbings.

The truckdriver spins away from her and breaks for
the door. He looks out the window for a moment. The
attackers still beat at the truck, wildly trying to
tear it apart. The truckdriver flings open the door
and leaps off of the porch. The two men look up ...
for the first time we see the faces of the attackers ... They are dead things ... the flesh on their
faces is rotting and oozing ... their eyes bulge from
deep sockets ... their hair is long, and their clothing

rotten and in tatters. They are ghoulish beings,
staring up at the truckdriver ...
He starts for them slowly, with building vengeance.
He moves steadily at first ... with controlled
power ... he speaks as he advances ... wielding his
jack-handle ...

TRUCKDRIVER: COME 'N GIT IT ... COME 'N GIT SOME O' THIS JACK-
HANDLE ..."

He concentrates on his attack ... moving stolidly toward the two creatures ... he breaks almost into a
run. But the two, rather than backing off, move toward the man ... as though drawn by some urge. The
man pounds into them, swinging and thrashing with
arms and jack-handle. They are buffeted by his
blows ... they seem weak compared to him ... but his
powerful blows don't really stop them ... it is like
beating a rug ... he flings them back and they advance again. It is a violent, brutal struggle. But
the big man finally beats the two into the ground,
and for a great while continues to pound at their
limp forms. He breaks into almost a sobbing with
each of his blows. He beats at them and beats at them
as the girl watches in shock from the porch ... he
thrashes and beats until she starts to scream again.
Her screams pierce the night. The man stops.
Breathing heavily, he stands, enveloped in the quiet
of the night.
The girl stands in the doorway. The truckdriver
turns to face her. He is out of breath.
Suddenly, a noise behing the girl. She spins ... and
walking toward her from the kitchen is another of the
hideous creatures ... the truckdriver leaps toward
the thing ...

TRUCKDRIVER: "LOCK THAT DOOR!"

Barbara slams the door and locks it, backing against
it, as another equally brutal struggle ensues in the

living-room. The big man again beats the attacker down ... but another appears at the kitchen door. The truckdriver leaps toward it, and with powerful jack-handle blows drives it out beyond the door so that he can fall against it, shutting it. He bolts it and stands leaning against the frame trying to breathe ...

Long silence ... the truckdriver just stares down at the floor ...

TURCKDRIVER: "THEY KNOW WE'RE IN HERE, NOW ... THERE AIN'T NO USE DISPUTIN' THAT."

Outside the house, the fourth ghoul stands staring at the back door. Another slowly walks up behind it ... and another. At the front of the house, three more stand near the bodies of the first two.

Pull off and follow focus from the front yard of the house, through the curtains at the front door, to the face of the girl as she spins to face the camera. Her face twitches in fright, and her eyes are wide with a non-blinking stare. As she spins, her eyes fall on the floor, where the dead humanoid lies. The thing is askew on its back, its right arm extended toward the girl with fingers twisted as though to grab.

(Cut to MCU. Camera is trucking in slowly.)

There is a slight movement in the thing's hand. It twitches ... the whole body twitches slightly ... the bent, broken neck has the being's head twisted up-ward, in an open-mouthed glassy stare ... Barbara steps toward the thing. The fear in her face bears the beginnings of a sick frown. The hand twitches again. The girl moves closer, drawn toward it, star-ing down at it with over-powering curiosity.

The thing is something dead, with the beginnings of decay on its face and neck. Barbara moves closer. The thing still twitches ...

She is staring right down into the thing's eyes ...

her hands come up to her mouth ... the urge to be ill,
to scream, to run must all be fought ... the glassy
stare from bulging eyes ... right back up at her ...
(Camera shoots back and forth at her face and the
staring eyes of the dead thing ... zoom in on the
thing ... it seems as though the body is going to
stand again ... its face holds as much life as it did
when it walked ...)

Suddenly, with a rustling sound, the thing moves ...
(Cut back.) The big truckdriver has a hold on the
thing's legs and is dragging it across the floor.

TRUCKDRIVER: "SHUT YOUR EYES, GIRL ... I'M GITTIN' THIS DEAD BE-
HOPPER OUTTA HERE ..."

He is sweating. His face shows anger and anguish as
he drags the body across the floor. Barbara just
stands, her hands still at her mouth, watching. The
sounds of the man's breathing, and his struggle, fill
the room. With the body, he reaches the back door
and lets the legs fall ...

TRUCKDRIVER: "YOU ... FILTHY ..."

(He cuts himself short. Cut-in for close-up.) The
stark light on the big man's face makes him shine in
his sweat. His eyes are alert, and afraid. He turns
quickly to see through the small window panes in the
door.

Outside, lurking in shadow from the huge trees, the
three beings watch and wait, their arms dangling and
eyes bulging, as they stare at the truckdriver's activities. With a swift move, the big man unbolts the
door, flings it open, and bends toward the inert thing
at his feet. The ghoulish things begin to move toward
him. With one great heave, the dead form is flopped
outside the door. It lies across the threshold. The
things advance silently ...

TRUCKDRIVER: FILTHY ...

Another great effort shoves the body almost clear.

From inside the house, the big man's efforts cannot
be clearly seen by the girl, because the door-frame is
blocking her view. She moves into the kitchen. The
truckdriver flops the body down onto the edge of the
porch. The three figures are close upon him, are
starting to reach out. The big man shudders. He
fumbles into the breast pocket of his work shirt. The
things advance. He produces a pack of matches, manages to strike one ... and touches the burning tip to
the clothing of the dead thing, and with almost a pop-
ping sound the clothing catches fire ...
The things in the yard stop in their tracks ... the
fire blazes slowly. Shaking, the truckdriver touches
the match to other aspects of the thing's clothing.
His fingers burn, and he snaps them, throwing the
match into the heaped form. He is breathing hard.
Standing, he kicks the burning thing off the edge of
the porch ... watches it roll down three small steps
onto the grass, where it lies still, the flames licking
around it. The three beings step back slightly ... the
big man clings to the bannister around the little
porch ... his fists clench and his face is fiery in the
glow of the flames. His voice quivers ...

TRUCKDRIVER: "AH'LLGIT YOU ... AH'M GONNA GIT YOU ... ALL OF
YOU ..." (his voice grows stronger in his violence)
"ALL OF YOU ..."
He stands defiantly on the little porch, the flaming
corpse separating from the things that wait. He
spins suddenly ... the girl stands inside the kitchen
door. His face is a fury of sweat and quivering
anger. His eyes meet the girl's ... she steps slowly
back into the room. The big man, in great strides,
re-enters the kitchen and slams the door, bolting it
again. His breathing, still loud, is even more rapid
than before. His eyes dart quickly about the room in
search of something.

He rushes to the cabinets and throws them open, beings rummaging through them: standard kitchen uten-
sils and supplies. He does not speak, just
frantically ransacks the room ...

TRUCKDRIVER: "SEE IF YOU CAN FIND THE LIGHT SWITCH."

Barbara falls back against a wall, and her hand
gropes to a switch. The light from an overhead fix-
ture comes on, providing dim illumination. The big
man continues to clatter about frantically. The
light coming on makes the girl blink. She remains
against the wall, her hand still touching the switch.
It is as though she dare not move. She watches
silently. The man flings open drawers and spills
contents onto the shelfing and onto the floor. His
hands fall to the silverware drawer, still open from
when Barbara first discovered it. He pulls it out
until it stops itself with a crash. He roots through
it, pulls out a large knife and, sucking his breath in,
stuffs it under his belt. Then he reaches into the
drawer again and produces another knife. Taking
Barbara by surprise, he strides toward her. He
shoves the knife at her, handle first, but she falls
back slightly. Her action stays his franticness ...
breathing heavily through his words, he speaks to
her ...

TRUCKDRIVER: "... NOW ... YOU HANG ON ... TO THIS ..."

She hesitates, but she takes the knife. She seems
weak, almost apathetic, as though she is losing control of herself. She stares at the weapon in her
hand, then her eyes come up to meet the man's intense
face.

TRUCKDRIVER: "ALL RIGHT."

He pulls away from her and continues to rummage, but
he speaks periodically now, between great breaths,
and between the brief times when his interest is
wrapped in something he finds in his rummagings.

His search is not without control; it has a coordi-
nated purpose; it is selective, although frantic and
desperate. He looks for nails and strips of wood or
planks that he might nail around doors and windows.
His actions are hurried, and intent after these defensive ends; at first, his search has his full attention. Gradually, as he moves about, and begins to
come up with several key items that he needs, his efforts pace down into a more deliberate flow ... he
starts putting up boards and tables against the vulnerable parts of the old house. The mood relaxes in
intensity, becomes calmer, more analytical ... the
barricading instills a feeling of greater security.
And the knowledge of some security begins to over-
take the girl, bringing her out of her shock and pas-
sivity. The scene procedes as follows:
... the girl looks at her knife, recedes against the
wall. The noise of the search is ever-present. The
man mutters occasionally, and spills his findings
about the room. At first, as new cabinets and drawers fail to turn up what he is looking for, he grows
impatient and more violent ... spools of thread, buttons, maincure implements, shoe-shine materials ...
Another drawer ... immediately, as the drawer is
flung open with a clatter, the big man sees what he
needs ... he almost leaps into the drawer ...

TRUCKDRIVER: "TELL ME ... YOU AIN'T THE SWEETEST THING ..."
His big hand comes out of the drawer with an old
pipe-tobacco tin, and in one gesture he spills its
contents onto a shelf ... nails and screws and washers and tacks spill out onto the wooden shelf. A few
roll too far and clatter onto the floor. His fingers
scoop them up. He fumbles through the little pile of
things and selects the longest nails in the batch, and
stuffs them into the breast pocket of his work-shirt.
Even as he stuffs the nails into his pocket, he is al-

ready moving, his eyes seeking for his next need ...

TRUCKDRIVER: "SEE IF THERE'S ANY WOOD AROUND THE FIREPLACE OUT THERE!"

His hands explore the shelfing surface. The girl does not respond immediately. His impetus carries him toward another shelf, but in turning he notices the girl, still motionless.

TRUCKDRIVER: "LOOK ... YOU ..." (angry at first, he stops himself, then speaks still frantically, but with less harshness)

"... YOU'RE SCARED ... AH'M SCARED ... AH'M SCARED, TOO ... JIST LIKE YOU ... NOW ..." (he composes himself even more) "WE AIN'T GONNA BE WORTH A PLUGGED NICKEL IF WE DON'T DO SOMETHIN' ... AH'M GONNA BOARD UP THESE DOORS AND WINDOWS ... BUT YOU GOTTA PITCH IN ... WE GOTTA HELP OURSELVES, 'CAUSE THERE AIN'T NOBODY AROUND TO HELP US ...'N WE'RE GONNA BE ALL RIGHT ... OK? ... NOW ... AH WANT YOU TO SCAMPER OUT THERE 'N SEE IF THERE'S ANY WOOD IN THAT FIREPLACE ..."

He stops, still breathing hard. The girl just looks at him. She starts to move, very slowly, away from the wall.

TRUCKDRIVER: "OK?"

The girl is still for a long moment; then nods her head weakly.

TRUCKDRIVER: "OK"

The girl leaves the room and he continues his search. She moves quickly into the living room area. The darkness stops her for an instant, slowing her pace. From the kitchen, come the clattering sounds of the man's search. She looks ahead. The white curtains on the windows seem to glow, and every shadow seems suspect. Barbara shudders.

(Shot of the foreboding room. Closer shot on her face.) On a table is a bowl of large, rounded flow-

ers ... a breeze causes them to stir--in sync with a
sound from the kitchen. The effect startles the girl;
she dives for a table lamp, clicks it on, and dull illumination fills the room. The room is empty. She
starts slowly toward the fireplace. Near it, is a
stack of logwood, and a few planks that might be
large enough to nail across the windows. Still
clutching her knife, she bends over the pile and
gathers up the planking. She stands with her awkward load, and the foreboding room faces her again,
stopping her. She bolts and hurries toward the
kitchen.

Bursting through the door, she finds the big man
pounding with his jack-handle at the hinges on a tall
broom-closet door. One final swipe and a great yank
frees the wooden door, and the man stands it against
the wall next to the broom-closet. In the recesses of
the closet, the man spots other useful items and pulls
them out ... an ironing board, three center boards
from a dining table, and some old scrap lumber.

He motions for Barbara to follow, as he grabs the
closet door and moves to the back door of the house,
which he had previously bolted against the beings
outside. He slaps the closet door up against the
paned portion of the kitchen door and finds that with
this same piece he can cover the kitchen window. He
leans against the piece of wood and gropes in his
pocket for nails. The door starts to slip slightly; it
does not completely cover the adjoining window, but
it leaves slots of glass at top and bottom; however, it
does cover the glass part of the entrance door. It
slips, and he nudges it back into position, as he continues to grope for nails. Barbara drops her burden
and moves swiftly, helping the man by holding an end
of the barrier in position. The truckdriver accepts
her help automatically, without recognition, and

gives the barricade a cursory inspection as he deter-
mines where to sink the nails; pulling several nails
from his pocket, he places them and drives them in
with his jack-handle. He drives two on his side
through the door and moulding until they grab, then
moves to her side and drives two more. When four are
in, he whacks at them with the jack-handle until they
are completely sunken, then begins to add more.
Now he starts to talk. The first decisive steps are
taken.

Quite a lot of relief comes with it. Most of the house
is still vulnerable, but the measures taken instill
confidence. While he talks, though, he keeps working
rapidly, his pace as intense as ever ...

TRUCKDRIVER: "THERE, BY GOD ... THIS OUGHTTA HAMP THEIR
CRIMPER ... THEY AIN'T THAT STRONG ... THERE ..."
Two more nails, in position, driven to the moulding.
He tests the barricading wood with two good yanks.
It holds.

TRUCKDRIVER: "THEY AIN'T COMIN' THROUGH THAT."
He drives the last two nails in all the way.

TRUCKDRIVER: "GOTTA FIGURE OUT HOW MUCH NAILS WE GOT."
He sees the parts of the window that remain uncov-
ered.

TRUCKDRIVER: "AH'LL LEAVE THAT FOR NOW. WE'LL FIX THE REST."
He turns quickly from the barracade and looks around
the room. No other doors or windows except the door
that leads to the living-room.

TRUCKDRIVER: "WELL ... THIS PLACE IS FAIRLY SECURE ..."
He examines planks and table extensions.

TRUCKDRIVER: "NOW ... IF WE HAVE TO ..."
The girl just stands and watches him.

TRUCKDRIVER: "IF WE HAVE TO ... WE JUST RUN IN HERE ... AND NO
DRAGGIN NOW, OR FUSSIN' WITH YOUR MAKE-UP, OR I
LEAVE YOU OUT THERE. WE RUN IN HERE AND BOARD UP
THIS DOOR."

The door between the kitchen and living-room has
been open all the time. The big man closes it; tests
it; it shuts tight. He opens it again. He quickly
chooses several of the lumber strips and stands them
against the door frame. He gropes in his pocket and
notices that his supply of nails is dwindling. He
checks the pile spikled from the can; he empties the
can completely and fingers the contents for all of
the longest nails, and tosses just these back into the
can. He hands the can to the girl ...

TRUCKDRIVER: "YOU TAKE THESE."

This time she reacts quickly and takes the little to-
bacco tin from his big hand. As she does so, the man
gathers as much of the lumber as he can into his arms
and starts out of the room. Barbara follows. They
are in the living-room.

TRUCKDRIVER: IT AIN'T GONNA BE TOO LONG, THEY BE TRYIN' TO HAMMER
THEIR WAY IN HERE. THEY'RE AFRAID NOW.

He drops his load of wood in the middle of the floor
and walks over to the largest front windows, talking
as he moves. His speech is rapid.

TRUCKDRIVER: THEY'RE SCAIRT OF FIRE TOO, I FOUND THAT OUT ...

His eye measures the size of the big windows. He
looks all around the room. Finally, his eyes fix on
the large dining table, and he moves quickly toward
it, talking as he moves, resuming his train of
thought ...

TRUCKDRIVER: THERE MUST'VE BEEN FIFTY ... A HUNDRED OF 'EM DOWN
IN CAMBRIA WHEN THE NEWS BROKE ...

Barbara watches, almost transfixed. At his mention
of the number of the things, her eyes reflect amazement, and frightened curiosity. The man reaches the
table, walks around it studying its size, then hoists
one end and turns it onto its side. Bracing it
against himself, he heaves on one of the legs and
tries to break it free. With a great ripping sound,

the table leg is torn off, and the man drops it onto
the rug. He continues talking, punctuating his remarks with vengence on the table as he rips all the
legs off.

TRUCKDRIVER: I SEEN THIS BIG GASOLINE TRUCK, YOU KNOW ... DOWN
BEEKMAN'S ... BEEKMAN'S DINER ... AND I HAD HEARD
THE RADIO ... I GOT A RADIO IN MY TRUCK ...
He wrenches at the second table leg ... it cracks
loudly but does not come free. He moves to where his
jack-handle lies on the floor.

TRUCKDRIVER: ... THIS GAS'LINE TRUCK COME SCREAMIN' OUTA THE
DINER LOT ONTO THE ROAD ... MUST BE TEN ... FIFTEEN
OF THEM THINGS CHASIN' IT ... AND IT LOOKS FUNNY TO
ME, BUT I DON'T SEE THE THINGS RUNNIN' BEHIND IT
RIGHT AWAY ...
He picks up the jack-handle and hammers at the table
leg. The second powerful swat frees the leg. He
moves on to the third.

TRUCKDRIVER: I JUST SEE THIS BIG TRUCK ... AND IT LOOKS FUNNY, YOU
KNOW, HOW SLOW TRUCKS'LL START ... AND IT'S PULLIN'
OUT ONTO THE ROAD ... AND WEAVIN' ... THEN I SEE THEM
THINGS ... AND THE TRUCK'S MOVIN' SO SLOW, THEY'RE
CATCHIN' UP ... AND GRABBIN' ... JUMPIN' ON ...
Another table leg falls loose to the rug.

TRUCKDRIVER: AND THAT TRUCK JUST CUT RIGHT 'CROSS THE ROAD ...
THROUGH THE GUARD RAIL, YOU KNOW. I'M STARTIN TO
THROW ON MY BRAKES, AND THE TRUCK SMASHES INTO THIS
BIG SIGN AND INTO THE PUMPS IN THE ESSO STATION
DOWN THERE ... I HEAR THIS CRASH ... AND THAT BIG
THING STARTS BURNIN' ... AND IT'S STILL MOVIN' ...
RIGHT THROUGH THE PUMP STAND AND ON INTO THE STA-
TION ... AND I'M STOPPED, STOCK STILL ... AND I SEE
THEM THINGS ... AND THEY ALL STARTIN' TO BACK OFF ...
SOME OF 'EM RUNNIN' ... OR AT LEAST IT LOOKS LIKE
THEY'RE RUNNIN', BUT THEY MOVE KINDA LIKE THEY'RE
CRIPPLED ... BUT THEY KEEP BACKIN OFF ... AND IT'S

LIKE ... IT'S LIKE THEY GOTTA GET AWAY FROM THE
FIRE ... AND THE GUY DRIVIN' THE TRUCK CAN'T GET OUT
NOHOW ... HE GOT THE CAB OF THE TRUCK PLOWED
HALFWAY INTO THE WALL OF THE STATION ... THAT
THING'S FRYIN' HIM IN THERE AND HE'S SCREAMIN' ...
SCREAMIN' LIKE HELL ...

Barbara's eyes deepen and her face wrinkles in anxiety. The continuing nightmare grows more and more complex. The man swats the last leg from the table, and the table-top starts to drop. He regains control of it and struggles, trying to move it into the next room. Barbara automatically moves to his assistance and they walk together, each burdened by the heavy table.

TRUCKDRIVER: I DON'T KNOW WHAT'S GONNA HAPPEN, YOU KNOW? I
MEAN ... I DON'T KNOW WHAT THE WHOLE PLACE GONNA
EXPLODE ... OR FLY TO PIECES ... OR WHAT'S GONNA
HAPPEN ... I START DRIVIN' FOR THE GAS STATION ...
AND ... AND THE CAT IN THE TRUCK IS SCREAMIN' AND
SCREAMIN' ... AND AFTER A WHILE HE JUST STOPS ...

The man sets down his end of the table, and wipes beads of sweat from his forehead. His breathing is still heavy from his previous exertion. He wipes his hand on his shirt. His eyes are wide and angry ... it almost seems as though he might weep.

TRUCKDRIVER: ... AND THERE'S THEM THINGS STAND IN'BACK ...'CROSS
THE ROAD ... STANDIN' LOOKIN' LIKE ... LOOKIN'
LIKE ... LIKE THEY JUST COME BACK FROM THE GRAVE OR
SOMETHIN' ... AND THEY'RE OVER BY THE DINER ... AND
THERE'S CARS AND BUSES IN THE DINER LOT, AND LOTS OF
WINDOWS IS SMASHED. AND IT'S FOR SURE THEM THINGS
DONE THE PEOPLE IN THE DINER IN ... AND MORE IS OUT-
SIDE, ALL OVER THE PLACE, JUST BIDIN' THEIR TIME FOR
A CHANCE TO MOVE IN. SO I START MY TRUCK UP, AND I
BARREL IT RIGHT AT SOME OF THEM THINGS ... I'M
STEAMIN' DOWN RIGHT ON 'EM ... (His face grows more

intense with the memory) AND I GET A GOOD LOOK AT
'EM ... I SEE THEM FOR THE FIRST TIME IN MY LIGHTS ...
AND THEN ... I JUST RUN RIGHT DOWN ON 'EM ... I JUST
GRIND DOWN DOWN HARD AS I CAN ... AND I KNOCK A COU-
PLE OF 'EM ABOUT FIFTY FEET, FLAILIN' INTO THE
AIR ... AND I JUST WANT TO SMASH THEM ... CRUSH THEM
FILTHY THINGS. AND THEY'RE JUST STANDIN' THERE.
THEY AIN'T RUNNIN'. THEY AIN'T EVEN TRYIN' TO GET
OUTA THE ROAD. SOME OF EM IS EVEN REACHIN' OUT, AS
IF THEY CAN GRAB ME. BUT THEY'RE JUST STANDIN'
THERE, AND THE TRUCK IS RUNNIN' THEM DOWN ... LIKE
THEY WAS BUGS OR SOMETHING' ... THEY ...

Barbara is wide-eyed, staring in disgust, her hands
still clutched to the table-top. She says nothing.
The man sees her fear and stops himself.

TRUCKDRIVER: ... I ... I'M ...

He refocuses his attention on the table-top, and
starts to lift it again. Barbara is practically motionless. As he tugs the table, her hands fall away
and she slowly pulls them against herself. He drags
the table away from her, and she walks numbly behind,
having forgotten to assist. She just watches the
man's face.

TRUCKDRIVER: ... I'M JUST ... I GOT KIDS, YOU KNOW ... AND ... I
GUESS THEY'LL DO ALL RIGHT ... THEY CAN TAKE CARE OF
THEMSELVES ... BUT THEY'RE STILL ONLY KIDS ... AND
I'M BEIN' AWAY AND ALL ... AND ...

Perspiring heavily, he tugs the twists at the table-
top, trying to fit it through the doorframe and into
the living-room.

TRUCKDRIVER: I'M JUST GONNA DO WHAT I CAN ... AND I'M GONNA GET
BACK ... AND I'M GONNA SEE MY PEOPLE ... AND THINGS
IS GONNA BE ALL RIGHT ... AND ... I'M GONNA GET
BACK ...

He has started to almost babble ... he sees the girl
intently watching him, and he stops. He composes

himself with some effort, and starts to speak a little
more slowly. His voice is almost a monotone, with enforced calm, but he does, beneath his anger, seem as
confident as could be expected of anyone under the
circumstances.

TRUCKDRIVER: NOW. YOU AND ME IS GONNA BE ALL RIGHT, TOO. WE <u>CAN</u>
HOLD THEM THINGS OFF. I MEAN ... YOU CAN JUST ...
JUST SMASH 'EM. ALL YOU GOT TO DO IS JUST KEEP YOUR
HEAD AND DON'T BE TOO AFRAID. WE CAN MOVE FASTER
THAN THEY CAN, AND THEY'RE AWFUL WEAK ... AND IF YOU
DON'T RUN AND JUST KEEP SWINGIN' ... YOU CAN SMASH
'EM. WE'RE SMARTER 'N THEY ARE. AND WE'RE STRONGER
'N THEY ARE. WE'RE GONNA STOP 'EM. OKAY?

The girl stares.

TRUCKDRIVER: "ALL WE GOT TO DO IS JUST KEEP OUR HEADS."

They look at each other for a moment, until the big
man turns and picks up the table again. As he starts
away with it, the girl speaks, quietly and weakly ...

BARBARA: "WHO ARE THEY?"

The man stops in his tracks, still supporting the
heavy table-top and looks with amazement at Barbara's anxious face. Slowly, it dawns on him that the
girl has never really been aware of the thing that
has been happening. She had not heard the radio announcements, the bulletins ... she had been existing
in a state of uninformed shock.

TRUCKDRIVER: (incredulously): "YOU AIN'T HEARD <u>NOTHIN'</u>?"

She stares blankly, silently, her eyes fastening on
his. Her reply is in her silence.

TRUCKDRIVER: "YOU MEAN YOU AIN'T GOT NO IDEA ABOUT WHAT'S GOIN'
ON HERE?"

Barbara starts to nod her answer ... she begins to
tremble ...

BARBARA: "... I ... I"

Her trembling increases, she begins to shake violently, and suddenly she flings up her arms and flails

them about, sobbing wildly ... she begins to walk in panic, wildly and aimlessly, in circles about the room ...

BARBARA: "NO ... NO ... NO ... NO ... I ... I CAN'T ... WHAT'S HAPPENING ... WHAT'S HAPPENING TO US ... WHY ... WHAT'S HAPPENING ... TELL ME ... TELL ... ME ..."

The man grabs her, shakes her to bring her out of it, and her sobbing jerks to a halt, but she remains staring ... right through him, her eyes seemingly focused beyond him, at some far distant point ... her speech, still nearly hysterical, becomes a little more coherent ...

BARBARA: "WE WERE IN THE CEMETERY ... ME ... AND JOHNNIE ... MY BROTHER, JOHNNIE ... WE BROUGHT FLOWERS FOR ... THIS ... MAN ... CAME AFTER ME ... AND JOHNNIE ... HE ... HE FOUGHT ... AND NOW ... HE ... HE'S ..."

TRUCKDRIVER: "... AWRIGHT ... ALL RIGHT!"

He tightens his grip. She wrenches against him.

BARBARA: "GET YOUR HANDS OFF ME!"

She flings herself away from him, beating him across the chest, taking him by surprise. But in her momentum, she stumbles over an end table, barely regains her balance, and stands facing the front door ... poised as if to run out into the night ...

BARBARA: "WE'VE GOT TO HELP HIM ... GOT TO GET JOHNNIE ... WE'VE GOT TO GO OUT AND FIND HIM ... BRING HIM ..."

She comes toward the man, pleading with tears, the desperate tears of a frightened child ...

BARBARA: "... BRING HIM HERE ... WE'LL BE SAFE ... WE CAN HELP HIM ... WE ..."

The man steps toward her. She backs away, holding one hand toward him defensively, and the other toward her mouth ...

BARBARA: "NO ... NO ... PLEASE ... <u>PLEASE</u> ... WE'VE GOT TO ... WE ..."

He takes one deliberate stride for her.

TRUCKDRIVER: "NOW ... NOW YOU CALM DOWN ... YOU'RE SAFE HERE ...
NOW WE CAN'T TAKE NO CHANCES ..."

BARBARA: "WE'VE GOT TO GET JOHNNIE ..."

TRUCKDRIVER: "NOW ... COME ON, NOW ... YOU SETTLE DOWN ... YOU
DON'T KNOW WHAT THESE THINGS ARE ... IT AIN'T LIKE
NO SUNDAY SCHOOL OUT THERE ..."

BARBARA: "PLEASE ... PLEEEEESE ... NO ... NO ... NO ..."

She is sobbing, violently ... her words become
screams. She is verging toward complete hysteria.
The man struggles to calm her, she wrenches from
him--but his grip remains, so that her arms jerk her
whole body in the act of wrenching away. She stares
at the man, their eyes meet in an instant of calm ...
but only an instant, before she screams ... she kicks
him again and again, as he struggles to pin her arms
at her sides and shove her against a wall. At the
same time, he does not want to hurt her. With brute
force, he shoves her backwards, propelling her into a
soft chair ... but she is up again, screaming and
slapping at his face. He is forced to grab her again,
and practically slam her into a corner. He brings up
one powerful fist and punches the girl ... but her
head recoils and the blow is misplaced, it does not
put her out of commission. But it shocks her into
dumb, wounded silence. He hits her again,
squarely ... her eyes fall sorrowfully on his and she
begins to crumple ... she falls limp against him, as
he supports her weight, easing her into his arms.
Holding her, he looks dumbly about the room. His eyes
fall on the sofa. He does not carry, but almost walks
her to the sofa, permits her dead weight to fold onto
it, and eases her head onto a cushion.

Next to the couch is a cabinet-radio. The man stabs
at a button, clicking it on; while the radio warms up,
he looks around for the tin of nails, finds it where
Barbara had dropped it, takes nails and slides them

into his pocket. The radio hisses and crackles with static. He returns to it and searches with the tuning dial. At first, just static ... then it spins past what sounds like a voice, and he adjusts carefully, trying to find the spot. The tuner finds a metallic, monotone voice ...

VOICE: "... ERGENCY RADIO NETWORK. NORMAL BROADCAST FACILITIES HAVE BEEN TEMPORARILY DISCONTINUED. STAY TUNED TO THIS WAVE LENGTH FOR EMERGENCY INFORMATION. YOUR LAW ENFORCEMENT AGENCIES URGE YOU TO REMAIN IN YOUR HOMES. KEEP ALL DOORS AND WINDOWS LOCKED OR BOARDED SHUT. USE ALL FOOD, WATER AND MEDICAL SUPPLIES SPARINGLY. CIVIL DEFENSE FORCES ARE ATTEMPTING TO GAIN CONTROL OF THE SITUATION. STAY NEAR YOUR RADIO, AND REMAIN TUNED TO THIS FREQUENCY. DO NOT USE YOUR AUTOMOBILE. REMAIN IN YOUR HOMES. KEEP ALL DOORS AND WINDOWS LOCKED."
A long pause. A crackle. The message repeats. It is obviously a recording.

VOICE: "OUR LIVE BROADCASTERS WILL CONVEY INFORMATION AS RECEIVED FROM CIVIL DEFENSE HEADQUARTERS. THIS IS YOUR CIVIL DEFENSE EMERGENCY RADIO NETWORK. NORMAL BROADCAST FACILITIES HAVE BEEN TEMPORARILY DISCONTINUED. STAY TUNED TO THIS WAVE LENGTH ..."
The big man waves his hand in disgust--at the repetition of the radio--and moves away as it continues its announcement. He resumes his efforts with the heavy wooden tabletop; this time he drags it to the livingroom window. He leans it against the wall and pulls back the curtain to peer outside. There are now four figures standing in the yard. The voice of the distant radio recording continues. The figures stand very still, their arms dangling, aspects of their silhouettes revealing tattered clothing or shaggy hair. They are cold, dead things. Something in the distance suddenly startles the truckdriver.

From across the road, a figure is moving toward the
house. The man spins himself away from the door and
rushes to the fireplace. He reaches for his matches.
In the little stand near the couch, where Barbara lies
unconscious, there are old magazines. The man grabs
them, rips pages loose, and crumples them into the
fireplace. He piles kindling wood and larger logs,
then touches the paper with a lighted match and a
small fire takes hold. There is charcoal-light on the
mantle. He sprays the glowing fire and it whooshes
into a larger blaze, almost singeing the big man's
face as he works. The larger logs begin to burn. He
returas to the window. The recorded message repeats
itself continously. The man hoists the table-top to
the window-sill, and braces it there while he places a
nail in position. He pounds with the jack-handle ...
driven by desperation ... another nail ... and another. With the table secure, he checks it hastily
and practically leaps to another window, where he
can peer out between its nailed-up boards.
The new figure is just reaching the place where the
others stand silently. The man rushes to the fire,
where the biggest logs have now begun to blaze. He
seizes the discarded table-legs and saturates them
with charcoal-light, then holds their largest ends
into the fire until he has two good flaming torches.
Then, a torch in each hand, he moves toward the door
again. He nudges a big padded armchair ahead of him
to the door and, taking both torches in one hand,
pulls the curtain aside for another look at the yard.
The figures still stand silently.
With charcoal-light, he drenches the padded armchair
and touches it with a torch. It catches instantly,
and flames lick and climb, casting flickering light
throughout the house. The heat on the man is severe,
but he has to fight it. He lunges for the door, un-

bolting it, and flinging it wide open.

From the yard, as the door bangs open, the flaming chair is visible. It throws eerie, irregular illumination onto the lawn. The waiting figures step back slightly.

The man shoves the chair through the doorway; it slides across the front porch. It topples over the edge, and the flaming bulk tumbles down the steps onto the front lawn. In the rolling motion, flames lick and fly, and small particles of the chair's stuffing leap and glow in the night wind. The bonfire rages in the tall grass. The waiting figures back further away.

Inside the house, the front door bangs shut, and the man fastens the bolt. He hurries again to window, puts more nails into the table-top, fastening it securely, then surveys his surroundings, seeking out possible vulnerability. (The camera moves with him seeing the task that lies ahead.) There is a side window in the living room, a window in the dining room at the other side of the house, the front door and the flanking glass panels.

He turns, still inspecting, and his eyes reflect startlement.

The girl is sitting up on the couch. Her demeanor is startling (as we cut to her). Her face is bruised, and she sits in silence staring at the floor. The radio drones on. The fire plays on her face, and reflects in her eyes. The man takes off his jacket and moves toward her. He fixes his jacket over her shoulders and looks sympathetically into her face. She just stares at the floor. The man feels dumb and helpless. Forlornly, he moves to the pile of lumber, chooses a table-board, and goes to the side window. The radio voice continues ...

The truckdriver boards up the two side windows, then

moves to the front door. He gets an ironing board,
and places it across the door horizontally; it extends
over the flanking glass panels leaving cracks at the
top and bottom, but they are too small for anything to
get through. He drives nails through the board into
the moulding and tests the barricade for strength;
finding it sufficient, he leaves it and goes on to the
next. In the dining-room there are two closed doors.
He tries one, finds it locked, examines it and finds
no latch; it has been apparently locked with a skeleton key. The other door is unlocked and leads into a
den, which contains several windows. The man is disappointed at the added vulnerability; he thinks for a
moment, then leaves the room, shutting the door behind him. It is clear that he has decided to board up
the door rather than try to secure the bay windows.
He checks his remaining lumber; the supply is dwindling; but he selects the best piece for boarding the
den door. He is about to start hammering when an
idea strikes him--he opens the door again and enters
the room. There are chairs, a desk, a bureau ... he
steps to the desk and starts to rummage through the
drawers. He pulls out paper, a stack of pencils and
pens, a compass--a hundred little odds and ends. Another drawer ... a hundred more things ... he leaves
it open. The bureau contains mostly clothing; he rips
out the big drawers and hurls them through the doorway and into the dining area. One drawer ... two ...
their contents spilling onto the floor ... he looks
beck at the bureau ... a final idea hits him. He
shoves the great piece of furniture through the door,
walking it through the tight opening until it clears
the doorway. Then the desk, which warrants another
struggle, as the man attempts to secure all things of
possible value before he finally nails the door shut.
In the closet, there is a lot of old clothing; the man

finds a good warm coat and jacket and flings them over his shoulder. High on the shelves are piles of old boxes, suitcases, hatboxes, an old umbrella. He looks for an instant, debating their worth, or the possible worth of what they might contain. At his feet, he sees still more clutter: boxes, umbrellas, dust, shoes and slippers. He picks up a pair of ladies' flats, and examines them, thinking of the barefoot girl out on the couch, and tucks them under his arm. As he pulls away, something catches his eye ... within the dark recess of the closet, something shiny: the sheen of a finished piece of wood, a familiar shape, lying under a pile of dirty clothing. He reaches eagerly, and his hand finds what he had hoped: a rifle. He sets everything down and rummages even more eagerly all over the floor of the closet ... through shoe boxes, under things, items come flying out of the closet. A shoe box contains old letters and postcards. But, in a cigar box, clattering around with pipe cleaners and cleaning fluid, there is a maintenance manual and a box of ammunition. He flips open the box and finds it half full. He shoves manual and cartridges into his pocket, then decides to take the whole cigar box full of material; he tucks it under an arm, gathers jackets and shoes, and leaves the room.

In the dining room, he drops the load of supplies on the bureau, and the sight of the girl in the living room stops him short. She is sitting as before, not moving.

TRUCKDRIVER: "WE'RE ALL RIGHT NOW ... THIS PLACE IS GOOD AND SOLID. AND I FOUND US A GUN--A GUN AND SOME BUL-LETS."

He looks at Barbara from across the room. She doesn't seem to take any note of his talking. He turns to his work, but continues to speak ...

TRUCKDRIVER: "SO, WE GOT US A RADIO ... AND SOONER OR LATER SOME-
BODY'LL COME AND GET US OUTTA HERE ... WE GOT FOOD
IN THERE ..." (he starts to board up the door to the
den) "OH ... AND I GOT YOU SOME SHOES ... WE'LL SEE IN
A MINUTE IF THEY FIT ... AND SOME WARM CLOTHES FOR
YOU ..."

He pounds at the nails. The pounding and the repetition of the radio message are the only sounds. The
last nail in, the check for sturdiness, the big man
turns toward the girl again ...

RADIO VOICE: "... ERNMENT TO STAY IN YOUR HOMES. KEEP ALL DOORS
AND WINDOWS LOCKED ..."

Other than her upright position, the girl shows no
sign of life. Her wide eyes just stare through the
floor at some point beyond.

RADIO VOICE: "... PREFERABLY BOARDED SHUT ..."

TRUCKDRIVER: "WELL, THAT'S US ... WE'RE DOIN' ALL RIGHT ..."

He can't smile, and with the girl not looking at him
his attempt is half-hearted. He takes up the rifle,
the cigar-box, a coat and her shoes in one clumsy
armful. (As he leaves the frame, the camera lingers
for an instant. The alcove in the dining area is
cluttered with things from the den, the large pieces
of furniture obscuring the door that had been tried
and found locked; the camera lingers long enough to
make this door significant.) The man kneels with his
bundle in front of the girl; then drops the armful of
materials at her feet. He holds the shoes that he
found in the closet.

TRUCKDRIVER: "NOW, LET'S SEE ... HOW BIG YOUR FEET IS ..."

Looking up at her, he is unable to cope with her cata-
tonia. Her stillness makes him as gentle as he can
be, but he converses with her, still expecting her to
reply and react. She does not.

TRUCKDRIVER: "COME ON ..."

He holds one of the shoes near her foot, waiting for

her to lift her leg and slip into the shoe. She is
still. Finally, the man takes one of her ankles and
fumbles to put the shoe on her foot. It does not go on
easily, partly because it is too small, but mostly because of her limpness, but he gets it on, sets her foot
down and takes up the other one. He succeeds in getting the second shoe on, and leans back on his
haunches looking up at her. She is staring at her
feet.

TRUCKDRIVER: "WELL ... THAT'S ER ... THAT'S A REAL CINDERELLA
STORY, AIN'T IT?"
No response. The man reaches in reflex for his
jacket pocket, but he has given Barbara his jacket.

TRUCKDRIVER: "HEY ... YOU KNOW YOU GOT MY CIGARETTES."
He tries to smile again. Still no reaction. He
reaches toward her and his hand enters the pocket of
the jacket he has draped over her shoulders. His action makes the girl look directly at him, and her
stare makes him uncomfortable.

TRUCKDRIVER: "YOU GOT MY CIGARETTES."
He tries a gentler tone, as one would try to explain
some complex concept to a child. He pulls the cigarettes from the pocket and settles back from her
again. He fumbles for a cigarette, puts it in his
mouth and lights it, trying not to look at the girl.
Her gaze is still fixed on his face.

TRUCKDRIVER: (inhaling the first puff of smoke and blowing it
through his nose) "OK ... NOW ... MAYBE YOU OUGHT TO
LIE DOWN, YOU ..." (fumbling with the cigarette, a
thought occurs to him and he tries it) "YOU SMOKE?"
He holds up the burning cigarette. Her stare drops
from him back to the floor. He takes another drag
and blows the smoke out quickly. Another idea ...

TRUCKDRIVER: MAYBE YOU ..." (he stops, he is getting Nowhere, he decides that his time had better be spent in securing
the defenses of the old house) "OKAY."

His okay is more definite than his other talk, and he
scoops up the rifle and ammunition. He examines the
gun, dumps the shells onto the floor and methodically
loads them, one at a time.

TRUCKDRIVER: "NOW, I DON'T KNOW IF YOU'RE HEARIN' ME OR NOT ... OR
IF YOU'RE OUT OR SOMETHIN' ... BUT I'M GOIN' UPSTAIRS
NOW ... OKAY? ... NOW, WE'RE SAFE DOWN HERE. AIN'T
NOTHIN' GETTIN' IN HERE ... AT LEAST NOT EASY ... I
MEAN, THEY MIGHT BE ABLE TO BUST THROUGH THAT, BUT
IT'S GONNA BE SOME SWEAT, AND I COULD HEAR 'EM, AND I
THINK I COULD KEEP 'EM OUT. LATER ON, I'M GONNA FIX
THINGS GOOD, SO THEY CAN'T GET IN NOHOW ... BUT IT'S
GOOD FOR THE TIME BEIN' ... YOU'RE OKAY HERE ..."

He continues to load the rifle as he speaks, his cigarette dangling from his lip, causing him to squint
from the smoke that curls around his eyes.

TRUCKDRIVER: "NOW THE UPSTAIRS IS THE ONLY OTHER WAY SOMETHIN'
CAN GET IN HERE, SO I'M GONNA GO UP 'N FIX THAT ..."

He snaps the clip after the last shell, and is about to
stand when his glance falls on the girl again and he
tries to get through one last time ...

TRUCKDRIVER: "OKAY? YOU GONNA BE ALL RIGHT?"

She remains silent. The man stands, tucks the rifle
under his arm, grabs as much lumber as he can carry,
and starts for the stairs. The girl looks up at him,
and he is aware of it, but he keeps moving, and her
stare follows.

TRUCKDRIVER: "I'M GONNA BE RIGHT HERE. YOU'RE ALL RIGHT NOW. I'M
RIGHT HERE, UPSTAIRS."

He starts up the stairs. At the top of the landing he
is confronted once again with the body that lies
there torn and defaced. He sets down his supplies,
and the sight of the corpse is repulsive and he tries
not to look at it. The body is lying half across a
blood-soaked throw-rug, and a few feet away is another throw-rug, with oriental patterns and a fringe

sewn around its edge. The man grabs the second rug
and rips away one edge of the fringe. Once the initial tear is made, the rest of the fringe peels away
easily. He frees it and, taking the rifle, ties one
end of the fringe around the barrel and the other
around the narrow part of the stock, This done, he
slings the rifle over his shoulder. Then he leans
over the corpse and takes hold of one end of the rug
on which it lies, and begins dragging it across the
floor. On the landing is a long corridor with several
closed doors. He deposits the ugly load at one of the
doorways and throws open the door; inside is a bedroom. He tries the other doors and finds two more
bedrooms, one a child's room. He begins to remove
furniture into the hallway; his plan is to afterwards
board up the doors. The noise of his work fills the
old house ...

Downstairs, Barbara still sits dazed on the couch.
The fire flickers on her face, and the burning wood
pops loudly now and again. Objects in the room are
silhouetted and the atmosphere is stark. (The camera
moves slowly in to her face.)

RADIO VOICE: "... FACILITIES HAVE BEEN INSTRUCTED TO DISCONTINUE
PROGRAMMING. STAY TUNED TO THIS ..."

There is a sudden buzzing sound and crackling
static. Then, a hodgepodge of newsroom sounds (as
heard earlier by John on the car radio): typewriters,
ticker-tape machines, low voices talking in the background. The sound holds for a long while. The girl
does not seem to notice.

ANNOUNCER: "... ER ... LADIES AND GENTLEMEN ... WHAT? ... YEAH,
YEAH ... LA ... WHAT? YEAH, I GOT THAT ONE ...
WHAT? ... ANOTHER ONE? ... PUT IT THROUGH CEN-
TRAL ... OKAY, CHARLIE, I'M ON THE AIR NOW ...
YEAH ..." (the confusion of the broadcast headquar-
ters) "... LADIES AND GENTLEMEN, THE LATEST FROM

EMERGENCY CENTRAL ..." (the voice sounds tired, but the man is able to read his reports unemotionally, with the air of a professional commentator who has been covering a major event for forty-eight hours and is no longer impressed with the latest developments) "UP TO THE MINUTE REPORTS INFORM US THAT THE ... SIEGE ... FIRST DOCUMENTED IN THE MIDWESTERN SECTION OF THE COUNTRY IS INDEED SPREAD ACROSS THE NATION, AND IS IN FACT WORLDWIDE. MEDICAL AND SCIENTIFIC ADVISORS HAVE BEEN SUMMONED TO THE WHITE HOUSE, AND REPORTERS ON THE SCENE IN WASHINGTON INFORM US THAT THE PRESIDENT IS PLANNING TO MAKE PUBLIC THE RESULTS OF THAT CONFERENCE IN AN ADDRESS TO THE NATION OVER YOUR CIVIL DEFENSE EMERGENCY NETWORK."

(A long pause by the announcer. The camera studies Barbara's face. She is inert.)

ANNOUNCER: THE ... STRANGE ... BEINGS, THAT HAVE APPEARED IN MOST PARTS OF THE NATION, SEEM TO HAVE CERTAIN PREDICTABLE PATTERNS OF BEHAVIOR. IN THE FEW HOURS FOLLOWING INITIAL REPORTS OF VIOLENCE AND DEATH ... AND APPARENTLY DERANGED ATTACKS ON THE LIVES OF PEOPLE TAKEN COMPLETELY OFF GUARD, IT HAS BEEN ESTABLISHED THAT THE ... ALIEN BEINGS ARE HUMAN IN MANY PHYSICAL AND BEHAVIORAL ASPECTS. HYPOTHESES AS TO THEIR ORIGIN AND THEIR AIMS HAVE TO THIS POINT BEEN SO VARIED AND SO DIVERSE THAT WE MUST ONLY REPORT THESE FACTORS TO BE UNKNOWN. TEAMS OF SCIENTISTS AND PHYSICIANS PRESENTLY HAVE THE CORPSES OF SEVERAL OF THE ... AGGRESSORS, AND THESE CORPSES ARE BEING STUDIED FOR CLUES THAT MIGHT NEGATE OR CONFIRM EXISTING THEORIES. THE MOST ... OVERWHELMING FACT ... IS THAT THESE ... BEINGS ARE INFILTRATING THROUGH URBAN AND RURAL AREAS THROUGHOUT THE NATION, IN FORCES OF VARYING NUMBER, AND IF THEY HAVE NOT AS YET EVIDENCED THEM-

SELVES IN YOUR AREA, PLEASE ... TAKE EVERY AVAIL-
ABLE PRECAUTION. ATTACK MAY COME AT ANY TIME, IN
ANY PLACE, WITHOUT WARNING.

ANNOUNCER: REPEATING THE IMPORTANT FACTS FROM OUR PREVIOUS
REPORTS. THERE IS AN ... AGGRESSIVE FORCE ...
ARMY ... OF UNEXPLAINED, UNIDENTIFIED ... HUMANOID
BEINGS ... THAT HAS APPEARED ... IN WORLDWIDE PRO-
PORTIONS ... AND THESE BEINGS ARE TOTALLY AGGRES-
SIVE ... IRRATIONAL IN THEIR VIOLENCE ... CIVIL
DEFENSE EFFORTS ARE UNDERWAY ... AND INVESTIGA-
TIONS AS TO THE ORIGIN AND PURPOSE OF THE AGGRES-
SORS ARE BEING CONDUCTED. ALL CITIZENS ARE URGED
TO TAKE UTMOST PRECAUTIONARY MEASURES TO DEFEND
AGAINST THE ... INSIDIOUS ... ALIEN ... FORCE ...

THESE BEINGS ARE WEAK IN PHYSICAL STRENGTH ...
ARE EASILY DISTINGUISHABLE FROM HUMANS BY THEIR
DEFORMED APPEARANCE ... THEY ARE USUALLY UNARMED
BUT APPEAR CAPABLE OF HANDLING WEAPONS ... THEY
HAVE APPEARED, NOT LIKE AN ORGANIZED ARMY, NOT WITH
ANY APPARENT REASON OR PLAN ... INDEED, THEY SEEM
TO BE DRIVEN WITH THE URGES OF ENTRANCED ... OR ...
OR OBSESSED MINDS. THEY APPEAR TOTALLY
UNTHINKING ... THEY CAN ... I REPEAT: <u>THEY CAN BE
STOPPED BY IMMOBILIZATION</u>; THAT IS, BY BLINDING OR
DISMEMBERING. THEY ARE, ON THE AVERAGE, WEAKER IN
STRENGTH THAN AN ADULT HUMAN, BUT THEIR STRENGTH
IS IN NUMBERS, IN SURPRISE, AND IN THE SHEER FACT
THAT THEY ARE BEYOND OUR NORMAL REALM OF UNDER-
STANDING. THEY APPEAR TO BE IRRATIONAL, NON-
COMMUNICATIVE BEINGS ... AND THEY ARE DEFINITELY TO
BE CONSIDERED OUR ENEMIES IN WHAT WE MUST CALL A
STATE OF ... NATIONAL EMERGENCY. IF ENCOUNTERED,
THEY ARE TO BE AVOIDED OR DESTROYED. UNDER NO CIR-
CUMSTANCES SHOULD YOU ALLOW YOURSELVES OR YOUR
FAMILIES TO BE ALONE OR UNGUARDED WHILE THIS MEN-
ACE PREVAILS. THESE BEINGS ARE FLESH-EATERS. THE

PRINCIPAL CHARACTERISTIC OF THEIR ONSLAUGHT IS
THEIR DEPRAVED, IRRATIONAL QUEST FOR ... HUMAN
FLESH ...

At this, Barbara bolts from the couch in wild, screaming hysteria. She runs blindly toward the front
door. The truckdriver appears at the top of the
stairs. Startled, unslinging the gun, he leaps down
the stairs. The girl is clawing at the barricade, trying to break out of the house, she is sobbing in wild
desperation. The man is almost upon her, but she
writhes out of his reach, runs across the room--to-
ward the maze of heaped-up furniture. Suddenly,
from within the maze, strong hands grab her. She
screams in terror. The truckdriver rushes toward
her, and he is startled by the sight of the other man,
who is trying to contain the hysterical girl. Behind
him, an older man stands holding a length of pipe at
his side. They have come through the door that the
truckdriver had tried and found locked. The man
holding Barbara is dressed in coveralls; he is probably a farmer, he is big and powerful-looking.

TOM: (Still trying to calm the girl) IT'S ALL RIGHT ...
WE'RE FROM THE GAS STATION ... WE'RE NOT ...

Barbara sags against him and sobs sporadically, in
shock and semi-relief; she is still nearly catatonic.
The older man rushes to the radio. The truckdriver
just stares dumbly as Tom calms the girl and leads
her to a chair where she sits very still, numb with
expended emotion. The radio voice continues with its
information about the emergency. The older man,
Harry Tinsdale, crouches close to the radio, still
holding his length of pipe.

HARRY: LISTEN.

RADIO VOICE: ... PERIODIC REPORTS, AS INFORMATION REACHES THIS
NEWSROOM, AS WELL AS SURVIVAL INFORMATION AND A
LISTING OF RED CROSS RESCUE POINTS, WHERE PICK-UPS

WILL BE MADE AS OFTEN AS POSSIBLE WITH THE EQUIP-
MENT AND STAFF PRESENTLY AVAILABLE ...

The big truckdriver stands staring at the two NEW
men. He exudes an air of resentment, as though the
strangers have intruded on his private little
fortress.

TRUCKDRIVER: ... WHY ... MAN, I ...

TOM: LOOKS LIKE YOU GOT THINGS PRETTY WELL LOCKED IN.

TRUCKDRIVER: (almost in an aggressive tone) MAN, I COULD'VE USED
SOME HELP. HOW LONG YOU GUYS BEEN IN THERE?

HARRY: THAT'S THE CELLAR ... IT'S THE SAFEST PLACE.

TRUCKDRIVER: MAN, YOU MEAN YOU DIDN'T HEAR THE RACKET WE WAS
MAKIN' UP HERE?

HARRY: HOW WERE WE SUPPOSED TO KNOW WHAT WAS GOING ON UP
HERE? IT COULD HAVE BEEN THOSE THINGS, FOR ALL WE
KNOW.

TRUCKDRIVER: THAT GIRL WAS SCREAMIN'. NOW, YOU KNOW WHAT A GIRL
SOUNDS LIKE. THEM THINGS DON'T MAKE NO NOISE. ANY-
BODY'S GOT TO KNOW THERE'S SOMEBODY UP HERE COULD
USE SOME HELP.

TOM: YOU CAN'T REALLY TELL WHAT'S GOIN' ON FROM DOWN
THERE ...

HARRY: WE THOUGHT WE COULD HEAR SCREAMS, BUT THAT MIGHT
HAVE MEANT ... THOSE THINGS WERE IN THE HOUSE AFTER
HER.

TRUCKDRIVER: AND YOU WOULDN'T COME UP 'N HELP?

TOM: (a little shamed) ... WELL, I ... IF ... THERE WAS MORE
OF US ...

HARRY: THAT RACKET SOUNDED LIKE THE PLACE WAS BEING
RIPPED APART ... HOW WERE WE SUPPOSED ...

TRUCKDRIVER: YOU JUST SAID IT WAS HARD TO HEAR DOWN THERE. NOW
YOU SAY IT SOUNDED LIKE THE PLACE WAS BEING RIPPED
APART. YOU BETTER GET YOUR STORY STRAIGHT,
MISTER ...

HARRY: ALL RIGHT! NOW YOU TELL ME. I'M NOT GOING TO TAKE
THOSE KIND OF CHANCES WHEN WE GOT A SAFE PLACE ...

WE LUCK INTO A SAFE PLACE, AND YOU'RE TELLIN' US TO
RISK OUR LIVES JUST BECAUSE SOMEBODY NEEDS HELP ...

TRUCKDRIVER: SOMETHIN' LIKE THAT, YEAH.

TOM: (not knowing whose side to take) ALL RIGHT ... WHY
DON'T WE SETTLE ...

HARRY: (Ignoring everything but his own line of thought)
LOOK, MISTER ... (He shouts this, then calms his voice
for the rest of the line) ALL RIGHT ... WE CAME UP,
OKAY? WE'RE HERE. NOW I SUGGEST WE ALL GO BACK
DOWNSTAIRS BEFORE ANY OF THESE THINGS FIND OUT
WE'RE IN HERE.

TRUCKDRIVER: THEY CAN'T GET IN HERE.

TOM: YOU GOT THE WHOLE PLACE BOARDED UP?

TRUCKDRIVER: (his attitude softer toward Tom) MOST OF IT. ALL BUT
UPSTAIRS ... IT'S WEAK IN PLACES, BUT IT WON'T BE
HARD TO FIX IT UP GOOD ...

HARRY: YOU'RE INSANE ... THE CELLARS THE SAFEST PLACE IN
THE HOUSE.

TRUCKDRIVER: (lashes out) I'M TELLIN' YOU THEY CAN'T GET IN HERE!

HARRY: AND I'M TELLIN YOU ... THOSE THINGS TURNED OVER OUR
CAR. WE WERE DAMNED LUCKY TO GET AWAY AT ALL. NOW
YOU TELL ME THEY CAN'T GET THROUGH A PILE OF WOOD.

TOM: HIS WIFE AND KID'S DOWNSTAIRS. THE KID'S PRETTY
BADLY TORE UP.

This statement takes the truckdriver completely by
surprise. His face softens, he exhales a deep breath.
Nobody says anything for a long moment. Finally, the
truckdriver swallows and makes his point again ...

TRUCKDRIVER: "WELL, I ... I THINK WE'RE BETTER OFF UP HERE."

TOM: (glancing about at the barricades): "WE COULD
STRENGTHEN ALL THESE UP, MR. TINSDALE."

TRUCKDRIVER: "MAN, WITH ALL US WORKIN' WE COULD FIX THIS UP SO
NOTHIN' CAN GET IN HERE ... AND WE GOT FOOD ... THE
FIRE ... AND WE GOT THE RADIO."

HARRY: "WE CAN BRING ALL THOSE THINGS DOWNSTAIRS WITH US.
MAN, YOU'RE CRAZY ... YOU GOT A MILLION WINDOWS UP

HERE ... ALL THESE WINDOWS, YOU'RE GONNA MAKE
STRONG ENOUGH TO KEEP THEM OUT?"

TRUCKDRIVER: "THEM THINGS AIN'T GOT NO STRENGTH, MAN, I SMASHED
THREE OF 'EM AND PUSHED ANOTHER ONE OUT THE DOOR."

HARRY: I'M TELLING YOU THEY TURNED OUR CAR ONTO ITS ROOF."

TRUCKDRIVER: "OH, HELL, ANY GOOD FIVE MEN CAN DO THAT."

HARRY: "THAT'S MY POINT! ... ONLY THERE'S NOT GOING TO BE
FIVE ... THERE'S NOT GOING TO BE TEN. TWENTY ...
THIRTY ... A HUNDRED, MAYBE ... YOU KNOW? ONCE THEY
KNOW WE'RE IN HERE, THE PLACE'LL BE CRAWLIN' WITH
'EM."

TRUCKDRIVER: "WELL, IF THERE'S THAT MANY, THEY'RE GONNA GET US
WHEREVER WE'RE AT."

HARRY: "LOOK, IN THE CELLAR, THERE'S ONLY ONE DOOR, ALL
RIGHT? ONLY ONE. THAT'S THE ONLY PLACE WE HAVE TO
PROTECT. AND TOM AND I FIXED IT SO IT LOCKS AND
BOARDS FROM THE INSIDE. BUT ALL THESE DOORS AND
WINDOWS ... WHY, WE'D NEVER KNOW WHERE THEY WERE
GOING TO HIT US NEXT."

TOM: "YOU GOT A POINT, MR. TINSDALE, BUT DOWN IN THE CEL-
LAR THERE'S NO PLACE TO RUN ... I MEAN, IF THEY DO
GET IN, THERE'S NO BACK EXIT. WE'D BE DONE FOR."

This stops Harry for an instant.

TOM: "WE COULD GET OUT OF HERE IF WE HAD TO ... AND WE
CAN SEE WHAT'S GOIN' ON OUTSIDE ... DOWN THERE,
THERE AIN'T ANY WINDOWS ... IF A RESCUE PARTY DOES
COME WE'D NEVER KNOW IT ... WINDOWS ..."

HARRY: "BUT THE CELLAR IS THE STRONGEST PLACE!"

TRUCKDRIVER: "THE UPSTAIRS IS JUST AS MUCH OF A TRAP AS THE CEL-
LAR ... THERE'S THREE ROOMS UP THERE, AND THEY HAVE
TO BE BOARDED UP LIKE THIS STUFF DOWN HERE ... THEN
IF THEY DO GET IN THE WINDOWS THEY CAN'T GET PAST
THE DOORS ... AND THEY'RE WEAK, WE CAN KEEP THEM
OUT. I GOT THIS GUN NOW, AND I DIDN'T HAVE IT BE-
FORE, AND I STILL BEAT THREE OF THEM OFF ... NOW, WE
MIGHT HAVE TO TRY AND GET OUT OF HERE OURSELVES,

'CAUSE THERE AIN'T NO GUARANTEE THAT ANYBODY IS
GONNA SEND HELP ... SUPPOSE THEM THINGS COME IN
HERE ... WE CAN'T BUST OUTTA THE CELLAR, CAUSE WE
OPEN THAT ONE DOOR AND THEY GOT US ..."

TOM: "I DON'T KNOW. I THINK HE'S RIGHT." (he turns to the
truckdriver) "YOU KNOW HOW MANY'S OUT THERE?"

TRUCKDRIVER: "I FIGURE MAYBE SIX, SEVEN."

HARRY: "LOOK, YOU TWO CAN DO WHATEVER YOU LIKE. I'M GOING
BACK DOWN TO THE CELLAR, AND YOU BETTER DECIDE, BE-
CAUSE I'M GONNA BOARD UP THAT DOOR AND I'M NOT
GONNA BE CRAZY ENOUGH TO UNLOCK IT AGAIN, NO MAT-
TER WHAT HAPPENS.

TOM: "WAIT A MINUTE, MR. TINSDALE, LET'S THINK ABOUT THIS
FOR AWHILE ..."

HARRY: "NOPE. I'VE MADE MY DECISION. YOU MAKE YOURS. AND
YOU CAN STEW IN YOUR OWN JUICE."

TOM: (flashing anger): "NOW WAIT A MINUTE DAMMIT LET'S
THINK ABOUT THIS AWHILE ... WE CAN MAKE IT INTO THE
CELLAR IF WE HAVE TO ... AND IF WE DO DECIDE TO STAY
DOWN THERE, WE WILL NEED SOME THINGS FROM UP
HERE ... NOW LET'S AT LEAST CONSIDER THIS
AWHILE ..."

TRUCKDRIVER: "MAN, IF YOU BOX YOURSELF INTO THAT CELLAR, AND IF
THERE IS A LOT OF THEM THINGS THAT GET INTO THE
HOUSE, YOU HAD IT. AT LEAST UP HERE YOU CAN OUTRUN
THE THINGS."

Tom has gone to one of the front windows and is peer-
ing out through an opening in the barricade.

TOM: "YEAH, LOOKS LIKE SIX ... OR ABOUT ... EIGHT ..."

His hand goes to his temple, and he rubs nervously,
his demeanor a little shaken. The truckdriver joins
him at the window.

TRUCKDRIVER: "THAT'S MORE THAN THERE WAS ... THERE'S A BUNCH OUT
THE BACK, TOO..." (he pivots to check the kitchen)
"... UNLESS THEY'RE THE SAME ONES THAT WAS BACK
HERE."

He bursts into the kitchen, as the fringed rifle sling snaps and the weapon starts to fall; he twists to keep it on his back, and tries to grab it, reaching behind. His attention on the gun, he does not see the door as he moves toward it ... he regains control of the gun and looks up--and stops cold. Hands reaching through broken glass behind the barricades ... graying, rotting hands, scratching, reaching, trying to grab ... and through aspects of the glass ... the inhuman faces behind the hands. The barrier is being strained, no doubt about that, but it is holding well enough.

The man smashes with the rifle butt against the ugly extremities ... pounding ... once, twice. One of the grabbing hands is driven back with a shattering of the already broken glass it was reching through. The rifle butt smashes one of the hands against the door moulding solidly ... but the hand, unfeeling of pain, continues to claw after a hold. The man slides his finger to the trigger, and turns the rifle, smashing the barrel through another of the little broken glass areas, and two of the gray hands sieze the protruding metal. A dead face appears behind the hands ... ugly ... expressionless. The man's face looks directly through the opening into the dead eyes beyond, the man struggling desperately to control the weapon and the zombie thing outside trying to pull it away by the barrel. A brief instant when the muzzle points directly at the hideous face ... BLAM ... the report shatters the air, the lifeless thing is thrown back, propelled by the blast, its head torn partially away, its still outstretched hands falling back with the crumpling body. The other hands continue to clutch and grab.

Tom has rushed into the kitchen, and Harry is standing cautiously a few feet from the doorway, still in

the dining area. A distant voice, that of Harry's
wife, suddenly begins to cry out from the cellar:

HELEN: "HARRY ... HARRY ... HARRY ... ARE YOU ALL RIGHT?"

HARRY: "IT'S ALL RIGHT, HELEN ... WE'RE ALL RIGHT ..."

Tom immediately rushes to the door. The truckdriver
is pounding at a hand that is trying to work at the
barricade from the bottom. The blows seem ineffectual, as the hand, oblivious except for the physical
jouncing about from impact, continues to grab. Tom
leaps against the door and grabs the rotting wrist
with both his hands, and tries to bend the wrist back
in an effort to break it, but it seems limp and almost
pliable. Disgust sweeps over the young man's face.
He tries to scrape the cold thing against the edge of
the broken glass, and the absence of blood is immediately evident as the sharp edge rips into what looks
like rotting flesh. Another hand grabs at Tom's
wrist and tries to pull it through the glass. Tom
yells, and the truckdriver tries to swing the barrel
of the gun toward the thing struggling with Tom; but
another hand clutches at him even as he is trying to
help the younger man. A hand is clawing and ripping
his shirt ... but he focuses his attention on aiming
the gun. Another loud blast, and the hands Tom was
fighting jerk back, and fall into darkness. Foot
against the wall, the big man forces himself away
from the door out of the grasp of the hand still
clutching his shirt. The shirt tears away, and the
thing backs off, still with the fragment in its hand.
Badly shaken, Tom just stares through another opening in the door. The truckdriver takes careful aim
and pulls the trigger again; the blast rips through
the thing's chest, leaving a gaping hole in its
back ... but it remains on its feet, backing slowly
away.

TOM: "OH ... GOOD GOD!"

Panicked at the failure of the weapon, the big man
levels off again ... another loud report. This time
the shell rips through the thing's thigh, just below
the pelvis. The thing still backs away, but as it
tries to put weight on its right leg it falls to a heap.
The two men just stare in disbelief. The thing is
still moving away, dragging itself with its arms and
pushing against the ground with its remaining useful
leg.

TOM: "MOTHER OF GOD ... WHAT ARE THESE THINGS?"

The truckdriver wets his lips, takes a deep breath
and holds it, carefully sights down the barrel of the
rifle again. He pulls the trigger. The shell seems to
blow open the skull of the crawling form, and it falls
backwards.

TRUCKDRIVER: "DAMN ... DAMN THING FROM HELL ..." (his voice trem-
bles as he lets out his held breath)

Outside, the thing that has fallen limply, without the
use of its eyes, moves its arms in groping, clutching
motions, seemingly still trying to drag itself away.

HELEN: (from the cellar) "HARRY ... HARRY! ..."

After a moment of silence, the truckdriver turns from
the door.

TRUCKDRIVER: "WE GOTTA FIX THESE BOARDS."

He starts to move to gather supplies, when Harry
speaks.

HARRY: "YOU'RE CRAZY ... THOSE THINGS ARE GONNA BE AT
EVERY DOOR AND WINDOW IN THE PLACE. WE'VE GOT TO
GET INTO THE CELLAR."

The big truckdriver turns to Harry with absolute fury
in his eyes. His voice is deeper in his rage, and more
commanding.

TRUCKDRIVER: "GO'HEAD INTO YOUR DAMN CELLAR! GET OUTTA HERE!"

The shouting stops Harry for an instant, then his
adamancy returns. He has decided that he will go
into the cellar without the others if need be and is

now prepared to gather his supplies.

HARRY: "I'M TAKING THE GIRL WITH ME."

He moves toward the refrigerator in the kitchen, but the big man steps in front of him.

TRUCKDRIVER: "YOU KEEP YOUR HANDS OFF OF HER, SHE'S STAYIN' HERE WITH ME."

Harry is stopped again for a moment. Then he moves toward the refrigerator again.

TRUCKDRIVER: "AND YOU DON'T TOUCH NONE OF THAT FOOD." (his grip is still on the gun, and though he doesn't point it at Harry, we are aware of the power it implies) "NOW IF I STAY UP HERE I'M GONNA BE FIGHTIN' FOR WHAT'S UP HERE ... AND THAT FOOD AND THAT RADIO AND ALL THIS IS WHAT I'M FIGHTIN' FOR. AND YOU ARE STONE DEAD WRONG ... YOU'RE JUST WRONG, YOU UNDERSTAND ... NOW, IF YOU'RE MAKIN' IT TO THE CELLAR GET YOUR ASS MOVIN' ... GO DOWN THESE ... AND GET OUT OF HERE, MAN ... AND ... AND ... DON'T MESS WITH ME NO MORE ..."

HARRY: (turning toward Tom) "THE MAN IS CRAZY ... HE'S CRAZY ... WE'VE GOT TO HAVE FOOD DOWN THERE ... WE HAVE A <u>RIGHT</u> ..."

TRUCKDRIVER: "THIS IS YOUR HOUSE?" (he knows it isn't)

HARRY: "WE'VE GOT A RIGHT TO ..."

TRUCKDRIVER: (confronting Tom) "YOU GOIN' DOWN THERE WITH HIM?"

TOM: "... WELL ..."

TRUCKDRIVER: "NO BEATIN' AROUND THE BUSH ... YOU GOIN' OR AIN'T YOU. THIS IS YOUR LAST CHANCE."

There is a long moment of silence. Tom then turns to the older man ...

TOM: "HARRY ... I THINK HE'S RIGHT."

HARRY: "YOU'RE CRAZY."

TOM: "I REALLY THINK WE'RE BETTER OFF UP HERE."

HARRY: "YOU'RE CRAZY. I GOT A KID DOWN THERE. HE CAN'T TAKE ALL THE RACKET, AND THOSE THINGS REACHING THROUGH THE GLASS. WE'LL BE LUCKY IF HE LIVES AS IT

IS NOW."

TRUCKDRIVER: (more impersonal than ever before) "OKAY. NOW
YOU'RE HIS FATHER. IF YOU'RE DUMB ENOUGH TO GO DIE
IN THAT TRAP, IT'S YOUR BUSINESS. BUT I AIN'T DUMB
ENOUGH TO GO WITH YOU. IT'S JUST BAD LUCK FOR THE
KID THAT HIS OLD MAN'S SO DUMB ... NOW GET THE HELL
DOWN THE CELLAR ... YOU CAN BE BOSS DOWN THERE ...
AND I'M BOSS UP HERE ... AND YOU AIN'T TAKIN' NONE OF
THIS FOOD, AND YOU AIN'T TAKIN' NOTHIN'".

TOM: "HARRY ... WE CAN GET FOOD TO YOU ... IF YOU WANT TO
STAY DOWN THERE ... AND ..."

HARRY: "YOU BASTARDS!"

HELEN: (from the cellar): "HARRY ... HARRY!"
Harry looks toward the cellar door, looks back at the
two men, then quickly moves toward the door.

HARRY: "YOU KNOW I WON'T OPEN THE DOOR AGAIN. I MEAN IT."

TOM: "WE CAN FIX THIS UP HERE. WITH YOUR HELP, WE
COULD ..."

HARRY: "YEAH ... WELL. I THINK YOU'RE BOTH NUTS ... WITH MY
HELP! ..."

TRUCKDRIVER: (to Tom) "LET HIM GO, MAN, HIS MIND IS MADE UP, NOW
LET HIM GO."
Harry looks for a moment, then lunges for the cellar
door, opens it, and slams it behind him ... sounds of
his footsteps going down the steps ...

TOM: (rushes to the door) "HARRY, WE'D BE BETTER OFF UP
HERE!"
The truckdriver ties the broken fringe back onto the
rifle, then begins to reload the gun, replacing the
spent shells.

TOM: (shouting through the door) "HARRY, IF WE STICK TO-
GETHER, MAN, WE CAN FIX IT UP REAL GOOD ... THERE
ARE PLACES WE CAN RUN TO UP HERE ..."
We hear sounds of Harry boarding up the door. The
truckdriver straps the gun to his shoulder again,
then turns and moves toward the upstairs. In pass-

ing, his glance falls on Barbara; he steps backward off the stairs and looks at her. The radio has taken up again with the monotonous recorded message.

TOM: "HARRY ... WE'D BE BETTER OFF IF ALL THREE OF US WAS WORKIN' TOGETHER ..."

(sounds of Harry's barracading)

TOM: "WE'LL LET YOU HAVE FOOD WHEN YOU NEED IT ..." (he glances warily at the truckdriver, half-expecting reprisal for this) "... AND IF WE KNOCK: THOSE THINGS MIGHT BE CHASIN' US, AND YOU CAN LET US IN ..."

Barricading sounds stop. Footsteps can be heard as Harry walks down the cellar steps. Tom listens awhile, then retreats, disappointed and worried about the lack of Harry's efforts in the defensive measures that must lie ahead.

The truckdriver is with Barbara, stooping beside her chair; she stares into an unseeing void. The big man softens at seeing her.

TRUCKDRIVER: "HEY ... HEY, HONEY."

He brushes her hair back from her eyes. Tears well up and it almost seems as though she might acknowledge his tenderness, but she does not. The man feels very sorrowful, almost as he would feel for his child when it was very sick. He massages his forehead and eyes, tired from fear and exertion of the past hours. He bends to cover the girl with a coat that he had brought from the den, then steps away and feeds the fire, and stirs it to keep the blaze good and warm; his primary concern in this effort is for the girl. Behind him, Tom walks up; truckdriver senses his presence ...

TRUCKDRIVER: "HE'S WRONG, MAN."

Tom is silent.

TRUCKDRIVER: "I AIN'T BOXIN' MYSELF IN DOWN THERE NOWHOW." (he finishes with the fire and rises to go upstairs, to continue his work there) "WE MIGHT BE HERE SEVERAL

DAYS ... WE'LL GET IT FIXED UP ... HE'LL COME UP ...
HE AIN'T GONNA STAY DOWN THERE VERY LONG ... HE'LL
WANTA SEE WHAT'S GOIN' ON ... OR MAYBE IF WE GET A
CHANCE TO GET OUT ... HE'LL COME UP."
He turns and goes up the stairs ...

* * *

The cellar, with its stark grey walls and dusty clutter, seems cold and damp. Cardboard cartons tied
with cord and a hanging grid of pipe-work all look
dirty in the subdued light of bare light bulbs. The
cartons take up much of the space; they vary in size
from grocery boxes with faded brand names to large
packing crates that might have contained furniture.
The washing machine, an old roller type, sits off in a
corner of the cellar near a makeshift shower stall.
Lines for drying clothes are strung over the pipe-
work so low that Harry has to duck under them as he
walks from the stairs to the other side of the confin-
ing quarters.

There are stationary tubs and an old metallic cabinet
against one of the walls. Harry's wife, Helen, is at
the faucet over the tubs, wetting a cloth with cold
water. She looks up as Harry enters, but is more interested in what she is doing at the moment; she
wrings out the cloth and takes it to where a young
boy, their son, lies motionlessly atop a home-made
work table. On a peg-board above the table are hanging tools and cables, and built into the table itself
are drawers that probably contain smaller tools,
screws and bolts, washers, etc. The woman moves a
little stiffly in the coolness of the cellar; she is
wearing a dress and sweater, while a warmer coat is
spread on the table under the boy, its sides flopped
up and over him, covering his legs and chest. The
woman bends over her son and wipes his head with the
cool cloth.

Harry quietly walks up behind her. She concentrates
on caring for the boy, pulls the coat more securely
around him.

HELEN: (not looking up) "HE HAS A BAD FEVER."

HARRY: "THERE'S TWO MORE PEOPLE UPSTAIRS."

HELEN: (still primarily concerned with the boy's comfort)
"TWO?"

HARRY: "YEAH ..." (a long pause, then half-defensively) "I
WASN'T ABOUT TO TAKE ANY UNNECESSARY CHANCES."
Helen is silent.

HARRY: "HOW DID WE KNOW WHAT WAS GOING ON UP THERE?"
Harry nervously reaches to his breast pocket for a
cigarette. He produces an empty pack and, seeing
that it is empty, crumples it in his hand and pitches
it to the floor. He steps over to the work table where
there is another pack, snatches it up, and it too is
empty--with the same crumpling action, he discards
this pack, violently this time, the action spinning
him into a position facing his wife and boy. She continues to quietly swab the boy's forehead. Harry
stares at them for a moment.

HARRY: "DOES HE SEEM TO BE ALL RIGHT?"
Helen is silent. The boy is motionless. He is sweating to the point where beads of sweat are formed all
over his face. Harry waits and, seeing no answer
forthcoming, changes the subject.

HARRY: "THEY'RE ALL STAYING UPSTAIRS ... IDIOTS. WE SHOULD
STICK TOGETHER ... IT'S SAFEST DOWN HERE ..."
He goes to his wife's purse and rummages through its
contents; he pulls out a pack of cigarettes, rips the
pack open, and fumbles for a cigarette. He lights it
and drags in the first puff deeply; it makes him cough
slightly.

HARRY: "THEY DON'T STAND A CHANCE UP THERE ... THEY CAN'T
HOLD THOSE THINGS OFF FOREVER ... THERE'S TOO MANY
WAYS THEY CAN GET INTO THE HOUSE UP THERE."

Helen remains silent. On the floor, next to the workbench, is a small transistor radio. Harry's glance
falls on it and he stabs at it, scoops it up and clicks
it on.

HARRY: "THEY HAD A RADIO ON UPSTAIRS ... MUST'VE BEEN CIVIL
DEFENSE OR ... I THINK IT'S NOT JUST US, THIS THING IS
HAPPENING ALL OVER." The radio picks up nothing but
static. Harry plays with the tuning dial, listening
anxiously, but across the receiving band the transistor just hisses. Harry holds the radio up and turns
it into various positions, trying it for reception,
spining the tuner as he goes. Still nothing but hiss.
He walks around the room with still no results.

HARRY: "THIS DAMNED THING ..."
Still just static.
Helen stops wiping the boy's forehead and neatly
folds the cloth, and drapes it over her son's brow.
She gently places her hand on the boy's chest and
looks over toward her husband. He moves impatiently
around the cellar, his cigarette dangling from his
lip, waving the little radio around in the air. The
radio just emits static at varying levels.

HELEN: "HARRY ..."
He continues his fidgeting with the radio. He goes
near the walls and stairs, holding it high and still
spinning the dial.

HELEN: "HARRY ... THAT THING CAN'T PICK UP ANYTHING IN THIS
STINKING DUNGEON!"
Her rising tone of voice stops him; he turns and looks
at her; about to cry, she brings her hands to her
face. She bites her lip, and just stares at the floor.
Looking at her, Harry lets his anger take hold of him,
but he cannot think of words; his face twitches, his
emotion searching for some vehicle or expression,
until he pivots violently and flings the radio across
the room.

HARRY: (shouting) "I HATE YOU ... RIGHT? I HATE THE KID? I
WANNA SEE YOU DIE HERE, RIGHT? IN THIS STINKING
PLACE. MY GOD, HELEN, DO YOU REALIZE WHAT'S HAPPEN-
ING? THOSE THINGS ARE ALL OVER THE PLACE ...
THEY'LL KILL US ALL ... I ENJOY WATCHING MY KID SUF-
FER LIKE THIS? I ENJOY SEEING ALL THIS HAPPEN?"
Helen's head jerks toward him. She looks at him with
what is almost vengeance.

HELEN: "HE NEEDS HELP ... HE NEEDS A DOCTOR ... HE'S ... HE'S
GONNA MAYBE DIE HERE ... WE HAVE TO GET OUT OF HERE,
HARRY. WE HAVE TO."

HARRY: "OH, YEAH ... LET'S JUST WALK OUT. WE CAN PACK UP
RIGHT NOW AND GET READY TO GO, AND I'LL JUST SAY TO
THOSE THINGS, 'EXCUSE ME ... MY WIFE AND KID ARE UN-
COMFORTABLE HERE ... WE'RE GOIN' INTO TOWN. FOR
GOD'S SAKE ... THERE'S MAYBE TWENTY OF THOSE THINGS
OUT THERE. AND THERE'S MORE EVERY MINUTE ...'"

HELEN: "THERE'S PEOPLE UPSTAIRS. WE SHOULD STICK TO-
GETHER YOU SAID. ARE WE FIGHTING WITH THEM? UP-
STAIRS, DOWNSTAIRS ... WHAT'S THE DIFFERENCE? MAYBE
THEY CAN HELP US. LET'S GET OUT OF HERE ... LET'S GO
UPSTAIRS ... LET'S DO SOMETHING ... LET'S GET OUT OF
HERE ..."
A pounding sound interrupts her. They listen. The
sound is coming from the door, at the top of the
stairs.

TOM: "HARRY!" (from outside the door)
More pounding. Harry just stares up at the door, and
does not answer the call. Tears well in Helen's eyes.
More pounding. Helen looks at Harry. When he does
not respond, she gets up and goes for the stairs.

HELEN: "YES ... YES, TOM!"
Harry, running after her, grabs her shoulders from
behind and stops her.

HELEN: "HARRY ... HARRY ... IT'S TOM RYAN."

TOM: (through the door) "HARRY ... WE GOT FOOD, AND SOME

MEDICINE AND THINGS FROM UP HERE ..."

Harry stares up at the door speechlessly.

TOM: "THERE'S GONNA BE A THING ON THE RADIO ... IN TEN
MINUTES, HARRY ... A CIVIL DEFENSE THING ... TO TELL
US WHAT TO DO."

HELEN: (looking up at the door, shouts) "WE'RE COMING UP!
WE'LL BE UP IN A MINUTE!"

HARRY: "YOU'RE OUT OF YOUR MIND, HELEN. ALL IT TAKES IS A
MINUTE ... THOSE THINGS GET IN UP THERE AND IT'S TOO
LATE TO CHANGE YOUR MIND ... DON'T YOU SEE THAT? ...
CAN'T YOU SEE THAT WE'RE SAFE AS LONG AS WE KEEP
THAT DOOR SEALED UP?"

HELEN: "I DON'T GIVE A DAMN! I DON'T CARE, HARRY ... I DON'T
CARE ANYMORE ... I WANT TO GET OUT OF HERE ... GO UP-
STAIRS ... SEE IF SOMEONE WILL HELP US ... MAYBE
KEVIN WILL BE OKAY ..."

Her shouting stops and she takes control of herself.
She steps toward Harry and speaks in a calmer tone,
almost pleading.

HELEN: "HARRY ... PLEASE ... FOR JUST A MINUTE ... WE'LL GO
UP AND SEE WHAT'S UP THERE ... WE'LL HEAR THE RADIO,
AND MAYBE WE CAN FIGURE SOME WAY TO GET OUT OF
HERE ... MAYBE WITH ALL OF US WE CAN MAKE IT,
HARRY."

Harry, his adamancy weakening somewhat, takes the
cigarette from his mouth, exhaling the last puff, and
drops it to the floor. He rubs it out with his foot;
the smoke comes in a long stream through his pursed
lips. Startlingly, Tom's voice penetrates again.

TOM: "HARRY! ... HEY, HARRY! ... BEN FOUND A TELEVISION
UPSTAIRS! COME ON UP ... WE'LL SEE THE CIVIL DEFENSE
BROADCAST ON TV ..."

HELEN: (soothingly, to Harry, her tone an attempt to relieve
the onus Harry must feel in going against his original decision) "COME ON ... LET'S GO UP ... THERE'LL BE
SOMETHING ON TV THAT TELLS US WHAT TO DO. YOU CAN

TELL THEM I WANTED TO COME UP ..."

HARRY: (acquiescing, but with stolid misgivings, his eyes
fasten on her; he pronounces his words with what is
almost menace) "ALL RIGHT ... THIS IS YOUR DECI-
SION ... WE'LL GO UP ... BUT DON'T BLAME ME IF WE ALL
GET KILLED ..."

Her eyes fall away from his, and she leads as they go
up the stairs. The cellar door swings open. Helen
and Harry step into the hallway. Faltering, they peer
through the entrance-way into the living-room.

Harry, standing behind his wife, is hostile--partially
due to anger with himself because he has reneged on
his decision about the cellar. Helen, too, is over-
wrought, due to the emotional effect of the recent argument and to the fact that she is about to meet
strange people in an anxious circumstance.

But only Tom and Barbara are in the living-room, and
Barbara, overcome with nervous exhaustion, is sleeping fitfully on the couch.

TOM: "WE CAN SEE THE BROADCAST, I THINK ... IF THE TV
WORKS. I HAVE TO GO HELP BEN."

Helen has gone immediately to Barbara, looks down at
her sympathetically, brushes back her hair and pulls
the overcoat around her shoulders.

HELEN: "POOR THING ... SHE MUST HAVE BEEN THROUGH A LOT."

Harry, during these moments, has been flitting anxiously all over the house ... from door to window to
kitchen to living-room... . checking out the actual
degree of security and worrying about imminence of
attack at any second.

TOM: (to Helen) "I THINK HER BROTHER WAS KILLED OUT
THERE."

BEN: (yelling somewhat peeved from upstairs) "TOM! ... HEY,
TOM! ARE YOU GONNA GIVE ME A HAND WITH THIS THING?"

Tom startles, aware of his procrastination, and bolts
for the upstairs to help Ben. Harry, pausing momen-

tarily in his anxiety comes over to where his wife is
looking after Barbara.

HELEN: "HER BROTHER WAS KILLED ..."

HARRY: "THIS PLACE IS RIDICULOUS--THERE'S A MILLION WEAK
SPOTS UP HERE."

(We hear sounds from upstairs of Tom and Ben struggling with the television set. They are making their
way down the steps.)

HELEN: "I DON'T CARE ... THERE'S PEOPLE UP HERE. WHY DON'T
YOU DO SOMETHING TO HELP SOMEBODY?"

Harry, not really hearing her, is staring once more
into the gloom outside.

HARRY: "I CAN'T SEE A DAMN THING OUT THERE! THERE COULD BE
FIFTY-MILLION OF THOSE THINGS, I CAN'T SEE A THING--
THAT'S HOW MUCH GOOD THESE WINDOWS DO US ..."

The truckdriver, who with Tom has reached the landing with the heavy television set, has heard the last
part of Harry's remark; he glowers even as he moves
with his end of the burden, but says nothing, as he
and Tom gingerly deposit the TV in the center of the
room. They hunt for an outlet, find it, then slide and
walk the set until the cord is close enough to be
plugged in. Ben kneels behind the set to plug in the
cord.

HARRY: "WAKE THAT GIRL UP. IF THERE'S GOING TO BE A THING
ON THE TUBE, SHE MIGHT AS WELL KNOW WHERE SHE
STANDS. I DON'T WANT ANYBODY'S LIFE ON MY HANDS."

HELEN: "HARRY ... STOP ACTING LIKE A CHILD!"

BEN: (on his feet, finished with plugging in the set) "I
DON'T WANT TO HEAR ANYMORE FROM YOU, MISTER. IF
YOU STAY UP HERE, YOU'LL TAKE YOUR ORDERS FROM
ME ... AND THAT INCLUDES LEAVING THAT GIRL ALONE.
SHE NEEDS REST ... SHE'S JUST ABOUT OUT OF HER HEAD
AS IT IS NOW ... NOW WE'RE JUST GOING TO LET HER
SLEEP IT OFF. AND NOBODY'S GOING TO TOUCH HER UN-
LESS I SAY SO ..."

Ben stares Harry down for a moment, to ascertain
that he is at least temporarily silenced; then his
hand plunges immediately to the television set. He
snaps it on, the occupants of the room jockey for
vantage points, and there are a baited few seconds of
dead silence as they all wait to see if the set will
actually warm up. All eyes are on the tube. A hiss
begins, increases in volume, Ben cranks the volume
all the way. A glowing band appears and spreads,
filling the screen.

HELEN: "IT'S ON ... IT'S ON!"

There are murmurs of excitement and anticipation--
but the tube shows nothing. No picture, no sound.
Just the glow and hiss of the tube. Ben's hand races
the tuning dial through the clicks of the various stations.

HARRY: "PLAY WITH THE RABBIT-EARS ... WE SHOULD BE ABLE TO
GET SOMETHING."

Ben fusses with horizontal and vertical, with bright-
ness and contrast. On one station, he finally gets
sound; he adjusts the volume; the picture tumbles; he
plays with it and finally brings it in. Full-screen is
a commentator, in the middle of a news report ...
(The people in the room settle back to listen. During
the telecast, the camera studies look and reactions,
but these responses are sporadic and infrequent.
Predominant mood of all involved is to learn as much
as possible from the telecast.)

COMMENTATOR: "... ASSIGN LITTLE CREDIBILITY TO THE THEORY THAT
THIS ONSLAUGHT IS A PRODUCT OF MASS HYSTERIA. AU-
THORITIES ADVISE UTMOST CAUTION UNTIL THE MENACE
CAN BE BROUGHT UNDER ABSOLUTE CONTROL. EYEWITNESS
ACCOUNTS HAVE BEEN INVESTIGATED AND DOCUMENTED.
CORPSES OF VANQUISHED AGGRESSORS ARE PRESENTLY
BEING EXAMINED BY MEDICAL PATHOLOGISTS, BUT AU-
TOPSY EFFORTS HAVE BEEN HAMPERED BY THE MUTILATED

CONDITION OF THESE CORPSES."

"SECURITY MEASURES INSTITUTED IN METROPOLITAN
AREAS INCLUDE ENFORCED CURFEWS AND SAFETY PATROLS
BY ARMED PERSONNEL. CITIZENS ARE URGED TO REMAIN
IN THEIR HOMES. THOSE WHO IGNORE THIS WARNING EX-
POSE THEMSELVES TO INTENSE DANGER--FROM THE
AGRESSORS THEMSELVES, AND FROM ARMED CITIZENRY ...
WHOSE IMPULSE MAY BE TO SHOOT FIRST AND ASK QUES-
TIONS LATER.

"RURAL OR OTHERWISE--ISOLATED DWELLINGS HAVE
MOST FREQUENTLY BEEN THE OBJECTIVE OF FRENZIED,
CONCERTED ATTACK. ISOLATED FAMILIES ARE IN EX-
TREME DANGER. ESCAPE ATTEMPTS SHOULD BE MADE IN
HEAVILY-ARMED GROUPS, AND BY MOTOR VEHICLE IF POS-
SIBLE. APPRAISE YOUR SITUATION CAREFULLY BEFORE
DECIDING UPON AN ESCAPE TACTIC. FIRE IS AN EFFEC-
TIVE WEAPON; THESE BEINGS ARE HIGHLY FLAMMABLE.

"ESCAPE GROUPS SHOULD STRIKE OUT FOR THE NEAR-
EST URBAN COMMUNITY. MANNED DEFENSE OUTPOSTS HAVE
BEEN ESTABLISHED ON MAJOR ARTERIES LEADING INTO
ALL COMMUNITIES. THESE OUTPOSTS ARE EQUIPPED TO
DEFEND REFUGEES AND TO OFFER MEDICAL AND SURGICAL
ASSISTANCE.

"POLICE AND VOLUNTEER CITIZENS ARE IN THE
PROCESS OF COMBING REMOTE AREAS IN SEARCH AND DE-
STROY MISSIONS AGAINST ALL AGGRESSORS, THESE PA-
TROLS ARE ATTEMPTING TO EVACUATE ISOLATED
FAMILIES. BUT RESCUE EFFORTS ARE PROCEEDING
SLOWLY, DUE TO THE INCREASED DANGER OF NIGHTFALL
AND THE SHEER ENORMITY OF THE TASK.

"RESCUE, FOR THOSE IN ISOLATED CIRCUMSTANCES, IS
HIGHLY UNDEPENDABLE. YOU SHOULD NOT WAIT FOR A
RESCUE PARTY UNLESS THERE IS NO POSSIBILITY OF ES-
CAPE. IF YOU ARE FEW AGAINST MANY, YOU WILL ALMOST
CERTAINLY BE OVERCOME. THE AGGRESSORS ARE IRRA-
TIONAL AND DEMENTED. THEIR SOLE URGE IS THE QUEST

FOR HUMAN FLESH. "SHERIFF CONAN W. MCCLELLAND, OF
THE COUNTY DEPARTMENT OF PUBLIC PROTECTION, WAS
INTERVIEWED MINUTES AFTER HE AND HIS VIGILANTE PA-
TROL HAD VANQUISHED SEVERAL OF THE AGGRESSORS. WE
BRING YOU NOW THE RESULTS OF THAT INTERVIEW."
(Fade and segue to video-tape interview.)
Open on wide shot. A night scene. Dense woods.
Posted guards maintain the periphery of a small
clearing. Sporadic gunfire can be heard in the distance. Some of the men smoke; some talk in groups.
The area is illumined by a large bonfire. Sheriff Mc-
Clelland is the focal figure, MCU, so that as he talks
we catch glimpses of activity in the background. He
is shouting commands, supervising defense measures
and the burning of the bodies, at the same time trying to answer reporter's questions. We cut or zoom
closer. McClelland is pacing around, not straying
too far, because a lavelier microphone is hanging on
a cord around his neck. The crackle of the bonfire,
the shouts and the bustle of activity can be constantly heard behind his commentary. As he talks, he
frequently turns away, his primary concern being his
efforts in dealing with the aggressors and control-
ling his search party.

McCLELLAND: (taking up with a previously-asked question)
"... YEAH ... WELL, THIS IS ROUGH COUNTRY FOR AN ...
EVENING HIKE ..." (he smiles) "... BUT THINGS AIN'T
GOING TOO BADLY. THE MEN ARE TAKING IT PRETTY
WELL. WE KILLED NINETEEN OF 'EM TODAY, RIGHT
AROUND THIS GENERAL AREA. THESE LAST THREE WE
FOUND TRYING TO CLAW THEIR WAY INTO AN ABANDONED
MINE SHED ... NOBODY IN THERE ... BUT THESE THINGS
JUST POUNDING AND CLAWING, TRYING TO BUST THEIR WAY
IN ... IT'S FUNNY IN A WAY ... MUST'VE THOUGHT THERE
WAS PEOPLE IN THERE ... WE HEARD THE RACKET AND
CAME AND BLASTED THEM DOWN ..."

REPORTER: "WHAT'S YOUR OPINION, THEN? CAN WE DEFEAT THESE
THINGS?

McCLELLAND: "THERE AIN'T NO PROBLEM ... ONLY PROBLEM IS WHETHER
WE CAN GET TO 'EM BEFORE THEY KILL OFF ALL THESE
PEOPLE. BUT ME AND MY MEN CAN HANDLE 'EM OKAY ...
WE AIN'T LOST NOBODY, OR SUFFERED ANY CASUALTIES.
ALL YOU GOTTA DO IS SHOOT FOR THE EYES. YOU CAN
TELL ANYBODY OUT THERE ... ALL YOU GOTTA DO IS DRAW
A SHARP BEAD AND SHOOT FOR THE EYES ... OR BEAT 'EM
DOWN 'N' LOP THEIR HEADS OFF ..."

REPORTER: "THEN I'D HAVE A DECENT CHANCE ... EVEN IF I WAS
SURROUNDED BY TWO OR THREE OF THEM?"

McCLELLAND: "IF YOU HAD YOURSELF A CLUB ... OR A GOOD TORCH ...
YOU COULD HOLD 'EM OFF OR BURN 'EM TO DEATH. THEY
CATCH FIRE LIKE NOTHIN' ... GO UP LIKE WAXPAPER ...
BUT THE BEST THING IS TO SHOOT FOR THE EYES ...
DON'T WAIT FOR US TO RESCUE YOU ... CAUSE IF THEY
GET YOU TOO FAR OUTNUMBERED YOU'VE HAD IT ... WE'RE
DOIN' OUR BEST ... BUT WE ONLY GOT SO MANY MEN AND A
WHOLE LOT OF OPEN COUNTRY TO COMB ..."

REPORTER: "BUT YOU THINK YOU CAN BRING THINGS UNDER CON-
TROL?"

McCLELLAND: "WE GOT THINGS IN OUR FAVOR NOW. IT'S ONLY A QUES-
TION OF TIME. WE AIN'T FOR CERTAIN HOW MANY THERE
ARE OF THEM THINGS ... BUT WE KNOW THAT WHEN WE
FIND 'EM WE'RE ABLE TO KILL 'EM. SO IT'S A MATTER OF
TIME ... THEY'RE WEAK ... BUT THERE'S PRETTY MANY OF
'EM ... DON'T WAIT FOR NO RESCUE PARTY. ARM YOUR-
SELF TO THE TEETH, GET TOGETHER IN A GROUP, AND TRY
AND MAKE IT TO A RESCUE STATION ... THAT'S THE BEST
WAY ... BUT IF YOU'RE ALONE YOU GOT TO SET STOCK-
STILL AND WAIT FOR HELP ... AND WE'LL TRY LIKE HELL
TO GET THERE BEFORE THEY DO ..."

(Scene fades, segues back to live announcer)

McCLELLAND: (emphasising his point, even as scene fades out): TELL
'EM TO SHOOT FOR THE EYES ... THAT'LL STOP THESE BO-

JOBBERS!

COMMENTATOR: YOU HAVE HEARD SHERIFF CONAN W. MCCLELLAND, OF THE
COUNTY DEPARTMENT OF PUBLIC PROTECTION. THIS IS
YOUR CIVIL DEFENSE EMERGENCY NETWORK, WITH RE-
PORTS EVERY HOUR ON THE HOUR, FOR THE DURATION OF
THIS EMERGENCY. REMAIN IN YOUR HOMES. KEEP ALL
DOORS AND WINDOWS LOCKED. DO NOT UNDER ANY
CIRC ...

Ben reaches over and clicks off the television.

TOM: WHY'D YOU CLICK IT OFF FOR?

BEN: THE MAN SAID THEY ONLY COME ON EVERY HOUR ... WE
HEARD ALL WE NEED TO KNOW. WE GOTTA GET OUT OF
HERE.

HELEN: HE SAID THE RESCUE STATIONS HAVE DOCTORS AND MED-
ICAL SUPPLIES ... IF WE COULD GET THERE, THEY COULD
HELP TIMMY.

HARRY: (scoffing): HOW'RE WE GONNA BUST OUTTA HERE? WE GOT
A SICK BOY, TWO WOMEN ... ONE OF 'EM OUTTA HER HEAD--
AND THREE MEN. AND THERE'S A MILLION OF THEM
THINGS OUTSIDE.

TOM: WILLIARD! THE GUY ON THE TV SNIP THEY HAVE A CHECK-
POINT THERE ... ABOUT SEVENTEEN MILES FROM HERE.

BEN: (Excited) YOU <u>FROM</u> HERE ... YOU <u>KNOW</u> THIS AREA?

TOM: YEAH ... I WAS WORKIN' IN THE CEMETERY ACROSS THE
ROAD ... I'M THE CARETAKER ... TWO OF THEM THINGS
ATTACKED ME AND I HIGHTAILED IT OVER HERE ... FOUND
EVERYBODY WIPED OUT ... NOT TOO LONG AFTER, THESE
OTHER PEOPLE FOUGHT THEIR WAY IN HERE ... I WAS
SCARED BUT I OPENED THE BASEMENT DOOR AND LET--

BARBARA: (Unbeknownst to everybody else, has been sitting up,
listening; now she speaks, startling them and gathering their attention) YOU WORK IN THE CEMETERY ... MY
BROTHER IS OVER THERE. (She has come down from her
hysteria, but is very weak)

HELEN: YOU POOR THING ... (Rushes to Barbara, comforting) MY
BOY IS HURT TOO ... WE HAVE TO GET TO A RESCUE STA-

TION ... THE TELEVISION TOLD US ... WE HAVE TO TRY
AND ESCAPE.

HARRY: WELL, I THINK WE OUGHT TO STICK RIGHT HERE ... AND
WAIT FOR A RESCUE PARTY. HE SAID IF YOU'RE FEW
AGAINST MANY YOU DON'T HAVE A CHANCE ... WE CAN'T
TRAMP SEVENTEEN MILES THROUGH THOSE THINGS ...

BEN: WE AIN'T GOT TO TRAMP. MY TRUCK'S RIGHT OUTSIDE THE
DOOR. This stops Harry. There is a moment of silence.

BEN: ... BUT I'M JUST ABOUT OUT OF GAS ... THERE'S A PUMP
NEAR THE SHED OUTSIDE, BUT IT'S LOCKED.

TOM: (Becoming more enthused, seeing possibilities) THE
KEY OUGHT TO BE AROUND SOMEWHERE ... THERE'S A BIG
KEY-RING IN THE BASEMENT ...

HARRY: (Jumps up) I'M GONNA GO LOOK ... THE KEYS ARE LA-
BELED (He bolts for the cellar)

BEN: (Pressing) IS THERE A FRUIT-CELLAR?

TOM: YEAH ... WHY?

BEN: WE'RE GONNA NEED LOTS OF JARS ... WE CAN MAKE MOLO-
TOV COCKTAILS ... SCARE THOSE THINGS BACK ... THEN
FIGHT OUR WAY TO THE PUMP AND GAS UP THE TRUCK.

TOM: WE'RE GONNA NEED KEROSENE. THERE'S A JUG OF THAT
IN THE BASEMENT TOO.

HELEN: BARBARA AND I CAN HELP. WE CAN RIP UP SHEETS AND
THINGS.

HARRY: (Clomps up from the cellar) HERE'S THE KEY-RING. THE
PUMP KEY IS MARKED WITH A PIECE OF TAPE.

BEN: GOOD... . THAT SETTLES THAT QUESTION ... BUT WE
SHOULD TAKE A CROWBAR ANYWAY ... IN CASE THE KEY
DOESN'T WORK. THE CROWBAR CAN DOUBLE AS A WEAPON
FOR WHOEVER GOES WITH ME. BUT I DON'T WANT TO GET
ALL THE WAY OUT THERE AND FIND OUT THE PUMP WON'T
OPEN ...

TOM: I'LL GO ... YOU AND ME CAN FIGHT OUR WAY TO THE
PUMP ... THE WOMEN CAN STAY IN THE CELLAR AND TAKE
CARE OF THE KID. WE SHOULD HAVE A STRETCHER ...

BARBARA AND HELEN CAN DO THAT ...

BEN: HARRY, YOU'RE GONNA HAVE TO GUARD THE UPSTAIRS.
ONCE WE UNBOARD THE DOOR, THOSE THINGS CAN GET IN
HERE EASY. BUT ME AND TOM HAVE TO GET IN, TOO,
AFTER WE GET BACK HERE WITH THE TRUCK. YOU'VE GOT
TO GUARD THE DOOR, AND UNLOCK IT FOR US RIGHT AWAY.
THEN WE'LL BOARD IT UP FAST AS WE CAN, 'CAUSE THOSE
THINGS ARE GONNA COME FAST ON OUR HEELS ... IF WE
DON'T GET BACK, WELL THEN YOU'LL BE ABLE TO SEE
FROM UPSTAIRS, AND YOU CAN BARRICADE THE DOOR
AGAIN AND GO TO THE BASEMENT ... YOU AND THE REST
CAN SIT TIGHT AND HOPE FOR A RESCUE PARTY.

HARRY: I WANT THE GUN, THEN. IT'S THE BEST THING FOR ME TO
USE. YOU'RE NOT GOING TO HAVE TIME TO STOP AND AIM.

BEN: (Adamantly) I'M KEEPING THIS GUN ... NOBODY ELSE
LAYS A HAND ON IT ... I FOUND IT AND IT'S MINE.

HARRY: YOU DON'T CARE WHAT HAPPENS TO US ... HOW DO WE
KNOW YOU AND TOM WON'T JUST TAKE THE TRUCK AND CUT
OUT?

BEN: (Glowering, with controlled anger) THAT'S THE CHANCE
YOU HAVE TO TAKE. IF WE CUT OUT, YOU'LL HAVE YOUR
GODDAMN BASEMENT. LIKE YOU'VE BEEN CRYING ABOUT
ALL ALONG.

HELEN: WE'RE GOING TO DIE HERE ... IF WE DON'T ALL WORK TO-
GETHER.

BARBARA: MY BROTHER'S OUT THERE ... MAYBE WE CAN GET HIM AND
BRING HIM BACK. HE'S JUST WOUNDED ... HE'LL BE
OKAY ...

HELEN: (Understanding) THAT'S OKAY, HONEY ... WE'LL BE ALL
RIGHT ... MAYBE YOUR BROTHER WILL BE, TOO ...

BEN: LET'S GET BUSY. WE'VE GOT A LOT TO DO, IF WE'RE
GONNA BUST OUT OF HERE.
He is on his feet, taking command. We fade out of the
scene ...

... Fade into new scene, completion of escape preparations. Tom is pouring kerosene into fruit jars;

Helen is dipping twisted rag fuses in kerosene in the
bottom of a dish. Barbara comes from the kitchen
with more jars; drying them on the outside and then
setting them on the table. She and Helen begin working the kerosene-soaked fuses through holes which
Tom has cut in the caps of the jars.
CUT TO HELEN & BARBARA in the living room. In the
middle of the floor there is a crude stretcher, made
of broomsticks and torn sheets, this presumably for
the wounded boy, Timmy. The television is off, but
the radio drones lowly, repeating the recorded message ... The radio is on as a monitor only, that they
may work and still keep up with news that may affect
their situation.

BARBARA: I DON'T KNOW WHAT TO THINK ABOUT MY BROTHER ... WE
HAVE TO GET OUT OF HERE ... MAYBE WE'LL FIND HIM IN
WILLIARD ... MAYBE HE WAS ABLE TO CRAWL TO THE
CAR ... AND GET AWAY ...

HELEN: WE HAVE TO THINK OF OURSELVES NOW ... IT'S HARD FOR
YOU ... BUT IT'S ALL WE CAN DO ... MY BOY IS GETTING
WORSE, TOO ... I HAVE TO GET HIM TO A DOCTOR ...

HARRY: (Coming over, checking the stretcher, making sure the
makeshift straps will hold) BROOMSTICKS AND BELT-
BUCKLES ... AND OLD SHEETS IT SEEMS TO HOLD OKAY ...
I ALWAYS HATED THE BOYSCOUTS ...

TOM: IT'LL BE OKAY ... IS THERE ANYTHING OPEN UPSTAIRS?

HARRY: SOME WINDOWS IN THE ROOMS. BEN IS UNFASTENING THE
DOORS NOW.

TOM: WE'LL THROW THE COCKTAILS FROM UPSTAIRS ... JUST
SPLASH THE WHOLE AREA WITH THEM ... THAT SHOULD
KEEP MOST OF THEM AWAY ... WHILE WE MAKE A BREAK
FOR THE TRUCK.

HELEN: WE'RE READY ... HERE COMES BEN NOW ... (Hears him
coming down the stairs).
Ben, the gun strapped around his back, is carrying a
crowbar and claw-hammer. He walks around checking

preparations, smiles at Barbara, glad to see she's a little better.

BEN: THINGS ARE READY UP THERE. NOW ME AND TOM WILL UN-BOARD THE FRONT DOOR ... HARRY, YOU TAKE THE TWO WOMEN UPSTAIRS. CARRY ALL THE COCKTAILS WITH YOU ... SOON'S THE DOOR'S UNBARRED, YOU'VE GOT TO THROW THOSE THINGS ALL OVER THE PLACE ... MAKE SURE THEY CATCH FIRE GOOD ... THEN THE WOMEN BUST DOWN HERE AND GET IN THE CELLAR. DON'T FORGET THE STRETCHER ... WHEN WE HEAR YOUR FOOTSTEPS ON THE STAIRS ME AND TOM 'LL BE GONE. IT'LL BE UP TO YOU, HARRY ... YOU GOTTA WATCH THIS DOOR ... GOT YOUR-SELF A GOOD LENGTH OF PIPE?

HARRY: I HAVE A PITCHFORK.

BEN: GOOD ... OKAY.

Tom and Ben go over to the door. The others gather fruitjars, etc., and sneak quietly to the unboarded room upstairs. Tom and Ben are left alone. Tom is soaking a tableleg in kerosene, ready to light it for use as a torch.

They fall to work on the door ... the painstaking work of very quietly undoing the barricade. They do not want to give alarm to the lurking things outside.

With crowbar and claw-hammer, very carefully, both men working on each separate piece of lumber, they undo the barricade. Each nail-creak is a menace. They are alert to the constant danger.

They finish, and watch, posting themselves anxiously by the door. Shadowy figures lurk in the dark out-side. Tom and Ben wait for the molotov shower to begin ...

A cry is heard, a window flies open, the first fiery blaze lights in the yard. More follow, some aimed for the creatures themselves. One of two catch fire ... the others start to back away ... the entire field is lit up ... bombs shower from upstairs ...

HARRY: (Shouting, from upstairs, slamming the door to the
room he was in) THAT'S ALL, BEN ... RUN FOR IT!
His voice echoes, as Tom and Ben burst into the yard.
They are armed with torches, and with the gun. They
leap into the truck. Tom plunges a torch into the
chest of an attacker, who immediately catches fire
and goes down in a blaze, clutching the torch ...
The truck starts up, and careens, in a u-turn, for the
old shed. Attackers fall away as it starts out. Ben
aims, fires several shots, most miss as the truck
jounces toward the gas pump across the yard. But one
creature goes down, with part of its head blown away,
in front of the gas pump near the old shed. Tom and
Ben leap out. Attackers are starting to make their
way to them from across the yard. Tom fumbles with
the key to the locked pump. Ben shoves him back, hurriedly aims the gun, the gun fires, blowing the lock
to pieces ... gas spurts all over the place ... creatures advance ... gas still spurting, Tom crams the
nozzle into the mouth of the gas-tank in the back of
the truck. Ben crouches and levels off with his
weapon ... an approaching attacker goes down ... but
more are coming on ... Tom's torch has inadvertently
set fire to the doused truck ... the flames begin to
lick and spread ... the attackers gather in force ...
ever closer ... Tom leaps into the flaming truck, it
skids and lurches across the yard ... Ben shouts, to
no avail ... the flaming truck speeds away, driven by
the panicked Tom ... several of the things are upon
Ben ... he thrashes and pounds them with torch and
gun ... ignoring Tom, he has to try and fight his way
back to the house ...
From inside the house, the panicked and cowardly
Harry has seen only pieces of the action. He has been
darting back and forth from door to window, trying
to see what has been happening outside ... from his

viewpoint, the escape attempt has met with total
doom. He has seen the truck catch fire, driven away
by Tom. Ben appears to be overwhelmed.
Harry runs again to the door. He sees the truck, completely in flames, speeding away from the house, toward a small rise. Back to the kitchen window ... Ben
is about to be overcome ... things all around him ...
Harry does not see, as Tom jumps from the burning
truck to be seized by attacking ghouls. The truck
continues unmanned toward the far rise ... and explodes violently ... the noise and flame shattering
the night ...
Ben continues to battle his way nearer the house.
But several ghouls are at the front door, trying to
beat their way into the house. From inside, Harry is
in complete terror. He cannot hold out ... all is
lost ... he panics and bolts for the cellar ...
But Ben has slugged his way through the attackers on
the porch ... he is pounding for admission at the
front door. He turns, and with a powerful lunge,
kicks the last attacker off the porch; in the rebound,
he plows his shoulder against the door; it crashes
open, the lock broken, and Ben bursts through in time
to catch Harry at the cellar door ... but there is no
time. Ben frantically turns to re-boarding the door.
His eyes meet Harry's for an instant ... then they
both fall to work. They board up the door ... they are
temporarily safe ... they turn and look at each other,
sweat streaming from each face ... Harry knows what
is coming ... Ben's fist crashes against Harry's
face ... he is driven back, one punch following another, until Ben corners him, clenching his lapels,
against the wall ... Ben's words spit out, each word
punctuated by an additional slam of Harry against
the wall ...
BEN: YOU ... ROTTEN ... NEXT ... TIME ... YOU TRY

SOMETHING ... LIKE THAT ... I'LL KILL YOU ...

Ben slams him one final time, and he slides down the
wall, crumples on the floor. His face is swollen; he
is streaming blood. Ben is already at the cellar
door ...

BEN: (pounding) COME ON UP! IT'S US ... IT'S ALL OVER ...
TOM IS DEAD!

Fade out.

The people in the house still remaining are gathered
in the living-room. Barbara and Helen are slumped
on the sofa. Overwhelming mood of hopelessness and
despair. Harry sulks in a corner, his head slung
back, his face swollen; he is holding an ice-pack
against his eye. His good eye follows Ben, who is
pacing about the room; when Ben's pacing takes him to
the kitchen, or to some area out of Harry's sight, the
good eye nervously relaxes. Ben's movements make
virtually the only sound; he is checking the defenses,
by force of habit rather than hope; the rifle is slung
on his back. For a long time, we dwell on the scene,
on the absolute dejectedness of the prisoners within
the barricaded house ... Ben paces from door to
kitchen to window; he starts to go upstairs, stops,
checks himself, goes to the door again ... he looks at
his watch ...

BEN: TEN MINUTES TO THREE ... THERE'LL BE ANOTHER BROAD-
CAST IN TEN MINUTES ...

Nobody says anything. Ben pulls back the curtain,
his eyes grow suddenly wide; but he watches for a
long moment (WE SEE HIS VIEW OF THE OUTSIDE). There
are many ghouls, lurking in the shadows of the hanging trees. Some of the things are in the open, much
nearer the house than they dared come before. Remains of charred bodies are dimly apparent in various parts of the yard.

But Ben's eyes are fastened on a more grisly scene; at

the edge of the lawn, in the moonlight, several ghouls are devouring what was once Tom ... they rip and tear into aspects of his body ... ghoulish teeth ... biting into Tom's arms and hands ... Ben stares ... fascinated ... and repulsed ...

With a convulsive movement his fingers release the curtain; he spins, shaken, and faces the others ... beads of perspiration on his face.

BEN: OH, GOD! DON'T ... DON'T NONE OF YOU LOOK OUT THERE ... YOU WON'T LIKE WHAT YOU SEE ...

Harry's good eye fastens on Ben, watches him, satisfied and contemptuous to see the big man weaken.

Ben moves for the television, clicks it on.

Barbara's scream pierces the room ... Ben leaps back from the television ... she is on her feet, screaming, uncontrollably.

BARBARA: WE'LL NEVER GET OUT OF HERE ... NONE OF US! ... WE'LL NEVER GET OUT OF HERE ALIVE! JOHNEEEE! JOHNEEEE!... . OH! ... OH ... GOD ... NONE OF US ... NONE OF US ... HELP ... OH GOD ... GOD ... !

Before anyone can move to her, she chokes up as suddenly as she began, and slumps, sobbing violently, to the couch, her face buried in her hands. Helen tries to soothe her, but great sobs come wracking from deep within ... she grows gradually quiet, the sobs diminish, but she remains slumped on the couch, her face covered with her hands. Helen covers her with the overcoat but the action seems futile, Barbara makes no movement whatsoever

Ben allows himself to sink very slowly into a chair in front of the TV. Harry's good eye goes from Barbara to Ben; his eye fastens on the gun, which Ben lowers butt first to the floor and leans across his legs. Ben threads his arm through the fringed sling, and maintains his grip on the forepiece. Harry watches.

HELEN: (Getting up, announces) I'M GOING TO THE CELLAR TO

TAKE CARE OF TIMMY. (She bends over, places her hand
on Barbara) COME ON HONEY ... COME AND TALK TO
ME ... IT'LL MAKE YOU FEEL BETTER ...
But Barbara makes no response. Helen turns and
starts for the cellar door; she has to squeeze past
Harry's chair. Furtively, his eye on Ben, Harry
touches her and pulls her toward him. She, too,
watches Ben; she knows something is up. Ben remains
transfixed before the TV; he is lost in thought, his
mind in a total daze. Those in nothing on the
screen--just a dull glow and low hiss of scanning
lines and static. He has turned the set on too early.

HARRY: (Whispering, cautiously and quickly to Helen) I'VE GOT
TO GET THAT GUN ... WE CAN GO TO THE CELLAR ... YOU
HAVE TO HELP ME ...
He has let the ice-pack come away from his eye. We
see its swollen, blackened condition--- and the desperation in his face. Ben still gazes at the TV. Worried about the possibility that Ben might catch them
in the act, and not really sympathizing with Harry,
Helen pulls away; but she leans her face to Harry's
and whispers quickly ...

HELEN: I'M NOT GOING TO HELP YOU ... HAVEN'T YOU HAD
ENOUGH ... HE'D KILL US BOTH ...
She goes to the cellar, and on the way has to pass behind Ben's chair; she hesitates, her eyes fall on the
gun; the sling is wound around Ben's arm. We study
her face; it is not clear whether she would have taken
it or not. But she makes no attempt. She opens the
door and goes down into the cellar. Harry's eye follows her as she leaves.
As Helen reaches the bottom of the cellar stairs, she
looks up, and her face shows startlement ... a shaken
smile ... her son is sitting up, propped on his elbows,
on the workbench table.

HELEN: ... TIMMY ...

She starts for him, but stops ... there is something
strange ... his face turns slowly toward her ... we
see the ghoulish look in his eye ... he is dead. He begins to rise slowly, terrifyingly, his features
grotesque ... the coat that was his blanket begins to
fall away ... his eyes stare through Helen ... and beyond her ... slowly, agonizingly, he raises himself
from the table ...

Helen, terrified begins to back away, across the cellar, her hand falls on a knife, her son creeps toward
her ... she moves a large packing crate, trying to
block his path ... trying to stave the confronta-
tion ... but she is too late ... he springs. It appears
as though the knife will be driven into her breast.
But, on the spring, we cut to the upstairs ... where,
simultaneously, a scream pierces the room. An assault has begun, the things are beginning to break
into the house. They have gotten into the den ... and
are hammering at the barricaded door ... the walls
are starting to come apart ...

Ben is on his feet, trying to re-inforce the barricades; with hammer and crowbar, he works furi-
ously ...

BEN: HARRY! HARRY! ... GIVE ME A HAND OVER HERE!

Harry comes over, behind Ben, and instead of helping,
rips the gun from Ben's back. Holding the gun on Ben,
Harry backs toward the cellar. Ben turns around,
panicked, the things are breaking into the house ...

BEN: WHAT ARE YOU UP TO MAN ... WE'VE GOT TO KEEP THOSE
THINGS OUT!

HARRY: (Backing away) NOW WE'LL SEE WHO'S GOING TO SHOOT
WHO ... I'M GOING TO THE CELLAR ... AND YOU CAN ROT
UP HERE ... YOU CRAZY BASTARD ...

His hand goes behind him to open the cellar door ...
but at that moment the ghoulish Timmy leaps upon him,
with a great springing thud ... Timmy is at Harry's

throat. Ben is able to grab the gun ... he levels off,
trying to hit the kid ... but a sudden wrench of the
two struggling bodies ... and Ben misses ... Harry
screams ... a great clot of blood appears at his
chest ... clutching the wound, he begins to go down ...
he falls through the entranceway to the cellar
stairs ... he reels, grabs the bannister, and begins
to descend ... we see his stare as he falls ...
reeling ... head-first down the stairs ...
Ben ... meantime ... has flung the kid, Timmy, with
one heave against the wall ... but things have broken
into the house ... everywhere, the barricades are
coming apart.
Barbara, with the hysteria of revenge, has flung herself into the attack ... She smashes a chair against
one again & again she smashes and smashes it ... on
the floor ... until there is nothing left of the
chair ... she jumps up, still sobbing, fighting with
Ben against the things that have come into the house.
It is obvious they cannot hold out ... the attack
rages ... they are overwhelmed ... Ben grabs Barbara
and pulls her after him into the cellar ... she is
lashing and swinging, beating at an attacker, even as
he drags her away ...
Ben flings open the door to the cellar ... and Helen
is at his throat ... he brings the gun up between
their struggling bodies until the muzzle is against
her throat, and squeezes the trigger. she is blown
halfway across the room ... Ben and Barbara run down
the stairs ...
But Harry is sprawled in a pool of blood on the
floor ... he is dead ... but beginning to rise ... Ben
pushes Barbara back ... she turns her head away ...
Ben raises the gun and we study him as three evenly-
spaced shots rip the room ... Ben is almost glad to
kill Harry ... he turns to Barbara, breathing hard ...

she collapses against him, and begins to sob ...
We hear faint pounding against the barricaded cellar
door. But it is holding. The creatures cannot get
in ...
The screen is black. There are the sounds of
birds ... fainter sounds of dogs ... human voices ...
Fade up quickly ... sunrise ... the morning after the
siege. The sky is clear ... the rising sun is bright
and warm ... there is dew on the high grass of a
meadow.
Men with dogs and guns are working their way up from
the woods that surround the meadow. We do not see
the posse at first; we merely hear their sounds ...
shouts ... muffled talk ... panting and straining of
dogs against leashes ... Sheriff McClelland's posse.
A few men, some with German Shepherds on leashes, finally come up out of the woods and onto the edge of
the sunlit, dewy meadow. The wet grass has dampened
the boots and trouser-legs of the men.
McClelland is perhaps the third man up from the surrounding thicket. He is a heavy man, moustached,
breathing hard because of his weight and the difficult job of leading the posse through the night. He is
armed with shotgun and pistol, and a belt of ammunition strung over his shoulder. He pauses, looks back
into the woods, and mops perspiration from his brow
with a balled-up dirty handkerchief ...

MCCLELLAND: (Shouting back at the men still working their way to-
ward the clearing) COME ON ... LET'S STEP LIVELY
NOW ... NEVER CAN TELL WHAT WE'LL RUN INTO UP
HERE ...

He accosts a man just climbing out of the woods. The
man wears an improvised sweat-band, carries a rifle
and side-arm, and has a walkie-talkie strapped to his
side.

McCLELLAND: YOU KEEPING IN TOUCH WITH THE SQUAD-CARS, GEORGE?

GEORGE: (Breathing hard, adjusting the straps and burden across his back) YEAH ... THEY KNOW WHERE WE ARE ... THEY SHOULD BE INTERCEPTING US AT THE HOUSE ...

MCCLELLAND: GOOD ... THESE MEN IS DOG-TIRED ... THEY CAN USE SOME REST AND HOT COFFEE ... (He looks back, to the men moving up from behind) COME ON, MEN. (He shouts) LET'S PUSH ALONG, NOW ... THE SQUAD CARS 'LL BE WAITING WITH COFFEE AND SANDWICHES AT THE HOUSE ...

The men push on across the field ...

Inside the house, Ben and Barbara have been dozing on chairs in the basement. Ben wakes abruptly, thinking he has heard something; but he isn't sure ... he sits up and listens more closely ... from far off, there is the sound of a dog. Ben listens for a long time, but hears nothing more ...

Outside, the meadow has become the outskirts of a cemetry, the one Barbara and John had come to with the flowers for their father. The posse is advancing, threading its way among the grave-markers. A man finds John's skeletal remains near the spot where he had fallen. Down a dirt road, and up a short grade, is Barbara's car, with the smashed window.

MCCLELLAND: LOOKS LIKE THIS GUY'S CAR ... POOR FELLOW ... NEVER HAD A CHANCE ...

The men pass through the cemetery, and over the wall, where several squad cars are waiting on the road. There are also one or two motorcycle patrolmen. One of the men dismounts and hails McClelland ...

PATROLMAN: HI, CONNIE ... HOW'S THINGS GOIN'?

McClelland advances and shakes hands, mops his brow again. The men begin to catch up and regroup. The posse fills the bend in the narrow road.

MCCLELLAND: SURE GLAD TO SEE YOU FELLAS, CHARLIE ... WE BEEN AT IT ALL NIGHT ... BUT I DON'T WANT TO BREAK 'TIL WE GET TO THE HOUSE OVER THERE ... WE MIGHT BE LOLLY-GAGGIN' AROUND WHILE SOMEBODY NEEDS OUR HELP.

WE'LL SEE FIRST, THEN STOP AND GET SOME COFFEE ...

PATROLMAN: ANYTHING YOU SAY, CONNIE ...

... Inside the house, Ben has sneaked up to the top of the cellar stairs. He listens there, very intently, not wanting to open the door because creatures may still be in the house. This time, for sure he hears gunshots ... and mumbled sounds of what must be the voices of approaching men. There is even what sounds like a car engine ... Ben bolts excitedly down the stairs.

BEN: (Waking the girl) BARBARA ... BARB ... HEY, HONEY ... THERE'S MEN OUTSIDE ... I CAN HEAR THEM ... THEY MUST BE HERE TO RESCUE US ...

Outside, we see the cause of the gunshots. The posse is flushing out ghouls from the pumphouse and surrounding area. The squad cars have driven up. The posse is advancing across the lawn, guardedly, toward the partially-destroyed old farmhouse. The men crouch and sneak up slowly, keeping their eyes fastened on the house ...

A loud sudden noise stops them ... they watch, stopped in their tracks.

MCCLELLAND: SHOOT FOR THE EYES BOYS ... LIKE I TOLD YOU BEFORE. ALWAYS AIM RIGHT FOR THE EYES ...

Inside, ready to shoot or swing, Ben has slammed open the cellar door. The force of his shoulder against the door has carried him into the living room ... Nothing ... Only the ramshackle and destruction from the recent siege. He edges his way through the twisted wreckage and overturned furniture toward the front door. There is no light in the place. His hand finds what is left of the curtain. He pulls it back and starts to peer out ... but ... a shot rings out ... Ben reels, driven back ... a circle of blood on his forehead, right between his eyes ... Barbara's scream is heard, from downstairs ... simultaneously,

McClelland shouts, his face flushed with anger ...

MCCLELLAND: DAMN IT, WHAT'D YOU SHOOT FOR? I TOLD YOU TO BE
CAREFUL ... THERE MIGHT BE PEOPLE IN THERE ...

MAN WHO FIRED
THE SHOT: NAW, THIS PLACE IS DEMOLISHED, THERE AIN'T NOBODY IN
THERE ...

PATROLMAN: I'M SURE I HEARD A GIRL'S SCREAM ... FROM THE BASE-
MENT, MAYBE ...

Several men have advanced to kick in the front door.
They step back and peer cautiously inside. Their
faces search the room ... A patch of sunlight from the
opened door falls partially on Ben. He is dead. The
men look down at him, but step past him toward the
cellar. They do not know he was a man. From the cellar, they hear muffled sobs. McClelland enters and
begins to inch his way down the stairs.

MCCLELLAND: ANYBODY DOWN THERE? (He shouts)

He draws his pistol, inches his way down the stairs.
At the bottom, he confronts Barbara, sitting wide-
eyed in a chair. McClelland raised his pistol, aims it
for her head ... but something stops him ... a tear in
her eye ... he lowers the weapon ...

MCCLELLAND: IT'S ALL RIGHT MEN ... COME ON DOWN ... IT'S JUST A
GIRL DOWN HERE!

He goes to Barbara, bends over her, looks at her, begins to help her up ...

Closing scene, with titles and credits. Burning of
bodies in the yard of the old house. Perhaps the
burning of the house itself. In the background,
against scene of McClelland draping his jacket
around Barbara and bringing coffee to her lips, we
see Ben's body on a stretcher, carried by two men ...
they lift it into the rear of a station-wagon ...

MCCLELLAND: IT'S TOO BAD ... AN ACCIDENT ... THE ONLY LOSS WE
HAD, THE WHOLE NIGHT.

INDEX